The Dream of Success

*A Study of the Modern
American Imagination*

T H E
Dream of Success

A Study of the Modern
American Imagination

by

K E N N E T H   S.   L Y N N

GREENWOOD PRESS, PUBLISHERS
WESTPORT, CONNECTICUT

The Library of Congress has catalogued this publication as follows:

Library of Congress Cataloging in Publication Data

Lynn, Kenneth Schuyler.
    The dream of success.

    Bibliography: p.
    1. American fiction--20th century--History and
criticism. 2. National characteristics, American.
3. Success in literature. I. Title.
[PS379.L9 1972]   813'.03   76-176134
ISBN 0-8371-6269-6

The publishers wish to thank the following for permission to reprint selections which appear in this volume: MRS. HELEN DREISER — for selections from *Dawn; Newspaper Days; The Color of a Great City; Hey Rub-A-Dub-Dub; Tragic America,* and *Dreiser Looks at America,* by Theodore Dreiser. MRS. CHARMIAN K. LONDON — for selections from *War of the Classes; Revolution and Other Essays; The Sea Wolf; The Iron Heel; Martin Eden,* and *Burning Daylight,* by Jack London. MR. ROBERT MORSS LOVETT, Executor — for selections from *The World Decision; Together; The Gospel of Freedom; The Web of Life,* and *The Memoirs of an American Citizen,* by Robert Herrick. MR. H. L. MENCKEN — for selections from his *The Philosophy of Friedrich Nietzsche; A Book of Prefaces,* and *Prejudices, First Series.*

Also: APPLETON-CENTURY-CROFTS, INC. — for permission to reprint from *John Barleycorn,* by Jack London. Copyright 1913 by The Century Company; Copyright 1913 by The Curtis Publishing Company. *The Book of Jack London,* by Charmian London. Copyright 1921 by The Century Company. *The Fashionable Adventures of Joshua Craig,* by David Graham Phillips. Copyright 1909 by D. Appleton & Company; Copyright 1908 by The Curtis Publishing Company. *Light-Fingered Gentry,* by David Graham Phillips. Copyright 1907 by D. Appleton & Company; Copyright 1906–1907 by The Pearson Publishing Company. *Susan Lenox: Her Rise and Fall,* by David Graham Phillips. Copyright 1915–1916 by The International Magazine Company. DODD, MEAD AND COMPANY — for permis-
(Continued on following page)

Originally published in 1955 by Little, Brown and Company, Boston

Reprinted with the permission of Kenneth S. Lynn

First Greenwood Reprinting 1972
Second Greenwood Reprinting 1975

Library of Congress Catalog Card Number 76-176134

ISBN 0-8371-6269-6

Printed in the United States of America

For My Father and Mother

Contents

The Dream of Success
A Study of the Modern American Imagination

The exclusive worship of the bitch-goddess SUCCESS
. . . is our national disease.

> — William James, in a letter to
> H. G. Wells, September 11, 1906

Introduction

IN the decade before the Civil War, a new literature began to appear in quantity in the United States. Its forms were various, but it was dedicated to a single theme: life in America was a fluid, wide-open race in which everyone competed on an equal basis — winner take all.

To a people whose massive agricultural expansion proceeded apace with the acquisition of Texas and California and who yet at the same time accelerated the process of shifting from an agrarian to an industrial footing, books on success were no more than mirrors held up to nature. The success literature of the 1850's established a popularity which has since persisted. Indeed, success books have constituted "perhaps the most flourishing of all branches of American literature."

This popularity, however, is not the principal reason why the literature of success deserves attention. The primary significance of books entitled *There's Plenty of Room at the Top* or *Little Journeys to the Homes of Great Americans* is that they distill a scheme of values, a conception of the world, a way of life, which has in varying degrees been shared by the great bulk of the American people for over a century. Such books are the conscious, explicit rendition of that shadowy cultural

3

mythology — the mythology of success — which permeates the American imagination.

The present study, which traces the impact of the success myth on the consciousness of five American novelists, can begin profitably by a brief examination of the myth in the form afforded by the success books. Since the success literature is enormous and its message, over the hundred-year period, subject to changes in emphasis and detail, it will be most useful to begin with its classic expression in the work of Horatio Alger, Jr.

Alger was born in 1832 in Chelsea, Massachusetts. His father was a Unitarian minister who intended that his son and namesake should be the same. The decision was definitely unilateral. "His name will be Horatio, after me," the father announced when apprised that the baby was a boy, "not as a concession to any vanity of mine but rather as a reminder to him that I shall expect him to continue the religious endeavors I have begun."

Training for the life his father had chosen for him began as soon as possible. At the age of nine, Horatio was known for his mastery of Latin, his grave public manner, and his immaculate black clothes. That he had also acquired a bad stutter and the contempt of his schoolmates, who mocked him as "Holy Horatio," was of no moment to his father. Only his mother listened sympathetically to his confession that he didn't want to be anything when he grew up. His first story, "A Race up the Hill," written at the age of thirteen, tells of the loneliness of a small boy who has only the wind to play with.

At Harvard, Alger took courses in literature and began to dream of a writing career; he met a girl and hoped to marry her. But his father blocked the marriage and, after Alger had spent three desultory years teaching and writing free-lance for newspapers and magazines, finally browbeat his son into enter-

4

ing the Harvard Divinity School. Upon graduation, however, the worm turned. Alger refused to be ordained and fled to Paris, where, he was confident, he could lead a literary and a sexually liberated life (Alger was a devoted reader of Eugène Sue's *Mysteries of Paris*). After a year "marked by futile indiscretions and equally futile remorse," he returned ingloriously to Cambridge and began grubbing out a living as a private tutor. The outbreak of the Civil War provided Alger with his next opportunity to break free of his father. Organizing a group of Cambridge boys into a semblance of a military unit, he drilled and paraded them and allowed himself to be called captain; when playing with boys palled, he went off to enlist in the army, but broke his arm before he could be inducted. When the arm had healed, he set off for Washington with the renewed intention of enlisting, but en route he again broke his arm. A third and last attempt to get into the army also ended badly, when he came down with pneumonia on the very eve of his enlistment. After such a comedy of errors, it was no longer possible to resist his father, and in December, 1864, Alger was ordained at Brewster, Massachusetts.

His career as a minister lasted a year and three months. Then, like the boy heroes of the novels which would make him famous, he quit his job and ran away to New York. At the invitation of the director, Alger took up residence at the Newsboys' Lodging House, a refuge for homeless boys, and remained there most of his life. He entered immediately and enthusiastically into the affairs of the establishment, nursing the boys when they were sick and beating the drum in the band; between times he wrote the "Alger stories."

But despite his success as a writer, Alger was forever dissatisfied. The dream of his life was that he might some day become a serious author and write a great novel. To this end, he memorized passages from the novels of Henry James and other writers whom he admired, hoping that in this way he might acquire a good literary style; he affected a smock and rumpled his hair, hoping to look Bohemian; donning a wig and cape, he ambled along Broadway, hung around Pfaff's cellar — where Walt Whitman liked to hold forth — and dropped into the Astor House once a day, on the chance that he might strike up an acquaintance with a literary figure who might be staying there. But the great book never got finished, the inmates of Pfaff's ignored the timid, bald little man who neither smoked nor drank, and the Astor House celebrities never even looked his way. Alger's Bohemia was a solitary world.

Toward the end of his life, spurred on by a second visit to Paris and a love affair with a married woman, he put boys' books behind him and tried once again to write a serious novel. But the affair was broken off by the woman, Alger suffered a complete physical and mental breakdown, and the novel was abandoned. After a long convalescence in New York, Alger returned to a small town in his native New England, where he died in July, 1899.

In his own eyes, Alger was a failure. Yet by sitting down in his lonely room in the Lodging House and pouring out all his dammed-up ambitions and repressed desires into more than a hundred novels and countless short stories about adolescent boys who, beginning in poverty and obscurity, took the fabulous city of New York by storm, Alger became a famous man. Sublimating a lifetime which Alger himself judged to be ignominiously unheroic, he created the "Alger hero," and thereby became one of the great mythmakers of the modern world.

While Alger was not the first American success writer, it is nevertheless true that the Alger hero is the key to the meaning of the success mythology. Alone, unaided, the ragged boy is plunged into the maelstrom of city life, but by his own pluck and luck he capitalizes on one of the myriad opportunities available to him and rises to the top of the economic heap. Here, in a nutshell, is the plot of every novel Alger ever wrote; here, too, is the quintessence of the myth. Like many simple formulations which nevertheless convey a heavy intellectual and emotional charge to vast numbers of people, the Alger hero represents a triumphant combination — and reduction to the lowest common denominator — of the most widely accepted concepts in nineteenth-century American society. The belief in the potential greatness of the common man, the glorification of individual effort and accomplishment, the equation of the pursuit of money with the pursuit of happiness and of business success with spiritual grace: simply to mention these concepts is to comprehend the brilliance of Alger's synthesis.

Yet the fact that the Alger hero was a concrete embodiment of certain commonly held ideas does not in itself explain his popularity, for another mythic figure who embodied many of the same ideas was a firm fixture in the American pantheon long before the Alger hero appeared to displace him. This figure was the Western hero — the hunter, trapper, or scout who, from the legendary exploits of Captain John Smith to those of Daniel Boone, from Cooper's Leatherstocking Tales to the dime-novel adventures of Deadwood Dick and Mustang Sam, had an enormous appeal for nineteenth-century America. Self-reliant, intrepid, skillful, he possessed exactly the same personal qualifications as did the Alger hero.

In other respects, however, the Western hero was vastly different. The Westerner abominated the city and was fundamentally antisocial. At his most civilized, his residence was an agricultural community. He also distrusted the modern eco-

7

nomic system, preferring to kill game for food than buy in a market and scorning work for wages. Although in actuality the Western trapper or scout was usually the advance agent of land speculators, his mythic counterpart never was. And always he was of old American or British stock. In other words, despite his popular appeal, the Western hero increasingly lost touch with the facts of American life as the nineteenth century wore on. However admirable the values were which this mythic hero affirmed, they ceased "very early to be useful in interpreting American society as a whole because they offered no intellectual apparatus for taking account of the industrial revolution. . . . [and were] powerless to confront issues arising from the advance of technology."

Alger, however, confronted these issues. The Alger hero often began life in places as rural as those frequented by Cooper's Natty Bumppo, but the significant action of his life took place on the sidewalks and in the counting rooms of New York, Cincinnati or Chicago. Alger made no bones about the existence of poverty. The city of the Alger myth was a glamorous, wonderful place, but it had its seamier side, its tenements and flophouses and sweatshops. Money was in the forefront of every Alger novel — how much the hero earned in his first job, how much he spent on food and rent, how much of a fortune he eventually compiled. Finally, Alger's world was populated by Irish and Italians and Germans as well as by those whose ancestors were pioneers. The success myth, in the hands of its greatest expositor, was a grand and impossible dream, but part of its power derives from the fact that it was also a reflection of the contemporary world.

Alger's first success novel — *Ragged Dick; or Street Life in New York with the Boot-blacks* — was published in 1868; from that moment, he went on to become the most popular author in

American history. His publishers have estimated that between
the appearance of his first novel and the Great Depression
Alger's books sold the astounding total of ten million copies. In
his heyday — the thirty years between *Ragged Dick* and his
death — he was undoubtedly the most widely read author in
the world. (But not, however, the wealthiest. Alger apparently
sold his novels to his publishers for rather modest lump sums
and thus never collected a penny of the fabulous royalties
which rightfully should have been his.) Generations of American children were brought up on Alger; his version of the success myth was the way in which the world was interpreted to
them. His stories reached the zenith of their fame and popularity in precisely those three decades — the seventies, eighties
and nineties — when the rate of industrialization and urbaniza-
tion, the degree of social mobility, the absence of state control,
the power of individuals, reached levels never before attained
in American society. The Alger hero fired the American imagination at the instant of his maximum credibility.

But when children born in the year of *Ragged Dick* and
after began to come of age in the late eighties and early
nineties, they discovered that America's spectacular growth
had also spawned a host of problems too big to be ignored.
Industrial warfare, political explosions in the farm belt, rising
popular bitterness about monopolies and outbursts of xenophobic hatred were simply the most sensational signs of social
trouble. The soaring divorce rate and the increased concern of
the medical profession with nervous disorders and mental
breakdowns were evidence that the maladjustments generated
by the great race of American life were personal as well as
public. The death of the creator of the Alger stories at the end
of the nineties was a meaningful symbol of the fact that between the mythology of success and the reality of American

life there now yawned a palpable and an ever-widening gulf.

The world was, increasingly, out of joint, and as the nineteenth century drew to a close it devolved upon that Hamlet-figure, the American intellectual, to set it right — if not by raising the dead, then at least by reinterpreting American society to itself. This task of reinterpretation accounts for the tone of revaluation and re-examination that so dominates American thought at the turn of the century. Reconstructions in philosophy were launched, new ways of talking about psychology and economics appeared, the nature of the American novel altered radically. Truth was to be made known and justice done.

The trouble was, though, that personal problems immensely complicated attempts to deal with the affairs of state. The five novelists — Dreiser, London, Phillips, Norris, Herrick — who are considered in this study found that to adjust the success myth, on which they had grown up, to the reality which they saw around them was a complex, ambiguous and dramatic task. Each of the novelists considered herein was a very special case; none of them was a "representative man." Yet this study has a general significance, for the very deviations by which these novelists marked themselves off from their fellow citizens throw light across the general pattern of American experience in their time.

BOOK ONE

From Rags to Riches

CHAPTER I

Theodore Dreiser: The Man of Ice

On thinking back over the books I have written, I can only say: Ladies and gentlemen, this has been my vision of life. . . . You may not like my vision, ladies and gentlemen, but it is the only one I have seen and felt, therefore, it is the only one I can give you.

— THEODORE DREISER

THEODORE DREISER asserted, with a blunt directness which no other American writer at the turn of the century could match, that pecuniary and sexual success were the values of American society, that they were his values, too, and that they were therefore worthy of his total attention as a literary artist. The indebtedness to Dreiser expressed by later American writers is a formal acknowledgment of the fact that his was the most significant exploration made by any novelist in his generation of the themes of money and sex, the two themes which have become so very much the major concern of our modern literature.

Bright and energetic as any heroine out of Shaw, a woman who employed the pen name of Neltje Blanchan — and who was destined to figure importantly in Dreiser's life — was a perfect example of that *fin-de-siècle* phenomenon, the New American Woman. Being married and the mother of three

13

children did not swerve the strong-willed Miss Blanchan from the pursuit of her other interests — she had not come from the Midwest to New York simply to be a wife and mother. In the twenty-five years between the birth of her youngest child and her death in 1917, she published eight books, mostly scientific studies of birds and flowers, as well as numerous magazine articles on subjects ranging from antique furniture to the education of the American Indian, and was prominent in charity work in and around New York. It was a fitting climax to her life that she should die in Canton, China, while engaged on a special mission for the Red Cross. Her wide-ranging, independent career stands as a convenient symbol of the profoundly altered lives which American women had begun, from the 1880's on, to lead.

Thus the drift of population from the farms to the cities in the eighties and nineties was termed by one contemporary male "largely a woman movement." Yearning for neighbors and pretty clothes, "for schools, music, art, and the things tasted when the magazines came in," American women were fascinated by the thought of the metropolis. Once arrived in the cities, they spread out beyond their traditional routine of housework into jobs as telephone girls, bookkeepers, typists and clerks, with the result that by 1900 twice as many women were gainfully employed in the United States as had been twenty years before. On another class level, club activities and social work were the channels of expression of the new emancipation. The stepped-up agitation for political suffrage for women in this period was a simple reflection of the new facts of female life.

"What is this curious product of today, the American girl or woman?" asked a writer in the *Atlantic Monthly* in 1880. ". . . is it possible for any novel, within the next fifty years,

14

truly to depict her as a finality, when she is still emerging from new conditions . . . when she does not yet understand herself . . . ?" The question was a good one and, as it turned out, a perennial one. For the American novel in this century has been, perhaps more than anything else, a continuing study of the emergent, still-changing, ever-new American woman. Undine Spragg, Alice Adams, Carol Kennicott, Kitty Foyle, Rosemary Hoyt, Scarlett O'Hara, these have been the characteristic figures of our modern fiction, and their various ambitions have supplied its dynamic power.

The subject of our modern literature, the American woman has to a great extent also been its dictator, and this aspect of her new role in American society has never been more aptly illustrated than by, once again, Neltje Blanchan. In 1900, on the recommendation of Frank Norris and others, the firm of Doubleday, Page had decided to publish a first novel by Theodore Dreiser. Miss Blanchan, in private life Mrs. Frank Doubleday, read the page proofs and was horrified. "With a strength of purpose that had been a support to the firm in the past, she impressed her feelings upon her husband." The book was immediately suppressed.*

Neltje Blanchan was quite right to be horrified; this was not the kind of book Doubleday, Page wanted. The heroine of *Sister Carrie* was something new under the sun. A small-town girl on her way to Chicago with four dollars in her pocket and her lunch in a paper box, a "half-equipped little knight . . . venturing to reconnoitre the mysterious city and dreaming wild dreams of some vague, far-off supremacy," Carrie

---

* Because Dreiser had already signed a contract which called for publication, Doubleday actually printed one thousand copies of the book, but no effort was made to advertise or promote it. As a result, the novel had almost no sale and Dreiser's profit from the whole adventure was considerably below one hundred dollars.

Meeber manifested the arrival in our fiction of the freewheeling, unconnected female striking on her own into the urban jungles of America. But Miss Blanchan did not object to Dreiser's book on the grounds that the phenomenon of which she herself was a symbol was not a fit subject for literature. Her opposition sprang from her quite accurate opinion that this fictional representative of the New American Woman was utterly immoral. With a ruthlessness which Carrie herself would have admired, Miss Blanchan suppressed the novel. Why, what sort of novelist could it be who had such thoughts about American womanhood — who would write a book which quite plainly implied that "the wages of sin might easily be success"?

<h2 style="text-align:center">ii</h2>

Theodore Dreiser was driven all through his childhood and adolescence by the urgent desire to escape. The "peculiarly nebulous, emotional, unorganized and traditionless character" of his family life offered him very little to cling to. His father, John Paul Dreiser, had been the vigorous, prosperous owner of a woolen mill until a stunning series of disasters shortly before Theodore's birth broke him down completely. The uninsured mill was destroyed by fire; while rebuilding it, a beam fell on him, injuring his head and shoulders; some deeds and other valuable papers were stolen from his house; his three eldest boys died in rapid succession. In later years a wealthy mill owner told Dreiser that all his father had lacked in order to re-establish himself as a successful woolen manufacturer was "the courage to go ahead and organize another plant of his own," while as late as his eighty-first year his father was offered a salary of twenty thousand dollars a year to become an expert adviser for a large woolen company. But John Paul could not bring himself to capitalize on any of these opportunities; after the accidents which reduced him to poverty he was a beaten, terrified man. Dreiser remembered him only as "a morose and dour figure, forlorn and despondent, tramping about the house, his hands behind his back and occasionally talking to himself." A fanatical Catholic, Dreiser's father seemingly had only one remaining ambition — to subject his children to as severe a religious discipline as possible. Dreiser's mother, on the other hand, was a warmhearted, profoundly sympathetic woman, a great comfort to all the family, but equally ineffectual as a provider. An incorrigible optimist, her eye was "always on the future, where lay wonder and delight, if not fame and power," but she could never make ends meet in the present.

When Dreiser was eight or nine, his father's inability to locate even a part-time job, and the failure of the latest of his mother's perennial boardinghouse schemes, split the family, and Dreiser, in company with his mother and two of the other children, began a long hegira through a succession of Indiana towns. One summer and autumn in Sullivan, Indiana, a drab mining town, they were so poor that Dreiser had no shoes to wear. Winters always meant being cold and hungry, so that "for years, even so late as my thirty-fifth or fortieth year, the approach of winter invariably filled me with an indefinable and highly oppressive dread."

Out of the tangled mess of his broken family life, his rootlessness, his poverty, came the dream of escape, and the image of escape was the flight to the city. Several of Dreiser's older brothers and sisters had already fled, one brother to the West, another to New York, two sisters to Chicago. Their visits home and the stories they told fed Dreiser's imagination; in between their visits there was the daily sustenance of the pulp magazines — *Brave and Bold, Pluck and Luck,* and *Work and Win* — with their stories of poor small-town boys like himself who found happiness and affluence in the city. What Fred Fearnot could do, so could he. How much the success myth came to mean to Dreiser can perhaps be best sensed in his simple admission that "over half the glory" of life in these boyhood years was the visible arrival and departure of the trains — the highway of escape.

Although impractical herself, his mother constantly urged on Dreiser "the need of energy, study of a practical character, ambition, self-denial," if he were properly to prepare himself for "the battle of life." Like her, however, Dreiser was an optimist and a daydreamer. Alger's formula for rising from rags to riches was pluck and luck, but the youthful Dreiser was interested only in the latter half. "I was for mooning about and dreaming of how delightful it would be to do this and that, have this and that — without effort — by luck or birth, as it were." At the suggestion of his seventh-grade teacher, he read *Self-Help* by Samuel Smiles, which made him "see that there were many things to do and many, many ways of finding how to do them. Some people drifted into things, and most successfully; others thought them out." Thought and drift, pluck and luck: henceforth Dreiser believed with the mythology that the recipe for success had two essential ingredients, but for many years he would not relinquish the notion that there was a superior efficacy in luck.

In the summer of his sixteenth birthday, Dreiser left home and went, "like a boy hero out of a Horatio Alger, Jr., novel, to Chicago to seek his fortune." The city seemed to him "a land of promise, a fabled realm of milk and honey. . . . Here, as nowhere else, youth might make its way." The luxury of the magnificent city almost seemed to speak to him: "All that life or hope is or can be or do, this I am, and it is here before you! Take of it! Live, live, satisfy your heart!" As the formula for success had two parts, so the images of what success could mean, as they passed before his dazzled eyes, sifted down into two categories. "Burning with desire," he dreamed of "the mansions that should belong to me! . . . The beauties who should note and receive me." Pluck and luck meant success, and success meant wealth and women. These conclusions, arrived at in mid-adolescence, stained Dreiser's mind forever.

Although the opportunities for success were everywhere, Chicago brought to Dreiser a long chain of defeats. For a time he could not land a job at all; when he did succeed in getting one — cleaning a railway stable — he was fired after a half day. Hired next by a hardware store to clean stoves, he lasted exactly two hours before being told he was too weak for the job and dismissed. His connection with a household-furnishings company was abruptly terminated when he was caught stealing twenty-five dollars to buy himself a winter coat.

His relations with girls were equally unsatisfactory. When he measured his poor clothes, his lack of *savoir-faire*, and his homeliness against his own standard of the successful man, he found it impossible to believe that any girl could be interested in him. When occasions for sexual conquest arose, his insecurities rendered him completely and humiliatingly inadequate. In masturbation, as in his dreams of wealth, he found solace from the failures of the real world.

After four years in Chicago, Dreiser was still "without trade or profession, a sort of nondescript dreamer without the power to earn a decent living and yet with all the tastes . . . of one destined to an independent fortune." Then came the turning point, the crucial moment which the success myth had taught him every career contained. "The newspapers — the newspapers — somehow, by their intimacy with everything that was going on in the world, seemed to be the swiftest approach to all this of which I was dreaming." He hung around the city rooms in the hope that something might turn up, and finally he was taken on as a regular feature writer by the *Chicago Globe,* a "by no means distinguished paper."

In the seething caldron of the newspaper world, Dreiser shucked off the last vestiges of the moralistic qualms which, the heritage of his father's rigid Catholic discipline, had heretofore caused him to feel guilty as he ran after money and women. Most of his journalistic colleagues, Dreiser discovered, "looked upon life as a fierce, grim struggle in which no quarter was either given or taken, and in which all men laid traps, lied, squandered, erred through illusion." With their conclusions he now heartily agreed. He doubted in these newspaper years that any human being ever coveted success more completely than he did. "My body was blazing with sex, as well as with a desire for material and social supremacy — to have wealth, to be in society. . . ." The problem was how to get what he was after, no matter the means.

Moving to St. Louis, he angled for and got the post of drama reviewer on the *Globe-Democrat,* thus gaining access to the theatrical world, which, with its suavity and its glitter, exhilarated Dreiser beyond anything he had ever known. He affected Bohemian clothes and a dramatic air, and fantasied that he was just on the verge of a liaison with some beautiful actress. Wondering if becoming a littérateur might open the door to easy cash and easy women, he was immensely pleased and excited when someone told him he ought to write a play. One of his newspaper colleagues had written a novel about Paris which Dreiser was allowed to read in manuscript. It impressed him tremendously. The author had never been to Paris, but his novel's "frank pictures of raw, greedy, sensual human nature, and its open pictures of self-indulgence and vice" sounded wonderfully authentic to Dreiser. Definitely, "art" was the open sesame to success. "This world was a splendid place for talent, I thought. It bestowed success and honor upon those who could succeed. Plays or books, or both, were the direct entrance to every joy which the heart could desire." Dreiser had even been prepared "to accept socialism," if it would only bring him "a great home, fine clothes, pretty women, the respect and companionship of famous men," but now he was positive he had found a better way to achieve his desires.

Dreiser was also prompted in the direction of becoming a novelist by his fear of failure at newspaper work. "I was always driven," he said, "by haunting fear of losing this or any position I had ever had, of not being able to find another (a left-over fear, perhaps, due to the impression that poverty had made on me in my extreme youth)." Newspaper assignments sent him to the theater, but they also sent him to the slums. Such glimpses of life "in all its helpless degradation and poverty" caused him to break into a cold sweat when it occurred to him that the lot of the poor, "their hungers, thirsts, half-formed dreams of pleasure, their glittering insanities and broken resignations at the end," might be his lot, too. Owning a small-town paper seemed to offer security, so he quit St. Louis with the notion of looking for one. When nothing came of his search, Dreiser wandered East, picking up free-lance jobs on papers here and there. Out of a regular job and almost out of money, he was haunted — it is one of his key words — more than ever. "The most haunting and disturbing thought always was that hourly, I was growing older. . . . Some had strength or capacity or looks or fortune, or all, at their command, and then all the world was theirs . . . but I, poor waif . . . must go fumbling about looking in upon life from the outside." Although Arthur Brisbane soon hired him as a reporter on the glamorous *New York World,* Dreiser's fears of failure were fanned even higher by his awareness that in the brutally competitive big league of Manhattan journalism he was barely keeping his head above water. "I was haunted by the thought that I was a misfit, that I might really have to give up and return to the West, where in some pathetic humdrum task I should live out a barren and pointless life." Receiving only marginal assignments on the *World,* Dreiser knew he had to do something — to stand still was death. There were several men employed on the paper who in their spare time wrote fiction.* Their example helped Dreiser make his decision. "I began to think that I must not give up but must instead turn to letters, the art of short-story writing. . . ." In the spring of 1895 he took the plunge and resigned from the *World.*

His initial short stories earned him only rejection slips. When his funds had diminished to the point where the return to the West was imminent, Dreiser suggested to the sheet-music publishers with whom his brother Paul was associated † that they publish three or four new songs each month and surround them with the trappings of a magazine — articles, pictures, and criticism. They agreed, and Dreiser found him-

---

* One of the men was David Graham Phillips. See Chapter III.

† Paul Dreiser, or Paul Dresser, as he called himself, was the author of many popular songs of the day, including "On the Banks of the Wabash" and "My Gal Sal."

self "Editor and Arranger" of *Ev'ry Month. The Woman's Magazine of Literature and Popular Music.* An indifferent reporter, he was much better suited to the calmer, if occasionally froufrou, role of editor of a magazine for women.

He wrote many editorials (dramatically signed "The Prophet") for *Ev'ry Month,* commenting on everything from the phenomenon of mental telepathy to the social emancipation of women. These editorials served Dreiser as a kind of literary notebook, most of the topics of his fiction first appearing here in the guise of comments on contemporary events. An editorial in September, 1896, which began by commenting on the impending Bryan-McKinley election, quickly turned aside from politics to a reflection on how valuable reading was for the opportunity it gave to learn of the triumphant lives of great men. Contemplating such careers from the comfortable vantage of his editorial chair, Dreiser no longer found the struggle of life so overwhelming as it had seemed on the *World.* Nature was powerful, but man was even more so: "In the presence of such a creature pity has no mission. . . . Nothing can withstand him, for he is working in harmony with great laws which place splendid powers in his hand and assist him to rise." To the successful young editor of *Ev'ry Month,* the universe was really and truly the splendid place the success myth had always said it was.

The following month Dreiser began his column, in what would become his most characteristic vein as a novelist, by describing the lure of the metropolis. "To go to the city," he wrote, "is the changeless desire of the mind. . . . It is a magnet which no one understands." This reflection brought him to consider a tragic result of the city's magnetic appeal — the thousands of people who had been drawn to New York by its glamour, only to find themselves trapped in a world of long hours and low pay. But Dreiser's conclusion was that this pathetic condition was necessary and inevitable. "Oppression can be avoided, that is true," he conceded, "but the vine must have roots, else how are its leaves to grow high into the world of sunlight and air? Some must enact the role of leaves, others the role of roots, and as no one has the making of his brain in embryo he must take the result as it comes." Here, in this metaphor of roots and leaves, Dreiser first set forth his lifelong opposition to political and economic reform.

In February, 1897, Dreiser discussed the financial panic which was currently ruining many businessmen in New York, then switched to a lengthy analysis of the number of starving and freezing cases in the city that winter. Dreiser found these cases horrible to think about, but once more he concluded that such things must be:

> It is only the unfit who fail — who suffer and die. . . .
> They are unfit, because, unlike the fit ones, they lack these peculiarities which aid one to survive. They are too shy to complain openly, too thin-skinned to endure pity, too fearful of public opinion to seek refuge in a workhouse, and too timid and weak-bodied to risk seizing what is not their own.

Then followed one prophetic sentence: "In this world generally failure opens wide the gates to mortal onslaught, and the invariable result is death."

After two years with *Ev'ry Month*, Dreiser had become sufficiently confident of his abilities to crack the magazine market to go back into free-lancing, where there was just as much money as in editing, and more chance to build a writing reputation. Between 1897 and 1899 he sold enough articles to warrant being included in the first edition of *Who's Who*. His most important work in this period was done for Orison Swett

Marden, who had launched in the same year that Dreiser quit *Ev'ry Month* a new magazine bearing the bluntly descriptive name of *Success*. Marden had had a spectacularly successful career as the manager and then the owner of a chain of hotels, but fires and overconfident investments had wiped him out in the mid-nineties. He instantly started out for the top again by writing a book of inspirational essays. *Pushing to the Front, or, Success under Difficulties* had a fabulous sale; together with its sequels, Marden's book sold three million copies by the end of the century. *Pushing to the Front* relied for its power upon concrete descriptions of the mental and moral qualities most necessary to success, as evinced in the lives of iron-willed great men. By this "uplifting, energizing, suggestive force" Marden hoped to "encourage, inspire, and stimulate boys and girls who long to be somebody and do something in the world, but feel that they have no chance in life."

With the money from his book sales, Marden started *Success*. The Marden magazine formula called for writers who would interview the great business, political and artistic leaders of America for the stories of their careers. Dreiser, already on record as to the value of reading about the lives of the great and the strong, was perfectly suited for Marden's scheme. Beginning with the third issue of the magazine, which published his interview with Edison, Dreiser went on to become Marden's key writer. In the first two years of *Success*, an article by Dreiser appeared almost on the average of once a month. Interested in the newly liberated American woman, Dreiser did a series for Marden on women in the arts; but his principal work consisted of interviews with business tycoons, inventors, actors, and writers, including Philip Armour, William Dean Howells, Marshall Field and Anthony

Hope. Dreiser, with his fascinated belief in luck, asked Carnegie if he did not consider that his early promotion to superintendent of the western division of the Pennsylvania Railroad had been "a matter of chance." (Carnegie replied adamantly, "Never.") Through Thomas A. Edison, Dreiser first came across an aspect of the success myth which had never before occurred to him, but which would eventually constitute one of the great problems in his novels — what happens to a person after he succeeds? Edison told Dreiser that he had come to hate the thought of the inventions he had completed, the products he had finished. He liked the process of working, but when the invention was "all done and is a success, I can't bear the sight of it. I haven't used a telephone in ten years, and I would go out of my way any day to miss an incandescent light. . . . I continue to find my greatest pleasure, and so my reward, in the work that precedes what the world calls success." In both *Sister Carrie* and the Cowperwood series Dreiser would have occasion to remember Edison's words.

Marden thought Dreiser's interviews so superior that he paid him the supreme compliment of pirating them for the inspirational books he continued to turn out. No acknowledgments, either by credit line or in cash, ever recorded the fact that *Talks with Great Workers* and *How They Succeeded: Life Stories of Successful Men Told by Themselves*, both of which appeared under Marden's name, were in large part written by a man who was totally unaware that they had even been published. Ironically, these books appeared and sold well at precisely the time when Dreiser, sick and broke, and despondent over the suppression of *Sister Carrie*, was sinking into poverty and the contemplation of suicide.

iii

The last two of his articles on women in the arts were appearing in *Success* when Dreiser sat down, in the fall of 1899, to write a novel about a woman who rises from obscurity to become a famous actress. What made the novel so different that it can be said to have inaugurated the twentieth century in American social fiction is exactly what outraged Mr. Doubleday's wife: the character of the heroine, Carrie Meeber.

If Neltje Blanchan had no use for her, Carrie has had, over the years, a host of friends. Dreiser himself was very fond of his "little soldier of fortune," his "half-equipped little knight," as he affectionately called her. Pretty, but not a great beauty, natively intelligent, but nothing more, a poor, inexperienced girl who feels so sorry for the downtrodden people she encounters in Chicago, and who is herself seduced and deceived by two city slickers, Carrie has caused two generations of critics to melt into tears at the thought of her.*

The critics, however, should have listened to Mrs. Doubleday and saved their grief, for Carrie herself never wastes any tears on anyone. The sorrow she expresses for the poor is highly abstract and is constantly betrayed by her ruthless social selection, motivated by her desire to get ahead. As for her seductions, they have fazed the critics more than they ever did Carrie — never once in the novel does sex have any emotional effect upon her, except insofar as it leads to an aug-

---

* E.g., Van Wyck Brooks, *The Confident Years: 1885–1915* (New York, 1952), 303; Alfred Kazin, "American Naturalism: Reflections From Another Era," *The American Writer and the European Tradition*, Margaret Denny and William H. Gilman, eds. (Minneapolis, 1950), 125.

mentation of her living standard. Like Dreiser himself, who once admitted that he had never loved anyone, and that fame and power were the only objects of his heart, Carrie is characterized by a singular coldness of temperament. The author's sympathy for his heroine was the sympathy of self-recognition, not of pity — as the grief-stricken critics have assumed; and the real significance of Dreiser's affectionate nicknames for Carrie is that they are military terms.

Approaching from a distance the "gates" of "the walled city," Dreiser's little knight is indeed on an expedition of war. For a soldier, the ability to make decisions is of the essence; although Carrie is young and green at the beginning of the novel, her instinct for the main chance is already unerring. When Drouet, the salesman, tries to pick her up on the train bound for Chicago, she allows him to have her name and address — not simply because he is good-looking, but because he is so marvelously dressed:

> A woman should some day write the complete philosophy of clothes. No matter how young, it is one of the things she wholly comprehends. There is an indescribably faint line in the matter of man's apparel which somehow divides for her those who are worth glancing at and those who are not.

In a foreshadowing of the climax of the novel, Dreiser added, "Once an individual has passed this faint line on the way downward he will get no glance from her."

Walking along the fashionable streets of Chicago, Carrie is overcome by the glittering theaters, fancy shops and opulent restaurants. Through these glimpses of high living, Carrie realizes "how much the city held — wealth, fashion, ease — every adornment for women, and she longed for dress and beauty with a whole heart." Nowhere else in the novel is her heart so wholly engaged as in this moment of her discovery of luxury.

As it did to Dreiser, Chicago at first drags Carrie down to the bottom. The best job she can get is in a shoe factory. (Her selective powers, however, do not desert her, even here. Just as Dreiser's mother had taught him to feel "immensely superior" to the "poor scum" their poverty forced them to associate with in Indiana, so Carrie, noting their poor clothes, rigorously avoids her fellow workers, never even addressing a word to them.) When she falls ill with a cold, she loses her job. Coatless, she wanders the downtown streets in the wintry weather, vainly looking for work; in a few more days, she realizes, she will be compelled to give up and go back to her parents' home — a place to which Carrie, with her characteristic talent for cutting off previous associations with a ruthless finality, had hoped she would never have to return. Then, in a flash, luck strikes her; as Carrie is jostled by the crowd on the streets, Drouet suddenly stands before her. Recognizing her destitution, Drouet invites her to dinner and presents her with two "soft, green, handsome ten-dollar bills." The gift of the money leads Carrie to formulate the guiding principle of her life: "Money — something everybody has and I must get." Sizing up Drouet across the restaurant table, Carrie "felt that she liked him — that she could continue to like him ever so much. There was something even richer than that, running as a hidden strain, in her mind." The "hidden strain" is Carrie's unconscious realization that she can trade this man's desires for her own, her body for a life of fashion and ease. A few nights later she becomes his mistress.

"The most conspicuous characteristic of golddiggers," according to the evidence of psychoanalysis, is their emotional coldness. For them, feelings are something to be faked. They go through the act of sexual intercourse in a purely mechanical way. . . . The only time they show real emotion is when they are airing their grievances, complaining of how unjustly they are treated by others.

Thus, although Drouet buys her expensive clothes (all dressed up and looking at herself in the mirror, Carrie "caught her little red lip with her teeth and felt her first thrill of power") and establishes her in a nice apartment, Carrie is quickly dissatisfied.

When Drouet invites Hurstwood, the handsome, smooth manager of a well-known Chicago saloon, to accompany him and Carrie to the theater one evening, her dissatisfaction with the salesman immediately increases. When Hurstwood takes her out driving one afternoon along the fashionable North Side, the apartment Drouet had provided absolutely ceases to interest her. Looking over the fashion plate Hurstwood, she asks herself, "What, after all, was Drouet?"

Hurstwood's personality is a good deal like Carrie's. Shifty and clever, Hurstwood treats the men who patronize his saloon according to his estimation of their financial and social standing. Carrie has turned her back on her family and he wishes he could do the same; between Hurstwood and his wife there runs "a river of indifference," and he has no interest whatsoever in his two social-climbing children. Neither Hurstwood nor Carrie at any time throughout their long relationship feels any love for the other. He is attracted to her because she is physically desirable and hard to get, and Carrie is drawn to him because of his manners, his clothes and his obvious affluence. Beyond their exploitative calculations, there is nothing.

The coldness of Hurstwood's and Carrie's personalities, as contrasted with the warmth of Drouet's, is conveyed in the scene when the three of them again go to see a play together. Emerging from the theater, Carrie and Hurstwood are too busy talking to notice a beggar on the sidewalk pleading for the price of a bed. The generous, foolish Drouet, however, stops and hands him a dime, "with an upwelling feeling of pity in his heart." Hurstwood "scarcely noticed the incident, Carrie quickly forgot."

Deciding to make a break once and for all with his past, Hurstwood steals ten thousand dollars from the saloon safe and, by telling Carrie a series of lies, persuades her to go with him to New York. Stopping briefly in Montreal they are married, at Carrie's insistence. The coldness of both of them is never more manifest than at their marriage. "There was no great passion in her, but the drift of things and this man's proximity created a semblance of affection"; as for Hurstwood, he consents to the ceremony even though he knows (as she apparently does not) that it is bigamy.

Manhattan excites Carrie, but it distresses Hurstwood. He tries at first to hide his disquiet by a great show of his former aggressiveness, but whereas he had risen easily in Chicago, in New York he is unable to get started. His initiative and buoyancy desert him; just forty-three, he feels suddenly old. "The disease of brooding was beginning to claim him. Only the newspapers and his own thoughts were worth while." The same inexplicable paralysis of the will grips the former saloon manager as had seized Dreiser's own father. Hurstwood's decline becomes ever more swift and steep, for in a success society "the road downward has but few landings and level places."

New York has meanwhile been teaching Carrie dissatisfaction with her life with Hurstwood. A visit to the theater with a woman friend makes the apartment in which she and Hurstwood live seem a "commonplace thing." Dinner at Sherry's awakens her to the realization of "what a wonderful thing it was to be rich." As they grow poorer instead of richer, Carrie is "revolted," and she soon finds it impossible to regard Hurstwood any longer as her lover and husband. When he ceases even to pretend to look for work and sits around the house unshaved and in his old clothes reading the morning newspapers, she withdraws her sexual favors.

Carrie's refusal to sleep with Hurstwood marks only the beginning of his punishment at her hands. While Hurstwood tries and fails to find employment as a bartender, Carrie obtains a job as a chorus girl and soon thereafter wins a speaking part in a comic opera. Wishing "more and more that Hurstwood was not in the way," she throws her success in his face and lets herself be asked for household money before offering any. A few months later she deserts him; after a time she scarcely remembers him.

With a salary of one hundred and fifty dollars a week, a star dressing room, her picture in the magazines, a suite in a fashionable new hotel and expensive clothes, Dreiser's little knight finally enters through the "splendid gates" into the "walled city" of her dreams. The gates are opening for Hurstwood, too, but they are the dark portals to which Dreiser had referred in his *Ev'ry Month* editorial: "In this world generally failure opens wide the gates to mortal onslaught, and the invariable result is death." Living in a Bowery fleabag, suffering from hallucinations, Hurstwood barely manages to stay alive on the thin wages he receives as a handyman in a hotel basement. When pneumonia forces him to quit his job, Hurstwood has finally reached the point which Carrie had when Drouet ap-

32

peared to change her luck; in his hour of desperation Hurst-wood turns to Carrie for help. But in the grim warfare of their relationship neither Carrie nor Hurstwood had ever asked for quarter or given it, and it is too late to change. When he ac-costs her outside the theater where she is starring and begs for money, Carrie vouchsafes him all of nine dollars — eleven less than Drouet had given to the destitute Carrie years before.

Finally, "one day, in the middle of winter, the sharpest spell of the season set in." The icy nightmare of snow and freezing winds, which always haunted Dreiser's imagination, brings Hurstwood to the decision to kill himself. Heading for the Bowery and a cheap room where he can turn on the gas and lie down in the darkness, he passes Broadway and Thirty-ninth Street for one last look at Carrie's name blazing "in in-candescent fire" on the theater marquee. Through the heavily falling snow he makes his way down Fifth Avenue; in front of the Waldorf he slips in the wet snow and falls down. It is the hotel where Carrie lives. Dreiser's juxtaposition of Hurstwood prostrate in the slush of the street outside the blazing pin-nacle of Carrie's palatial hotel is appallingly unsubtle, but it pierces to the heart of his vision of American life.

Failure meant the Bowery and suicide; success meant the Waldorf — and one thing more. In her luxurious suite amidst all the things for which she has yearned, Carrie is bored and lonely. The realization of her dreams is somehow not as excit-ing as she had expected. Dreiser was unable, consciously, to say why this was so; he recorded Carrie's feelings, but he could not dredge to the surface of the novel any satisfactory explanation for them. All Dreiser was able to say in regard to her dissatisfaction was that Carrie has recently been told by a man she greatly respects that she should not be wasting her time in comedy, that true happiness for her lies beyond in the realm of — comedy-drama! The argument can be made that Dreiser's instinctive knowledge of his heroine led him to describe quite accurately an attitude of mind which he did not consciously understand, but which psychoanalysis explains is notably characteristic of golddiggers, namely, that they are "invariably severely neurotic . . . capable of achieving their conscious aim temporarily, only to find themselves depressed, dissatisfied, bored. . . ." But there is a sociological as well as a psychological explanation of Carrie's attitude, for which Dreiser himself supplied an important clue, although he was quite unable to apply it to the mystery of her behavior. In describing his bored heroine in her Waldorf apartment, Dreiser showed Carrie yawning over a copy of Balzac's *Père Goriot*.

Dreiser had read several volumes of *The Human Comedy* in the mid-nineties and had been tremendously excited by them. In Balzac's panorama of Paris, "a thoroughly amoral world in which greed and interest are 'squatting in every corner' and where money-values alone prevail," Dreiser encountered a vision of life very much akin to his own, while in the aspirations of Balzac's heroes to move up in the world Dreiser saw the reflection of his own hopes. Sister Carrie's career in some ways resembles that of the poor but handsome student, Eugène de Rastignac, the hero of *Père Goriot* — but there is one crucial difference between them. Rastignac, like Carrie, burns with a single overwhelming ambition: "Parvenir! *parvenir à tout prix*." Literally, success and *parvenir* are the same word, but the similarity breaks down on the functional level. When Dreiser's heroine reaches the Waldorf, she has reached the top of the American success ladder; but for Rastignac there is another entire range of success beyond the attainment of wealth — the dazzlingly complex, labyrinthine world of French society. Whether, in Balzac's words, Rastignac rends his way through the crowd like a cannon ball or creeps through it silently like a pestilence, his journey to the top will be a long one, and every day will be new and different. Whatever else he may feel, the hazards of the morrow will keep him from being bored, a fact which unlocks the mystery of Carrie's depression. Dreiser's heroine, to whom all of life was "dreaming wild dreams of some vague, far-off supremacy," wakes up at the end of the novel to find the word made flesh, the wild dreams become reality, but somehow it is an anticlimax — as Alexis de Tocqueville had observed a generation before Carrie was born, the charm of life to Americans consisted in *anticipated* success. If success in America meant something more than glittering hotels and expensive clothes, then the drama of yearning and struggling for the goal beyond could of course continue, and Carrie could find again the charm of anticipation that had made her life exciting. In democratically monotonous America, however, there is no vista of success beyond wealth, simply no equivalent occasion for the exciting adventures of a Rastignac. Like Edison, who hated the sight of a telephone, Carrie found process all, completion nothing; the Waldorf was incomprehensibly dull, and there was no other success image capable of re-engaging her dreams; she turned the pages of *Père Goriot,* and yawned, and was all the more dissatisfied.

iv

There is an island surrounded by rivers, and about it the tide scurries fast and deep. It is a beautiful island, long, narrow, magnificently populated, and with such a wealth of life and interest as no island in the whole world before has ever possessed . . .

And such waters! How green they look, how graceful, how mysterious! From far seas they come — strange, errant, peculiar waters — prying along the shores of the magnificent island; sucking and sipping at the rocks which form its walls; whispering and gurgling about the docks and piers, and flowing, flowing, flowing. . . . Here, when the great struggle has been ended, when the years have slipped by and the hopes of youth have not been realized; when the dreams of fortune, the delights of tenderness, the bliss of love and the hopes of peace have all been abandoned — the weary heart may come and find surcease. Peace in the waters, rest in the depths and the silence of the hurrying tide; surcease and an end in the chalice of the waters which wash the shores of the beautiful island.

Dreiser went down to the East River in the spring of 1903 to drown himself. Unable, ever since the suppression of *Sister Carrie*, to do any kind of sustained writing, he had slipped slowly and agonizingly into grinding poverty. Separated from his wife, and shunning contact with friends because of his shame over his shabby appearance, Dreiser gave up his small Manhattan apartment and sought lodging in a dollar-and-a-half-a-week room in Brooklyn. Uncannily, he began to re-enact Hurstwood's last years. In the winter of 1903 he thought of applying for work with a streetcar company, but found he was too weak. He began to suffer from hallucinations; everything appeared crooked and he had to keep turning in a circle to the right in an effort to restore the world to its proper alignment. He was, he knew, a complete and utter failure; the decision to kill himself followed from this. Only at the last minute, as he walked beside the chalice of the waters, did Dreiser change his mind.

After finishing *Sister Carrie*, Dreiser had begun a second novel. Put aside and taken up again several times across these

36

three years of failure, *Jennie Gerhardt* was abandoned altogether when Dreiser began to be plagued by hallucinations.
The novel lay fallow for seven years.

The man who brought *Jennie Gerhardt* to completion in
1910 was very different from the underweight, shabbily
dressed failure who had begun it. Seven years after his suicide
attempt, Dreiser looked down at the world through a rib-
boned pince-nez from an "enormous paneled office." Director
of the destinies of the Butterick "Trio" of magazines — the
Delineator, the *Designer* and *New Idea Woman's Magazine*
— his salary was ten thousand dollars a year. Sinclair Lewis,
noting that Dreiser wore waistcoats and that they were well
filled, said he looked "more like a wholesale hardware merchant than a properly hollow-cheeked realist."

From the day he walked away from the river, Dreiser had
gone up fast. A year after his near suicide he was fiction editor
of Street and Smith's *Popular Magazine.* Working for the publishers of the Alger stories, Dreiser was in his element. The
head of the firm was so impressed that he made Dreiser editor of *Smith's Magazine.*

Jumping from job to job, Dreiser leapfrogged toward a five-
figure income. After a year as editor of *Smith's,* he resigned to
become managing editor of the *Broadway Magazine,* where he
also remained for a year (during which time he at last found
an American publisher for *Sister Carrie*). Disagreeing with
the owner's desire to publish such popular stuff as muckraking
exposés of business corporations, Dreiser quit and went to
work for Butterick. Although running three magazines at once,
Dreiser was a very good editor; he increased circulation, beat
down a typographical union which wanted recognition and
built up a capable staff of writers. As much of a sucker as
Mark Twain had been for get-rich-quick schemes, Dreiser

invested his ample bank balance in such varied enterprises as apple orchards in the Yakima Valley, and real
estate in upstate New York. Always on the lookout for a
publishing deal, he considered plans for a daily, four-page
penny digest of the news and for a series of seventy-five cent
books.

The decision as to whether or not Dreiser would ever resume his writing was made for him. A combination of
quarrels with the publishers and an office scandal which developed when it became known that Dreiser (still married,
albeit unhappily) was having an affair with the daughter of a
woman who worked for the Butterick organization forced him
out of his job. Moving into a studio overlooking Riverside
Drive, Dreiser picked up the uncompleted manuscript of
Jennie Gerhardt. He finished it just to see what happened. "If
there is no money in the game," he wrote to his friend H. L.
Mencken, "I [am] going to run a weekly."

Mencken, who felt that *Sister Carrie* contained two distinct
plots (he failed to see that Hurstwood's and Carrie's careers
were both integral aspects of the same up-and-down process),
has said that Dreiser's first novel suffers from a "broken back."
Actually, it is *Jennie Gerhardt* which has the broken back, the
result of having been begun in desperation and finished in
complacence. The writer who conceived the novel believed
that life was a meaningless struggle in which man fought to
stay alive for his brief span and then died. Because of the
overwhelming nature of the struggle, man had a desperate
need — in his cheap room in Brooklyn, Dreiser knew just how
desperate — for comfort and reassurance. In the year of his
failure, Dreiser created Jennie Gerhardt, the antisuccess heroine, a woman who, like Dreiser's own mother — on whom
Jennie is based in part — could be a refuge for those fallen in

the struggle. The man who in 1910 brought *Jennie Gerhardt*
to a conclusion was cocksure that the world was an oyster
ready to be eaten.

Jennie as we first see her is, like Carrie, eighteen years old,
poor, and pretty. As a person, however, she is everything that
Carrie was not — generous, unselfish, warm, and possessed of
a sense of the possibility of a life of dignity in the face of poverty and disaster. As Carrie had been, Jennie is seduced by a
man of the world, but the *quid pro quo* which she seeks is not
clothes and money, but his influence to get her brother out of
jail. When her seducer suddenly dies, Jennie is left to bear
his child. Instead, however, of abandoning the baby, Jennie
finds serene fulfillment in caring for it.

Going out to work as a maid in order to help pay the bills at
home (her father is out of work), Jennie encounters a rich
young man named Lester Kane in the mansion where she is
employed. He is attracted to Jennie and persuades her to go
to Chicago with him where he sets her up in an apartment.
As the novel was originally planned, Jennie and Lester were
to marry, but as Dreiser looked at the novel from the stand-
point of Riverside Drive and 1910, he decided this would not
do. He had lost interest in Jennie and now wanted to write
only about Lester Kane.

Lester is the younger of two sons of Archibald Kane, a wonderfully vigorous old man who has "amassed a tremendous
fortune, not by grabbing and browbeating and unfair methods, but by seeing a big need and filling it." The older son,
Robert, is a rigid, hard-working machine of a man, good at
making profits but nothing else — the kind of successful
American businessman who in Dreiser's opinion was most
thoroughly represented by John D. Rockefeller. To an extent,
Dreiser admired the oil billionaire: "John D. knew how to out-

plot the best of them." But he disliked Rockefeller's narrowness and frugality and despised his Puritanic standards of art and morality. "As an individual, well, if he weren't intellectually and artistically so dull I could forgive him everything." Lester Kane combines the force of his father with a colorfulness that his brother and Rockefeller lacked. "Strong, hairy, axiomatic, and witty," Lester has a Rabelaisian appetite for good food and beautiful objects. Social conventions mean nothing to him — his motto is, "Hew to the line, let the chips fall where they may."

In order to concentrate on Lester and let Jennie slip into the background, Dreiser had to split up their relationship entirely. To do so, he was forced temporarily to violate the character of Lester as he had established it. Always a shrewd and resourceful businessman, Lester suddenly begins to lose money in financial deals and to fall far behind his robot brother in "the game of life." The scorner of all conventions is bothered equally suddenly by society's disapproval of his arrangement with Jennie. Succumbing to these social and economic pressures, Lester decides to leave Jennie.

"During the year or two which followed the breaking of his relationship with Jennie, a curious rejuvenation in the social and business spirit of Lester took place." With this sentence, Dreiser repaired the personality he had put asunder and focused all his attention on him. Lester becomes the director of nine of "the most important financial and commercial organizations of the West"; he marries a beautiful and dashing widow of his own social class; he — but now the novel had begun to run away with Dreiser. His interest in Lester Kane was making off with the book entitled *Jennie Gerhardt,* while the theme of the overwhelming nature of life had given way to a celebration of power.

So that he might stop dead in his tracks, Dreiser committed two calculated murders. As the novel was originally planned, it was not envisaged that Jennie's child should die, but in the revised version the child contracts typhoid fever and swiftly succumbs. The effect of this incident is to give the latter phases of Jennie's story a "poignancy" which the "original tone demanded but which [Dreiser] had not been able to maintain." To generate reader-sympathy for Jennie — a sympathy which he no longer shared — Dreiser simply killed off her little girl. To conclude as quickly as possible his increasingly disproportionate concentration on Lester, he killed him off as well. With the same abruptness that had characterized the child's sickness, Lester gets fat and sluggish; the curative waters of two continents are of no help and he falls mortally ill.

By means of this twin killing, Dreiser brought the novel to an end with some semblance of unity with its beginning. Jennie is reunited with the dying Lester long enough for him to tell her she is the only woman he ever loved; later, at his funeral, she sits humbly and unrecognized in the back of the church. An incorrigible homebody, Jennie has adopted two orphans to whom her life from now on will be dedicated. Like the heroines of Willa Cather of whom she is the forerunner, Jennie has constructed a mystique out of doing the dishes and raising children. Life is meaningless, but she accepts it all, in generous embrace. Although spuriously achieved, the tone of the novel's conclusion is consonant with its beginning and Dreiser's real attitude toward life is nowhere in sight. The book sold better than *Carrie* had, and Mencken thought it, with the single exception of *Huckleberry Finn*, "the best American novel ever done," but Dreiser himself was glad to be done with mystical acceptances and the qualities of sweet-

41

ness and mercy. Not for thirty years would he return to the original theme of *Jennie Gerhardt.*

Even while he was impatiently engaged in finishing *Jennie,* ideas for four other novels were boiling in Dreiser's brain — a three-volume study of the American business hero and a portrait of the artist. The trilogy was to be based on the career of a well-known American businessman, while the artist's portrait was to be palpably autobiographical, but in fact the heroes are essentially the same; both Frank Cowperwood of *The Financier, The Titan* and *The Stoic* and Eugene Witla of *The "Genius"* are full-scale embodiments of all that Dreiser had started to express through the character of Lester Kane.

Cowperwood and Witla, the business titan and the artist genius, are lonely individualists, cold of heart, like Carrie, but greatly exceeding Dreiser's first heroine in their ruthlessness of purpose and their will to power. Since his own considerable worldly success Dreiser had reversed his opinion as to the relative importance of pluck and luck — now he agreed with Carnegie that pluckiness was all. "That which places one being over another," Dreiser wrote, "and sets differences between man and man is . . . intellect . . . plus, other things being equal, the vital energy to apply them or the hypnotic power of attracting attention to them." Dreiser's heroes are lucky, too, but their possession of brains, energy and hypnotic power is what counts supremely. They occupy a superior position in regard to the rest of society because they are in fact superior. Cowperwood and Witla are, in sum, American versions of the Nietzschean superman.

Dreiser had not, before he wrote either *The "Genius"* or the business novels, read Nietzsche, but Mencken had sent him a copy of the book which he had written on the German philosopher and Dreiser had devoured it with great excitement. He and Nietzsche, he wrote to Mencken after finishing it, were "hale fellows well met."

Through Mencken's book, Dreiser learned that Nietzsche admired "the proud, stiff-necked hero who held his balance in the face of both seductive pleasure and staggering pain; who cultivated within himself a sublime indifference, so that happiness and misery, to him, became mere words, and no catastrophe, human or superhuman could affright or daunt him." In Nietzsche's eyes, according to Mencken, there were two classes, the slave class and the "small, alert, iconoclastic, immoral progressive master class." By an absurd code of morality, the slave class attempted to define as immoral any man

> who seeks power and eminence and riches — the millionaire, the robber, the fighter, the schemer. The act of acquiring property by conquest — which is looked upon as a matter of course by master-morality — becomes a crime and is called theft. The act of mating in obedience to natural impulses, without considering the desire of others, becomes adultery. . . .

The superman's proper attitude toward morality is one of defiance. He does not recognize slave values — he transvalues them. The target of slave pressure to conform, the superman takes as his motto, "Be hard!" The impact on Dreiser of the Menckenized Nietzsche is abundantly evident in his conception of both Witla and Cowperwood.

The "Genius" is a thinly veiled account of Dreiser's own life rendered in Nietzschean hard-guy tough talk. Eugene Witla, whose journey from a small Midwestern town to Chicago to New York paralleled Dreiser's own, is a painter. Because he is an artist, Witla is "not really subject to the ordinary conventions of life." For quite some time, however, he finds it difficult to live up to this "anarchistic" creed. He feels an "eager desire to tear wealth and fame from the bosom of the world. Life must give him his share. If it did not he would curse it to his dying day" — but he does not know how to do so. His pictures sell only indifferently well and he becomes depressed.

His sex life has an even worse effect. Possessed of an "insatiable" appetite, he finds the stress of his innumerable love affairs so intolerable as to "make life itself seem unimportant and death a relief." Finally, he has a nervous breakdown. Emerging from the shadow of death, he exploits his artistic ability solely to make money. His first job is in the art department of the *New York World*. "Surrounded by other men who were as sharp as knives," Eugene realizes that he must become "ruthless, superior, indifferent," or perish.

His appointment as art director of an advertising agency marks the turning point: "From a lean, pale, artistic soul, wearing a soft hat, he . . . straightened up and filled out until . . . he looked more like a businessman than an artist." Within a few years he has risen to the post of managing publisher of a string of magazines, is earning twelve thousand dollars a year and has a "very sumptuous studio apartment" overlooking Riverside Drive. If, however, Witla has become superiorly indifferent to the competition of the business world, he is still unable to control his love life. His domineering wife refuses to release him from the "dreary pit" of matrimony; at work, he is emotionally buffeted by an affair with a passionate girl. Unable to dominate the situation, Witla is powerless to prevent the scandal which costs him his job.

But with the loss of his position, Witla is at last "tempered for life and work." Completely hard, he turns again to his painting and in no time becomes a famous artist. His wife dead, he resumes relations with his erstwhile mistress, but this

44

THEODORE DREISER: THE MAN OF ICE

time he is in complete control, grinding her "under the heel of his intellectuality. . . . Now never again, should love affect him." He is "hardened intellectually and emotionally."

In addition to its basically Nietzschean tone, there is, in *The "Genius,"* a certain flavor of Mary Baker Eddy. Throughout his life, Dreiser was fascinated by Christian Science. He urged people he knew to adopt it, he was fond of talking about it, and many of his books contain either quotations from *Science and Health* or references to Mrs. Eddy. In *A Hoosier Holiday*, for instance, Christian Science "somehow hung over" Dreiser's trip back to Indiana. Eugene Witla completes the transformation of himself into a man of steel in the crucial period following his dismissal from his magazine directorship by reading *Science and Health* and by visiting a Christian Science practitioner who cures him of "Failure." The one paragraph from *Science and Health* which sticks in Witla's mind furnishes the explanation as to why Dreiser was interested simultaneously in Nietzsche and Mrs. Eddy:

> Become conscious for a single moment that life and intelligence are purely spiritual, neither in nor of matter, and the body will utter no complaints. If suffering from a belief in sickness, you will find yourself suddenly well. Sorrow is turned into joy when the body is controlled by spiritual life and love.

The Nietzschean superman, who realizes all struggle is eventually in vain, but whose superhuman immunity to all emotion, to all ideas of pleasure and pain, prevents him from ever being daunted, is quite close to the Christian Scientist's denial of pain. Buffeted by society and by his own emotions in his pursuit of sex and money, Witla finds Mrs. Eddy's spiritualizations as effective an instrument of his ambitions as the philosophy of the superman.

45

In Dreiser's favorite character, Frank Cowperwood, the influence of Nietzsche and Mrs. Eddy are readily discerned, but they play second fiddle to still another philosophy, one which Mrs. Eddy had denounced as leading to "moral and physical death," as "mental diabolism," in short, as "malicious animal magnetism."

Mencken had pointed out to Dreiser that "Nietzsche had read Emerson in his youth, and those Emersonian seeds which have come to full flower in the United States as the so-called New Thought movement — with Christian Science, osteopathy, mental telepathy, occultism, pseudo-psychology and that grand lodge of credulous *comiques,* the Society for Psychical Research, as its final blossoms — all of this probably made its mark on the philosopher of the superman, too." Despite Mencken's scornful attitude, this passage probably interested Dreiser as much as Mencken's ecstasies over the master race. For Dreiser was a thorough believer in the principles of New Thought; if he and the Menckenized Nietzsche were hale fellows well met, it was on this ground above all that they saw eye to eye.

New Thought came out of Emerson and out of the mesmerism of P. P. Quimby, on whom Mrs. Eddy had drawn so heavily. Recognizing the existence of matter, as Christian Science did not, New Thought held that matter could be spiritualized and dominated by thought (which was defined not as thinking, but as "mystical power"). "Not a church but a system of mental telepathy, which anyone might practice regardless of his creed," the disciples of New Thought gathered together throughout the country in informal "centers." The movement interested thousands, who were attracted to it largely because of New Thought's emphasis on prosperity. If through New Thought you knew how to "Make Your Mind A Mental

Mazda," you could read other people's minds, control their actions, make yourself a million. Dreiser's old boss Orison Swett Marden, with his emphasis on character and the power of the individual will, came naturally to be an advocate of New Thought, and by 1910 his books were beginning to reflect its doctrines. Marden's *Prosperity. How to Attract It* is typical of New Thought's equation of magnetism and money.

Dreiser's entire life had prepared him to accept the axioms of New Thought. From the moment of his birth, which had been attended, so his parents later told him, by three graces, Dreiser's family life was grounded in superstition. Portents, omens, prophecies were depended upon by both his mother and father for guidance, to the extent that when Dreiser fell ill with some childhood disease they called in a witch doctress who lived in the neighborhood to minister to him.

The son was the child of his parents. In his adolescence, Dreiser's aunt told him his fortune, which, he later remarked, "haunted me for a long time and which has since largely been realized." As a grown man, Dreiser consulted palmists, Ouija boards and soothsayers for advice on problems ranging from his personal life to which side was going to win World War I. Convinced that knowledge, direction, and control of life were within the grasp of the strongminded individual, Dreiser in his editorial days — it was the very time he was reading Mencken's *Nietzsche* — urged that some reputable spiritualist hold a test séance before "scientists, college professors, and newspapermen," so that everyone could become as convinced as he was. In the opinion of his widow, Dreiser "was a mystic, first, last and always."

His general susceptibility to spiritualism aside, Dreiser had

47

two unforgettable telepathic experiences during his young manhood which were responsible for his belief in mental magnetism. The first occurred when his mother died. Falling ill in the summer of 1890, she stubbornly hung on to life for some months, but one day, as Dreiser was helping her out of bed to the toilet, she suddenly

> slipped to the rug at the side of the bed, relaxed, very weak and pale, and then looked at me, at first with such sickly and weary eyes, a most exhausted and worn look. But in almost the same moment, as I noticed — in a trice, no more — a, to me, mystic thing appeared or took place. Her eyes cleared — that muggy yellowness that was in them before, gone, and as instantly and in its place a clear, intelligent, healthy light, quite remarkable and most arresting to me, even startling. For now it looked as though she were thinking or trying to say something to me, but through her eyes alone. But only for a second or two, and then, as suddenly, a heavy, grey dullness once more, almost fishy and unintelligent, and then complete blankness, no light or fire at all. And all was over.

From that moment, Dreiser believed in the mysterious power of the eye, the ineluctable modality of the visible. The eye could hypnotize, communicate, dissimulate, discern at will — if one had the power of will. The implications such power might have for the battle for success did not occur to Dreiser until a few years later, but the "mystic thing" which had passed from his mother's eyes to his was the rock on which he built his faith in mental telepathy.

The second of his two great experiences took place while Dreiser was a newspaperman in St. Louis. J. Alexander McIvor Tyndall, a famous mindreader, came to town and, wishing to get some free publicity, asked Dreiser's paper to appoint a man to ride with him in a carriage through the center of the city. Tyndall, blindfolded but driving, would attempt to follow the directing thoughts of the man on the seat beside him. Dreiser was the man appointed. Sitting beside the mind-reader, Dreiser thought of the house of a friend, of a particular room in the house, of a wardrobe in the room, of an object on top of the wardrobe. Driving pell-mell through crowded streets, the blindfolded Tyndall raced unerringly to the house, dashed into the room and dramatically lifted down the correct object. The climax of this event was capped that evening at the opera house, where Dreiser was sent by his newspaper to cover a contest between Tyndall and a rival medium, Jules Wallace. The high moment came when, as Tyndall was endeavoring to pick up someone's thought currents, Wallace suddenly stepped forward, "appeared to go into a trance, and with a demonic glare brought about Tyndall's complete physical collapse. The lights had to be turned out to quell the uproar that ensued. . . ."

The two episodes combined to impress Dreiser enormously. The whole thing

> astounded me and caused me to ponder the mysteries of life more than ever. . . . It gave me an immense kick mentally, one that stays by me to this day, and set me off eventually on the matters of psychology and chemic mysteries generally. . . . Once and for all, it cleared up my thoughts as to the power of mind over so-called matter.

All subsequent experience merely confirmed him in his conviction. He and some of his newspaper friends entered upon some mental experiments of their own with hypnotism and spiritualism "until we were fairly well satisfied as to the import of these things," while George du Maurier's story of Trilby and Svengali "had a strange psychologic effect" on

Dreiser when he read the novel a year or so after the Tyndall-Wallace affair.

Evidences of Dreiser's faith in these matters occur in his fiction from beginning to end. Several of his short stories are concerned with hallucination and hypnosis and the correlation between these phenomena and the winning of wealth and women. In *Sister Carrie* and *Jennie Gerhardt*, Dreiser dramatized sexual conquest almost completely in terms of mental magnetism and hypnotic eyepower. Thus when Drouet, who has "daring and magnetism," first accosts Carrie on the train, all the while he is talking to her he is "looking steadily into her eyes." At their first dinner together, "every little while her eyes would meet his, and by that means the interchanging current of feeling would be fully connected." Hurstwood, manager of a saloon frequented, as Dreiser made a point of remarking, by the mindreader Jules Wallace, has eyes of "cold make-believe." Wishing to win Carrie's confidence at their first meeting, Hurstwood takes back "the shifty, clever gleam" in his eyes and replaces it "with one of innocence." In their first evening at the theater, Carrie decides Hurstwood is the superior of the two men after having looked in his eyes "several times." Hurstwood's failure both as businessman and as lover is foretold when his eye loses "that buoyant searching shrewdness which had [formerly] characterized it."

Jennie Gerhardt, confronted by the intellectual, defiant figure of Lester Kane, is helpless before his gaze. He seduces her almost with a glance:

> He looked into her big soft-blue eyes with his dark, vigorous brown ones. A flash that was hypnotic, significant, insistent passed between them.
> "You belong to me," he said, "I've been looking for you. When can I see you?"

"Oh, you mustn't," she said, her fingers going nervously to her lips. "I can't see you — I — I —"

"Oh, I mustn't, mustn't I? Look here" — he took her arm and drew her slightly closer — "you and I might as well understand each other right now. I like you. Do you like me? Say?"

She looked at him, her eyes wide, filled with wonder, with fear, with a growing terror.

"I don't know," she gasped, her lips dry.

"Do you?" He fixed her grimly, firmly with his eyes.

"I don't know."

"Look at me," he said.

"Yes," she replied.

Like "a bird in the grasp of a cat" was Dreiser's admiring comment on this scene.

But it is the colossal figure of Frank Cowperwood who is the grand illustration in Dreiser's work of the power of the individual mind and will. He is the Nietzschean hard guy, the sexual Svengali and the Mental Mazda who magnetizes his way to millions, all rolled into one. Dreiser's "rebellious Lucifer . . . glorious in his sombre conception of the value of power," is basically an Alger hero, but with all the modern twists.

Frank Algernon Cowperwood is the son of a Philadelphia bank clerk whose mild and cautious character can be told at once from looking at his "vague grayish-green eyes." Cowperwood's father is prosperous, but he lacks "the two things that are necessary for distinction in any field — magnetism and vision."

Cowperwood, however, possesses these qualities in superabundance, a fact which can also be told by looking at his "large, clear gray eyes." (Occasionally, Dreiser described Cowperwood's eyes as blue, but most of the time he compromised by saying they were blue-gray — the same color eyes, significantly, as he himself had.)*

The young Cowperwood does not care for books; he acquires his education in another way. In probably the best-known episode in *The Financier*, Cowperwood visits the tank at the fish market for the source of all the knowledge he will ever need. The lesson he learns from watching the death struggle of a lobster and a squid which have been put into the tank "stayed with him all his life." The lobster's slow but inexorable destruction of the squid impresses Cowperwood for two reasons: first, because of its Darwinian lesson as to the bloody nature of the universe; and secondly, because it is a New Thought allegory on the conditions for success in such a world, where only the fittest survive.

"The lobster lay at the bottom of the clear glass tank on the yellow sand, apparently seeing nothing — you could not tell in which way his beady, black buttons of eyes were looking — but apparently they were never off the body of the squid . . . for by degrees small portions of [the squid's] body began to disappear, snapped off by the relentless claws of his pursuer." The squid, in turn, attempts to hide from the lobster's gaze by darting away and "shooting out at the same time a cloud of ink, behind which it would disappear." When the squid's ink bag is finally exhausted, the lobster closes in, "looking at him all the time," and devours the helpless squid. The entire battle, Dreiser remarked in a loaded phrase, "cleared things up considerably" for Cowperwood.

Having learned his lesson early, Cowperwood moves out into the warring world at the age of thirteen. He is a success

* According to his secretary, William Lengel, Dreiser's eyes were "a curious gray-blue." His mother's and his brother Paul's eyes were the same color.

right from the start. An auctioneer who has "an incisive eye" is "impressed by the boy's peculiar eye" and recognizes his bids on some cases of soap, which Cowperwood promptly resells at a profit. By his junior year in high school, he is making too much money to afford to remain a student and drops out. Applying for work in a commission house, he is hired because his eye is "so bright, and yet so inscrutable." The company's books, on which Cowperwood is assigned to work, are fairly complicated, but they prove to be "child's play to Frank."

For, like Alger's heroes, Cowperwood has been born old. Not only does he achieve business success in his nonage, but the only women in whom he has any interest are older than he. When Cowperwood is nineteen he meets a married woman, Lillian Semple, five years his senior. She, too, is a crucial part of his education. As we are told seven times in the course of the first four pages of the novel which concern her, Lillian Semple is "artistic"; like the lobster who had enlightened Cowperwood's business vision, she "cleared up certain of his ideas in regard to women." Henceforward, his will to conquer includes artistic women as one of his goals.

By the time he meets Lillian, Cowperwood has shifted his operations from the commission business to the stock market. He quickly realizes the significance of mental magnetism in his new occupation. "If you had a big buying or selling order, it was vitally important that your emotions, feeling, or subtlest thought should, by no trick of thought transference, telepathy, facial expression, or unguarded mood on your part be conveyed to any other person." Some men on the exchange are "psychic — clairvoyant," but Cowperwood is soon the mastermind of them all.

Eventually he marries the widowed Lillian Semple, not because he loves her, but because his stock-market successes now enable him to accumulate objects which he considers artistic. He sires two children — "because he liked it, the idea of self-duplication. It was almost acquisitive, the thought." Once they are acquired, however, he loses all interest in his son and daughter and they are almost never mentioned again in the vast length of the trilogy. Because "art from the very first fascinated him," Cowperwood sets out to amass a collection of paintings and sculpture with the same deliberateness with which he had collected his wife and children.

At this point, only one sixth of the way through the first novel, Cowperwood's mature personality is set. Magnetic, affluent, "physically urgent," "artistically minded" and utterly cold, he is Dreiser's most fully developed version of the hero whom he had adumbrated in the character of Lester Kane. "I satisfy myself" is Cowperwood's motto, and from here on until his death Cowperwood's life is dedicated to the proposition of more money, more paintings and more women, regardless of the consequences either to himself or to society.

Self-fulfillment through adultery begins with his affair with Aileen Butler, the beautiful daughter of one of Philadelphia's most powerful politicians. Realizing she is more artistic than his wife, Cowperwood decides he must have her as his mistress. While Aileen is a vivid, forceful personality in her own right (her eyes "were such a nice shade of blue-gray-blue"), Cowperwood magnetizes her into submission to him as easily as Kane had hypnotized the more passive Jennie.

Aileen's final submission to Cowperwood occurs one spring day when they have gone for a horseback ride through the countryside. Dismounting, they walk down to the bank of a tumbling stream.

"Baby mine," he said, "do you understand all about it?
Do you know exactly what you're doing when you come
with me in this way?"

"I think I do."

She struck her boot and looked at the ground, and then
up through the trees at the blue sky.

"Look at me, honey."

"I don't want to."

"But look at me, sweet. I want to ask you something."

"Don't make me, Frank, please, I can't."

"Oh yes, you can look at me."

"No."

She backed away as he took her hands, but came forward again, easily enough.

"Now look in my eyes."

"I can't."

"See here."

"I can't. Don't ask me. I'll answer you, but don't make
me look at you."

Magnetized, Aileen gives in to him.

All's fair in business as well as love; Cowperwood pulls
off his illicit financial deals in the same magnetic fashion in
which he has seduced Aileen. Deciding that the banking
house he now controls needs more money for its operations,
he cultivates the acquaintance of the city treasurer. Cowperwood has only to look at the man to realize he can
control him; soon he has magnetized the treasurer into
allowing him to use the city funds for his own financial
schemes.

The climax of *The Financier* involves a struggle for power
between Cowperwood and a politico-business alliance. For a
time Cowperwood believes he can beat the alliance, but
eventually he is convicted of misuse of city funds, forced to
surrender all his wealth and sent to jail. (When he is in-

carcerated, a bag is put over his head — the symbolic blinding of his omnipotent eyes.)

Freed after a short term, Cowperwood instantly attempts to exploit a financial panic, with the dual purpose of recouping his fortune and revenging himself on his enemies, who had profited from his ruin. Keeping his activities hidden, Cowperwood does not allow his opponents to suspect anything, then swiftly closes in, smashing them and winning another fortune for himself. On this triumphant note, the story ends.

Mencken, who read the novel in manuscript, liked *The Financier* well enough, but it did not compare in his eyes with the sequel, *The Titan*. Cowperwood in the former novel had not been completely hard — he had, after all, failed, the plot action had been more concerned with his rise to power than with his exercise of it, while despite his motto of self-indulgence, he had broken very few laws and committed adultery with only one woman. The Cowperwood of *The Financier*, Mencken said, was "still little more than an extra-pertinacious money-grubber and not unrelated to the average stockbroker or corner grocer." The Cowperwood of the second novel, however, the fabulous man who builds an enormous mansion and stocks it with art objects looted from two continents, who scores countless business victories and has mistresses by the dozen, and who is sublimely indifferent to the whips and goads of society ("a law unto himself," around whom other men swing "as planets around the sun"), was to Mencken "radiantly real," the "best picture of an immoralist in all modern literature."

Yet *The Titan* is a fabulous bore. The structure of the novel is, as the critic Stuart Sherman has remarked, "a sort of huge club-sandwich, composed of slices of business alternating with erotic episodes." The faster Cowperwood changes his money and his women, the duller the novel becomes. The locale of his operations shifts from Philadelphia to Chicago, where most of the action takes place, to Europe, then back to Chicago; at the end of the book Cowperwood is "rushing on to new struggles and new difficulties" in England. "Forever suffering the goad of a restless heart," Cowperwood eternally searches for new worlds to conquer. If, however, he can find "no ultimate peace," it is because of the absence, not the presence, of such worlds. The struggles and difficulties are always all too familiar, which is the reason for his restlessness — and the reader's boredom. As a superman, it is incumbent upon Cowperwood that he differentiate himself from the slave classes, that he "transvalue" the values of his society. But the character of American life itself conspires against him in this ambition. In a society collectively dedicated to the success myth, how in the world did an Alger hero go about shaking off his similarity to his surroundings?

If Dreiser had read between the lines of Mencken's *Nietzsche*, he could have foreseen the dramatic difficulties he would encounter with Cowperwood. Nietzsche's Utopia, in Mencken's account, is an ideal anarchy in which the supermen make their own laws at the dictates of their own desires. This was perhaps an accurate-enough rendering of Nietzsche's ideas, but when Mencken went on to say that this ideal anarchy would "insure the success of those men who were wisest mentally and strongest physically" he was not describing the *Übermensch* Utopia, but the world of Horatio Alger. The great irony of Mencken's book is that while Mencken despised grocers and stockbrokers, and used Nietzsche's philosophy to express his disgust, the success myth had colored his mind just as surely as it had the minds of the great mass of Americans against whom Mencken inveighed, with the result that when he distorted Nietzsche to accommodate the philosophy of the superman to his own way of thinking, Mencken was also making Nietzsche acceptable to any boob who had read the Alger stories.

Mencken was at least partially conscious of his predicament. When he asserted that "Nietzschean anarchy would create an aristocracy of efficiency" he hastened to add that the efficient aristocracy he had in mind was not what it sounded like to American ears. Distinctly, he said, he did not mean businessmen.

> It is an obvious fact that the men who go most violently counter to the view of the herd, and who battle most strenuously to prevail against it — our true criminals and transvaluers and breakers of the law — are not such men as Rockefeller, but men such as Pasteur; not such men as Morgan and Hooley, but sham-smashers and truth-tellers and mob-fighters after the type of Huxley, Lincoln, Bismarck, Darwin, Virchow, Haeckel, Hobbes, Machiavelli, Harvey and Jenner, the father of vaccination.

Lincoln, however, the only American Mencken could muster for his list, was the demigod of the American people; the boobs and the money-grubbers admired him as much as did Mencken; and Horatio Alger had written his most famous book, *From Log Cabin to White House,* about America's Great Transvaluer.

Finding it embarrassingly necessary to offer up a few more American examples of the superman, Mencken gave himself away completely when he admitted that "it is conceivable that a careful analysis might prove Mr. Morgan to be a [superman]" and justified the suggestion on the grounds that "it is evident that the man who, in the struggle for wealth and power, seizes a million dollars for himself, is appreciably more intelligent than the man who starves." What Mencken failed to add was that in a society dominated by the myth of success an aristocracy of millionaires not only did not "go most violently counter to the view of the herd," but was the perfect symbol of that society's highest aspirations.

In conceiving of Cowperwood, Dreiser chose as a model the robber baron Charles T. Yerkes, who had buccaneered his way to a traction fortune and whose collections of women and art were almost as notable as the size of his fortune. By choosing Yerkes rather than, say, Rockefeller, as his model, Dreiser tried to create in Cowperwood a protagonist who was more than just the dry-souled bookkeeper he and Mencken felt Rockefeller to be. In *The Titan*, Dreiser drew far loftier comparisons to Cowperwood than the Yerkes parallel in an attempt to heighten his hero's stature beyond that of a businessman. Cowperwood is a Prometheus, a Renaissance prince, a Hannibal, a Hamilcar Barca, a "great personage of the Elizabethan order," a "colossus," a "half-god or demi-gorgon." Dreiser constantly emphasized in both *The Financier* and *The Titan* that finance was not merely a business, but an art which "presents the operations of the subtlest of the intellectuals and of the egoists. Your true prince is primarily a financier as well as a statesman."

But try as Dreiser might, the unavoidable fact remained: an artistic titan was still, after all, just a corner grocer who had made good. Unfortunately for a would-be transvaluer in America, the difference between him and the rest of society was merely one of degree, not of kind. If Cowperwood is hounded by lesser businessmen and politicians, it is not because they are slaves attempting to make a master conform, but because, like Cowperwood, they are rival Alger heroes

59

competing in the race for the top. No matter how out-
rageously he acts, Cowperwood cannot gainsay the fact that
in a nation where there was only one morality — success —
and everyone dreamed of becoming a superman, the Nietzschean immoralist and sham-smasher was a victim of sociological unemployment. Cowperwood moves about furiously,
trying to differentiate himself, his values, his class, from the
society around him, but all the time he is running in place,
caught on the treadmill of a society in which the universal
acceptance of Alger reduced Nietzschean distinctions to nonsense.

Cowperwood in *The Titan* tries for five hundred and fifty
pages to be different; the effort, albeit abortive, is understand-
ably exhausting; at the end of the novel he is beginning to
feel somewhat old and tired — he is a little sick of trying. So
too, for that matter, was Dreiser. As originally planned, the
Cowperwood series was to have been a trilogy, but to pile
another club sandwich on top of *The Titan* was unthinkable.
What to do with a hero who could not be demoted from his
pinnacle of power for the sake of fresh plot interest, else he
lose all his prestige as the world's champion hard guy, yet
whose continued presence at the top of the heap could only
lead to ever more dully repetitious and frustratingly inconclusive attempts to prove that he really was a superman, baffled Dreiser completely. Although *The Titan* was published
in 1914, Dreiser did not even start *The Stoic* until the beginning of the twenties. The passage of years, however, had not
solved the dilemma, and he worked on the novel only spo-
radically during that decade. He thought of it again during the
thirties, but not until the mid-forties, in the last months of his
life, could Dreiser bring himself to take up Cowperwood again
and finish out his career.

v

The success story, from Carrie to Kane to Cowperwood, had brought Dreiser's imagination squarely up against a baffling blank wall. Between 1911 and 1915 he published four novels; in the next nine years he published volumes of autobiography and travel, but not a single novel. When *An American Tragedy* finally appeared in 1925, it became evident that Dreiser had solved his dilemma by avoiding it, for in *An American Tragedy* Dreiser returned to the Hurstwood theme, the anatomy of failure.

Mencken had never liked Hurstwood, objecting that his story diverted attention from Carrie; his review of *An American Tragedy* in the *Mercury* called the book "dreadful bilge" and "a colossal botch." (There was something about the idea of failure that profoundly disquieted the solid bourgeois from Baltimore.) Despite Mencken, the novel outsold all of Dreiser's other books by a wide margin. An expensive limited edition was issued and sold right along with the booming regular edition; the novel was dramatized and produced on Broadway; twice in twenty years *An American Tragedy* was made into a film by Hollywood.

One reason, at least, for its popularity was the fact that Dreiser was here dealing, as he had in *Sister Carrie*, with a new and significant phenomenon in American life. Dreiser's chronicle of the adventures of a white-collar hero appealed to many Americans because in the story of Clyde Griffiths they recognized an image of their own increasingly bureaucratized lives.

White-collar people slipped quietly into American life. Nonetheless, by the time the dust of World War I had settled it was obvious that they were here to stay. Their arrival, says the sociologist C. Wright Mills, utterly transformed, and is still transforming, "the tang and feel of the American experience." With a population consisting of four times as many wage workers and salary workers as independent entrepreneurs, American society in the middle decades of the twentieth century has ceased to be a nation of small businesses run by their owners and has instead become "a great salesroom, an enormous file, an incorporated brain, a new universe of management and manipulation." If, however, the white-collar worker has made over American society in his own image, he has not been able to control it.

> He is more often pitiful than tragic . . . fighting impersonal inflation, living out in slow misery his yearning for the quick American climb. He is pushed by forces beyond his control, pulled into movements he does not understand; he gets into situations in which his is the most helpless position. The white-collar man is the hero as victim.

This new kind of American hero has produced alterations in the success mythology, alterations which are reflected in the shift of emphasis in the success literature of the last thirty years. The message

> is still focused upon personal virtues, but they are not the sober virtues once imputed to successful entrepreneurs. Now the stress is on agility rather than ability, on "getting along" in a context of associates, superiors, and rules, rather than "getting ahead" across an open market; on who you know rather than what you know.

The tone of our social fiction has changed, too, and nowhere is that change more strikingly evident than in *An American Tragedy*.

The theme of the novel grew out of Dreiser's recognition of "the determination of so many young Americans, boys and girls alike, to obtain wealth quickly by marriage." If the glorious days of Rockefeller and Cowperwood were over, the "yearning for the quick American climb" nevertheless remained; marrying one's way to wealth had become, Dreiser felt, the supreme ambition of the younger generation. He was aware, too, that the magazines and newspapers continued to insist that "we are all Napoleons, only we don't know it," whereas most people in the new age, he felt, were "weak and limited, exceedingly so." Out of these reflections came the story of the white-collar hero, Clyde Griffiths.

In some respects Clyde is the typical Dreiser hero. Characteristically, he is burning with desire, yet his soul is ice cold. "As vain and proud as he . . . [is] poor," he considers the other bellboys in the hotel in Kansas City where he is employed to be beneath him; so concerned is he with his clothes and his physical appearance that he can lie to his parents with complete cold-bloodedness about the size of the salary he is receiving, although they are desperately in need of money. Like Cowperwood and Carrie, Clyde has the instinctive faculty for sensing what he must do in order to capitalize a given situation to his advantage.

But in some respects Clyde is quite different from Dreiser's earlier protagonists. The general strategy for advancement which he formulates for himself while still in his teens is not, significantly, the lobster-eat-squid battle plan decided on by young Cowperwood, but the white-collar strategy of personality-selling. "For the first time in his life, it occurred to him that if he wanted to get on he ought to insinuate himself into the good graces of people." Clyde is plucky and lucky, but to an insufficient degree; under pressure he tends "to show tenseness and strain." Although clever at ingratiating himself with people who count, he is easily tempted into imprudent behavior, the unfortunate consequences of which he does not have the courage to face.

Clyde yearns to get up in the world, but until he is twenty the only jobs he is able to secure are menial and without a future. The turning point in his career comes when Clyde is working at the Union League Club in Chicago. There one day he encounters his wealthy uncle, Samuel Griffiths, a collar manufacturer of Lycurgus, New York, and charms him into giving him a job. "Very much thrilled," Clyde believes he is at last on the way to the top.

Arrived in Lycurgus, however, he finds himself assigned to a lowly position in the shrinking department. He remains there until his ingratiating personality succeeds in influencing the right people. Invited to dinner at the home of his aunt and uncle, Clyde is completely winning; a considerable promotion at the plant follows immediately. Because of whom, rather than what, he knows, Clyde is placed in charge of a manufacturing department, overseeing the work of hundreds of women.

Asked by his cousin, Gilbert Griffiths, who has general charge of the plant, if he can be trusted to do his work conscientiously and not to have his head turned by the fact that he will be supervising "a lot of women and girls," Clyde soberly says he can. But when his aunt and uncle do not follow up their first dinner invitation with a second, Clyde begins to look around him at work, his eye finally falling on Roberta Alden.

Roberta is young and pretty, but like Clyde, she considers her past life "a great disappointment." The daughter of an impoverished, extremely religious farmer, Roberta had been compelled throughout her youth "to hear of and share a depriving and toilsome poverty." Yet, "because of her innate

64

imagination, she was always thinking of something better. Maybe, some day, who knew, a larger city like Albany or Utica! A new and greater life." Aspiring to a white-collar career, she had worked first in a dry-goods store and then in a hosiery mill in an effort "to bring together the means for some further form of practical education — a course at a business college . . . which might fit her for something better — bookkeeping or stenography." More charitable, however, than Clyde, Roberta had found it impossible not to share her money with her poverty-stricken family, and her savings were dissipated. Finally deciding that she must leave home and strike out on her own, she moves to Lycurgus. Here her faded aspirations bloom again. "This big city. This fine Central Avenue with its stores and moving picture theaters. These great mills. And again Mr. Griffiths, so young, attractive, smiling and interested in her."

Clyde's "passing glimpse" of the Griffiths's household has made him ache to move in their glamorous circle, but, he decides, "plainly he was not to be allowed to share in it." Lonely, confused, resentful, he breaks the rules and begins to take out Roberta. Like most of Dreiser's portrayals of relations beween the sexes, the romance in *An American Tragedy* is an utterly heartless business. Far from falling in love with her, Clyde's seduction of Roberta simply causes him to speculate on the possibility of further sexual conquests. "If now Roberta was obviously willing to sacrifice herself for him in this fashion, must there not be others?" Nor does his relationship with her reconcile Clyde, even for a moment, to the failure of his material ambitions. "For after all, who was she? A factory girl! The daughter of parents who lived and worked on a farm and one who was compelled to work for her own living."

Thus when Sondra Finchley, a society girl whom Clyde had

met the night he had had dinner at his uncle's house, suddenly becomes interested in him, he drops Roberta without a qualm. Sondra is the daughter of the owner of the Finchley Electric Sweepers Company — in that simple fact Clyde sees his golden opportunity. He sees to it that he and Sondra get along very well together. Through her influence, he is invited to all the right parties, at which his talent for getting along with people wins him a considerable social success. Clyde's dream world of big cars, big houses and beautiful women, of splendid, careless living, seems suddenly and thrillingly almost within his grasp.

But Roberta, the respectable girl with the white-collar ambitions, discovers she is pregnant. In a situation demanding suavity and sophistication, Clyde is hopelessly upset. Scared and ignorant, he finds it impossible to arrange for an abortion; when Roberta begins to hound him with the demand that he marry her, he becomes more and more panicky. He is horrified to think that

> unless he could speedily and easily disengage himself from her, all this other splendid recognition would be destined to be withdrawn from him, and this other world from which he sprang might extend its gloomy, poverty-stricken arms to him and envelop him once more, just as the poverty of his family had almost enveloped and strangled him from the first.

Driven to desperation, he decides to drown Roberta. But even in this brutal act Clyde's lack of the ruthlessness which had carried Dreiser's earlier protagonists to success manifests itself. At the last moment, in the solitary rowboat on the lake, he cannot bring himself to act; when the boat accidentally overturns, he lets Roberta drown, but, in keeping with his whole life, he has not brought about her death by his own

66

efforts. The final irony is that Clyde's preparations for the murder which he did not commit have been so inept that they are immediately uncovered and are so damning that he is convicted of murder and electrocuted. If the white-collar man is the hero as victim, then Clyde Griffiths, who through his inadequacies finally becomes his own executioner, is the quintessential expression of bureaucratic America.

That Dreiser could call the story of Clyde a tragedy has scandalized certain critics, particularly F. O. Matthiessen, who has insisted that Clyde has none of the stature or the greatness of an authentic tragic hero. To make such a criticism is, however, to miss the point. Dreiser's title does not stem from any false illusions of greatness which he entertained about his hero, nor did he intend any parallel to the Greeks. The title did not attempt to convey the idea that Clyde himself was great, but rather was intended to suggest how enormous his anguish was as the law closed in on him and he finally realized that the life he had dreamed of, and almost had, would never be his. In the glittering twenties the dream of success was to Dreiser as alluring as ever; therefore, the story of *any* American who had failed to succeed was, inevitably, a tragedy.

To realize how overwhelmingly success continued to appeal to Dreiser in these years it is only necessary to take a look at the author of *An American Tragedy* after the book was published. For the novel's popular success put Dreiser in the big money for the first time in his life. In an era of conspicuous consumers, he made as much noise spending it as anyone. George Jean Nathan and other Broadway bystanders of the decade were blinded by the apparition of Dreiser as he emerged from the Ansonia, dressed to the eyes, twirling a cane, and with a Russian wolfhound in leash. Nathan noted in particular his "Caribbean blue shirts, vanilla ice-cream socks, and pea-green bow ties." In addition to his new wardrobe, Dreiser acquired a duplex apartment in the West Fifties, a cable address, and a country place near Mt. Kisco. Life, Dreiser affirmed, was good.

> I like this sharp, grasping scheme of things, and find that it works well. Plainly it produces all the fine spectacles I see. If it had not been for a certain hard, seeking ambition in Mr. Woolworth to get up and be superior to his fellows, where would his splendid tower have come from?

Dreiser took two trips to Europe in the twenties, but it was the United States that really interested and excited him. No other country was "so wonderful, so fully representative of the natural spirit of aspiration in man, his dreams, hopes, superior constructive possibilities." If there was anything wrong with his native land, it was primarily that the America of Clyde Griffiths was not quite so exciting as that of Frank Cowperwood had been. New York in the twenties was not the town it had been before 1914. Then, "the city . . . was more varied and arresting and, after its fashion, poetic and even idealistic . . . than it is now." Nostalgically, Dreiser recalled the tremendous social and financial contrasts that had existed before the war, the splendor of Fifth Avenue,

> the sparkling personality-dotted Wall Street of 1890–1910 as contrasted with the commonplace and almost bread and butter world that is today. (There were argonauts then.) The astounding areas of poverty . . . as contrasted with the beschooled and beserviced east side of today.

New York now was "duller because less differentiated" than formerly. And although Dreiser wrote no Nietzschean novels in this period, he looked at his country from what he hoped was Nietzsche's point of view and found one other shortcoming. Just as at the time of *The Titan's* publication, when he had decried democracy and come out for an "intellectual aristocracy," so now he said that what America needed was more leadership, and that if democracy was to justify itself it must be as efficient as autocracy.

In spite of its flaws, however, life in the American twenties was still pretty wonderful to Dreiser. Perhaps the clearest-cut expression of his approval of the American system during this period of his greatest success came in 1927, upon the occasion of his visit to the U.S.S.R. at the invitation of the Soviet Bureau of Cultural Relations. "I am an incorrigible individualist — therefore opposed to Communism" are the opening words of *Dreiser Looks at Russia,* but certain aspects of Soviet life Dreiser thoroughly admired. He was, almost inevitably, enthusiastic about the Russian government's encouragement of free love, praising it as a "wholesome attitude toward sex." Remembering the hated Catholic schooling of his youth, which he blamed for filling his mind with false ideas about life, Dreiser admired the Russian system of education, which had divorced religion from the curriculum and concentrated on teaching the children to think. The Communist effort "to give every living human being an equal start in the life race" was also applauded by Dreiser.

His disapproval, however, far outweighed Dreiser's enthusiasm for Communist ideas. The admirably antireligious Soviet education system, for example, aimed to eliminate from the human brain the principle of self-interest, a goal which Dreiser felt was probably impossible of achievement and in any event highly undesirable. If the Communist theory of an equal start in the race for all appealed to an old Alger boy like Dreiser, the theory of an equal finish for all struck him as ridiculous. "The human mind cannot be Communistically or otherwise equalized or prorated at birth," he proclaimed.

To Dreiser, whose suspicion of workingmen extended back to his earliest days in Chicago, when he had considered them "not quite as *nice* as I was, not as refined and superior in their aspiration, and therefore not as worthy or at least not destined to succeed as well as I," the Soviet labor policy seemed very dubious. It was his opinion that

> a little too much was being done for labor and too little for the brains necessary to direct it; that labor was being given an undue share of the fruits of the land; and that the elimination of the old-time creative or constructive businessman, with all that his self-interest and consequent industry, ingenuity, etc., implied, was likely to result in a kind of slowness or seeming indifference or quiescence which would not be likely to work out for the best interests of all concerned.

The man who had hated to see New York's old-time gulf between rich and poor narrow down naturally considered Moscow "the dullest city in the world." Moscow society, Dreiser objected, was simply nonexistent; he missed a "particular zest and go" in the Communist state.

> There appeared to me to be a kind of trudging resignation, based, I felt, on an absence of that "kick" which lies, for so many, in the hope of financial advancement or dread of failure. For what intellect is so dull that it cannot grasp the significance of financial gain?

On the broadest level, Dreiser's critique of Communist Russia was based on what in his opinion was its completely fallacious view of human nature. Russia, wrote Dreiser, wants all for one and one for all; "yet is not the temperament of man naturally greedy, cruel, this, that? And unless his evil heart is taken into consideration will not any society or organism fail?"

Dreiser Looks at Russia was published in 1928. Its adverse judgment of the Soviet experiment and its celebration of the principles of the success society were consistent with the vision of life to which Dreiser had given expression ever since he had assumed the editorship of *Ev'ry Month* some thirty-three years before. Then the crash of 1929 came and knocked the stuffing out of Dreiser and his life vision.

vi

The depression absolutely convinced Dreiser that capitalism was through, that the American atmosphere of "zest and go" which he so loved was now only a memory. The great race up the ladder of success had been permanently canceled because someone had removed the ladder. *Tragic America*, published in 1931, shows how profoundly the depression had shaken Dreiser in just two years' time. The hard, grasping scheme of things which had worked so well a few years before had now suddenly produced "the monopoly of everything by and for the few." Big businessmen, whom in 1920 he had acclaimed as "the most useful of all living phenomena," he now bitterly denounced for having reduced the average American citizen to a tortured and confused failure. Believing that the end of equality of opportunity had been reached, Dreiser no longer found the idea that the efficient ought to rule society quite so wonderful. In 1931 the question was not one of efficiency, but

71

whether an individual, however small or poor, shall retain his self-respect and his life, or whether a commercial oligarchy shall at last and finally take charge and tell all the others . . . how they shall do and what they shall think and how little (not how much) they may live on, while a few others (the strong and the cunning) exercise their will and their pleasure as they choose.

Turning his back on the faith of his whole life, Dreiser categorically denounced "the Pluck and Luck, Work and Win theory of achievement." In place of Alger, he hastily substituted Marx. "America needs a uniform, scientifically planned system which will divide work and the means of life's enjoyment and improvement among the people." Would such a system destroy "the restless and creative individualism" of the American people? To back up his negative answer to this question, Dreiser pointed to the Soviet Union: "I saw no lack of individualism in Russia; creative or otherwise." On the record of *Dreiser Looks at Russia*, this was either a deliberate lie or amnesia — or the hysteria of a man who was dead certain that the end of the only world he had ever known was "almost here and now."

The depression was not merely something he read about in the newspapers. As the breadlines lengthened, Dreiser's own financial security was wiped out by the failure of his publisher; the Hoovervilles mushroomed while Dreiser's country place burned to the ground. The effect on Dreiser's art was catastrophic — in such a world a man whose only values were success values had nothing to say. For the first time since the beginning of the century, a decade passed without a book from Dreiser's pen. An isolationist polemic, *America Is Worth Saving*, appeared in 1941, but even this was partially ghostwritten for Dreiser. The book's only significance was its further evidence that Dreiser still was convinced that the success dream had vanished from America forever. On into the forties, the river of his imagination ran drier and drier. Finally, in the last year of his life, Dreiser spoke again. Reaching back more than a quarter of a century into his past, he picked up the uncompleted manuscripts of two novels, *The Bulwark* and *The Stoic,* and finished them.

They are curious, hollow shells of books, utterly lacking in conviction. In the former, a rags-to-riches businessman with "clear bluish-gray eyes" forsakes success for the peace and tranquillity which he finds in the contemplation of nature and in the Quaker doctrine of the Inner Light. The message of *The Bulwark* is partly, as Lionel Trilling has said, that "the sad joy of cosmic acceptance goes hand in hand with sexual abstinence," and partly that happiness can never be achieved on a big income.

In *The Stoic,* Dreiser put the tired, aging Cowperwood through his paces once again. Although he had been an Episcopalian in *The Financier,* Dreiser now without explanation referred to him as a Quaker, nor was this the only sea change his hero had suffered across the years. For while Cowperwood's mind is "ever-telepathic," he finds it is no fun to win any more, no thrill to smash any more shams. Having lost his will to power, the Cowperwood of *The Stoic* shortly loses his will to live. Sick and weary, he is told by his doctor that only his mind can save his health, but Cowperwood is profoundly uninterested. After his death, Berenice, the most beautiful and artistic of all his mistresses (her eyes are an "inciting and compelling blue"), picks up a copy of the Bhagavad-Gita with the intention of brushing "completely out of her consideration the whole Western materialistic viewpoint which made money and luxury its only god." Like Dreiser's second wife,

73

who was his constant companion in his last years and who took up the study of Oriental philosophy because everyone she knew was "suffering from satiation, too much of everything, too much luxury, too much love, too much material comfort," Berenice finds spiritual ease in the East. Like his dead hero, however, Dreiser seemed to have no real heart for what he was writing; the theme of acceptance had never really been his genre. With a final chapter of *The Stoic* still to be written, he died.

In death, as he had for most of his life, Dreiser chose success. At his request, he was buried in Southern California in the most glamorous of American cemeteries, the place where all Hollywood moguls go when they die, Forest Lawn. Dreiser had visited Forest Lawn shortly before his death and, impressed as always by opulence, had declared it the most "beautiful resting place" he had ever seen.

CHAPTER II

Jack London: The Brain Merchant

> There is in America a general conviction in the minds of
> all mature men, that every young man of good faculty and
> good habits can by perseverance attain to an adequate estate;
> if he have a turn for business . . . he can come to wealth.
> — RALPH WALDO EMERSON

> I guess I'm the only man in America who is making money
> out of socialism!
> — JACK LONDON

In LENIN's last days, it became the chief pleasure of the dying
Soviet ruler to lie in bed and listen to his wife read aloud to
him. "Two days before his death," she later recalled,

> I read to him in the evening a tale of Jack London, *Love
> of Life* — it is still lying on the table in his room. It was a
> very fine story. In a wilderness of ice, where no human
> being had set foot, a sick man, dying of hunger, is making
> for the harbour of a big river. His strength is giving out,
> he cannot walk but keeps slipping, and beside him there
> slides a wolf — also dying of hunger. There is a fight be-
> tween them: the man wins. Half dead, half demented, he
> reaches his goal. That tale greatly pleased Ilyich. Next
> day he asked me to read him more Jack London. But Lon-
> don's strong pieces of work are mixed with extraordinarily
> weak ones. The next tale happened to be of quite another
> type — saturated with bourgeois morals. . . . Ilyich

75

smiled and dismissed it with a wave of the hand. That was the last time I read to him. . . .

If Lenin's judgment was aesthetically sound — and "Love of Life" is undeniably Jack London at his best — his ideological perception was decidedly cloudy. For the memorable story of the struggle between the man and the wolf, with its attendant glorification of free-for-all competition, survival of the fittest and the power of the individual will, was surely no less "bourgeois" than the tale which Lenin had so labeled and dismissed accordingly. Indeed, despite London's repeated public announcements that he was as Red as it was possible to be, the entire corpus of his work is "saturated with bourgeois morals," a fact which has been instinctively understood by the general reading public of the Soviet Union, even though it eluded Lenin. Soviet society is, we now know, profoundly committed to the worship of success, and it has apparently recognized in Jack London an author after its own collective heart. Since Soviet readers are fond of London's work precisely because it reflects the morality to which they themselves subscribe — morality which measures all things in terms of effort and accomplishment — Lenin's erroneous distinction between what is bourgeois in his writing and what is not simply never occurs to them. Vastly and indiscriminately fond of all his books, they have made Jack London as popular today in Russia as he was in the United States thirty or forty years ago.*

The question of why London should appeal so strongly to the readership of the world's most powerful Communist state probably must await a full-scale analysis of the cult of suc-

* In 1917, a reprint of *The Call of the Wild* sold a million and a half copies in this country; by the early thirties, London's novels and stories rivaled Lenin's works in popularity in the Soviet Union.

cess in the Soviet Union, and lies outside the scope of this study. What can concern us here, however, is a more modest but none the less interesting question: just why should a writer saturated with bourgeois morality have insisted on describing himself as a revolutionary socialist?

ii

Born a bastard, reared in poverty, a newsboy at the age of eleven, Jack London had, from the point of view of the success mythology, the perfect background for a successful career. In later years, London remembered his childhood as a nightmare time of unending deprivation. "I had been born poor. Poor I had lived. I had gone hungry on occasion." He suffered psychologically even more acutely than he did physically — he was ashamed of being a bastard and ashamed of being poor. Thus when he was eight years old he was given an undershirt which had been purchased in a store, unlike "the awful homemade things" he had worn up to that time. London was "so proud of it that I insisted on wearing it without any outer garment. For the first time I mutinied against my mother — mutinied myself into hysteria, until she let me wear the store undershirt so all the world could see." So all the world could see: it is the story of his life.

London's mother fought against poverty with get-rich-quick schemes — lottery tickets and stock speculations — but they were no more successful than the boardinghouse ventures of Theodore Dreiser's mother. The efforts of London's foster father to earn a decent living, first as a grocer in San Francisco, then as a farmer outside the city, and finally as the operator of two Oakland boardinghouses, were continually thwarted by his wife's expansive plans. Eventually, her schemes ruined the family completely; it was at this point that London became a newsboy.

After four years of selling newspapers and other odd jobs, London went to work full time in a cannery. Barely turned fifteen, he put in at least ten hours a day in the factory, sometimes as many as eighteen or twenty hours. Dragging home in the evening, too exhausted for anything but to go to bed, London asked himself "if this were the meaning of life — to be a work-beast?" To ask the question was to answer it; at the first opportunity he abandoned the proletarian life for a more lucrative career of crime.

With borrowed money, London bought a sailboat and became an oyster pirate. Every night he sailed down San Francisco Bay to raid the oyster beds, returning the next morning to sell his loot in the saloons of the city. Quick with his fists — or, if they failed, with a double-barreled shotgun — and ready to sail in any kind of weather, London made crime pay handsomely indeed. Earning up to one hundred and eighty dollars for a single night's work, London conveniently forgot his family's economic plight and spent his money wildly on his water-front mistress and, even more wildly, on whisky. In the volume of autobiography which he entitled *John Barleycorn,* London confessed that he "became pretty thoroughly alcohol-soaked during this period. I practically lived in saloons; became a barroom loafer, and worse." But exhilaration, as it always would with London, was succeeded by depression, particularly when he thought of the circumstances of his birth. One night, at the conclusion of three uninterruptedly drunken weeks, he decided to drown himself in the bay. After hours of drifting, the cold water sobered him and he changed his mind. At daylight, a Greek fisherman came upon a numb and exhausted sixteen-year-old boy battling the swift water off Mare Island and picked him up. London had licked poverty by desperate means, but not all the money or all the whisky in the world could gainsay the shameful fact of his illegitimacy.

When he was seventeen London went to sea, shipping out on a seal hunter bound for the coast of Siberia. Returned to San Francisco, he once again went to work in a factory, this time in a jute mill. The pay, however, was as miserable as the hours were long and he soon quit. London was now eighteen years old; the experience which would alter his whole life was about to begin.

As a child, London "had pored and thrilled over" Alger's famous biography of President Garfield, *From Canal Boy to President*. From that book London had acquired a literal belief "in the old myths which were the heritage of the American boy when I was a boy." London learned from Alger that even

> a canal boy could become a president. Any boy who took employment with any firm, could, by thrift, energy, and sobriety, learn the business and rise from position to position until he was taken in as a junior partner. After that the senior partnership was only a matter of time.

Although Alger had not so intended it, London felt that his account of Garfield's life implied that the rise to the top required only the exercise of inherent virtues, strength, conscientiousness, and so on; education, formal training of any kind, was completely irrelevant. Therefore when London reached the decision, shortly after leaving his job at the jute mill, that it was time he began to make his way in the world, it never occurred to him to return to the classroom he had forsaken some five years before. As a way of getting ahead, he "didn't think much of schools." London considered it much wiser to get a position somewhere — the sooner he began at the bottom, the sooner he would reach the top. With blind confidence in his eventual success, he applied for a job to the superintendent of a power plant in Oakland. "I told him that I wanted to begin right at the bottom and work up, that I wanted to devote my life to this one occupation." Sizing up the young man's gullible eagerness, the superintendent made London a shrewd proposition. For passing coal ten hours a day, seven days a week, he was to receive thirty dollars a month. London accepted immediately.

The proposition proved even worse in practice than it had seemed in theory, for, as it turned out, London's workday averaged closer to thirteen hours, bringing his wage under eight cents an hour, less than he had earned at the cannery at the age of fifteen. After a few exhausting months, London learned from another employe that he had been hired to do two men's work at less than the wages normally received by one, and that the superintendent had no intention of bringing this arrangement to an end by promoting him. So cruel had the work been that for a year after he left the job he was compelled to wear straps on his wrists, but the most important effect of the experience was that it blackened London's whole conception of the world. It revealed to him that literature was not life: the rewards which Alger had taught him to expect were the certain result of hard work had proved to be a mockery. Enormously shaken, London ran away from his job, his family, his native state. He had to see the world without Alger's rose-colored glasses and figure things out all over again.

Riding the rods and blind baggages, London bummed his way across the continent. He joined Coxey's Army for a time, begged on the streets of New York and was arrested and jailed for thirty days in Niagara Falls on a vagrancy charge. His friends during this fateful period of his life were all down-and-outers,

> what sociologists love to call the "submerged tenth" . . .
> sailor-men, soldier-men, labor-men, all wrenched and dis-
> torted and twisted out of shape by toil and hardship and
> accident, and cast adrift by their masters like so many
> old horses. I . . . slammed back gates with them, or
> shivered with them in box cars and city parks, listening
> the while to life-histories which began under auspices as
> fair as mine, with digestions and bodies equal to and bet-
> ter than mine, and which ended there before my eyes in
> the shambles at the bottom of the Social Pit.

So vividly did the horrid vision of the Pit impress itself upon London's mind that there were moments when he actually saw it as "a concrete thing," with high, slippery walls and a heap of broken humanity at the bottom. Even more appalling than the sight of its frightful depths was his sensation that he, too, was about to become a victim of the Pit. As he felt himself "slipping down, down, into the shambles at the bottom," London wrote later, "I confess a terror seized me."

> What when my strength failed? when I should be unable
> to work shoulder to shoulder with the strong men who
> were as yet babes unborn? And there and then I swore a
> great oath. It ran something like this: *All my days I have
> worked hard with my body, and according to the number
> of days I have worked, by just that much am I nearer the
> bottom of the Pit. I shall climb out of the Pit, but not by
> the muscles of my body shall I climb out.*

The only way to get out of the Pit and get up in the world was by using one's head; from this realization flowed his resolve "to sell no more muscle, and to become a vender of brains." But in order to do this he must read, he must go to school. Almost literally, London "ran back to California and opened the books."

London's belated and frantic pursuit of knowledge began with his enrollment as a freshman at Oakland High School. Spurred on by his fear of the Pit, he studied hard, submitted several literary efforts to the school magazines, kept "half-a-dozen membership cards working in the free library" and "dallied with little home clubs wherein we discussed poetry and art and the nuances of grammar," all at the same time he was working as the school janitor. After one furious year, he dropped out of high school and entered a cram school to prepare for the entrance examinations for the University of California. Five weeks later the authorities of the school discovered that London was endeavoring to cram their two-year cram course into four months and expelled him, on the grounds that he was discrediting the institution. Undaunted, London proceeded to prepare for the examinations on his own, studying an appalling nineteen hours a day for three months.

This titanic effort was sufficient to get him past the examinations, but once London was admitted to the university he remained there for only one semester. Desperately anxious to convert what he had learned into cash, he returned to Oakland during the winter of 1896–1897, locked himself in his room and wrote for fifteen hours a day, "pouring out ponderous essays, scientific and sociological tracts, short stories, humorous verse, tragic blank verse, and elephantine epics in Spenserian stanzas." London buoyantly sent off his manuscripts to the big eastern magazines. Every one was rejected.

Despite all he had done to escape it, London was driven back to manual labor, to "the old familiar work-beast condition," first of all in a laundry at a fashionable boys' school near San Francisco and then in the gold fields of the Klondike. After failing to make his fortune in the gold rush, London returned to California for one final, last-ditch effort to become — as he phrased it — a "brain merchant." He cut his sleeping time down to five hours a night, ate in nothing flat, and wrote.

Nine months later, in July of 1899, the twenty-three-year-old London had stories and articles appearing simultaneously in five different periodicals; by December of that year he had a contract with a Boston publisher for a book of short stories. His heroic feats of reading and writing had justified themselves, after all; the gods had begun to stand up for bastards. Before London was through he would become the first millionaire novelist in American history.

iii

"While thus equipping myself to become a brain merchant . . . I discovered that I was a socialist." On the surface, this statement of London's would seem to mean that in the hurried course of his education he had read some socialist books and was thereby converted. Indeed, London himself said exactly that. In an essay entitled "How I Became a Socialist," he stated that what he called his "rampant individualism" was "pretty effectively hammered out of me, and something else as effectively hammered in," on the day when "I first saw the walls of the Social Pit rise around me." Just what the "something else" was, he went on to say, he discovered when he got back to California and began opening books. In Marx and other writers London found a "lucid demonstration of the

logic and inevitableness of Socialism," which gave a philosophy and a name to his feelings.

The story is, however, not nearly that simple. The key to
the complexity of London's conversion to socialism is contained in his assertion that it was his vision of the Social Pit
which inspired him to accept the new faith. This is significant, because the Pit, for London, was not something to be
entered and organized in the name of the proletarian future,
but a horrid trap to be avoided at all costs. London, clutching his as-yet-unnamed faith, fled *away* from the Pit and back
to the books: the conversion of Jack London to the philosophy of Marx had more to do with rising in the world than
with world revolution.

The crucial phase in the process of London's acceptance of
socialism began with his discovery, shortly after he entered
Oakland High School, that around the San Francisco Bay
Area socialism was an avenue to culture, a highway to the
world of high thinking and high living to which he aspired.
In order to become "a vender of brains," London had joined
the "little home clubs" which studied poetry and art; he
joined the socialist local in Oakland for precisely the same reason. The other members of the local were not workingmen,
but intellectuals, whose announced purpose was to study "political economy, philosophy, and politics," and who in practice
met together in the evenings "for music and a glass of beer"
and "cultural" talk. His fellow members furnished London
with the names of books and authors with which they said
he should be familiar; they taught him how to think logically,
urged him to speak and write, and corrected and encouraged
him in both activities.

Socialism also served London as a social entree. Thus when
he joined the Ruskin Club of San Francisco, an organization

which believed in dinner parties as well as in Ruskin, London came to know "the cream of the Bay region intellectuals." Through a debating society which contained a number of his socialist acquaintances, London struck up a friendship with Edward Applegarth, the son of a cultivated and well-to-do English family which had settled in Oakland. Invited to visit his new friend's home, London promptly fell in love with Applegarth's sister, a young woman whose "manners were flawless," who had a "profound sense of breeding," and whose "constant companions" were "art and culture." In the best Alger tradition, which permits young ladies to aid heroes who must otherwise help themselves, she loaned London books, corrected his speech and his table manners, and took him to tea parties where he met still more "cultivated young ladies whose dresses reached the ground."

Socialism also helped to establish London, in the period before he had made a name as a writer, as something of a local celebrity. A talk which he delivered before the socialist local in Oakland led to an invitation to give some Sunday-night lectures in an educational series the club was sponsoring. This in turn led to his remarks being written up in the Oakland newspapers "in a serious, friendly fashion." As one of London's biographers has observed, "Socialism and Jack London had become respectable together!"

The special and complex nature of London's socialism is further revealed on the level of doctrine. For, almost inevitably, the social formulations of a man who had exploited socialism as a way of getting ahead in a capitalist world bear little resemblance to orthodox socialist ideology. London's socialism clearly reflects the success aspirations of an ex-newsboy; stated more abstractly, it reveals the impingement of the life outlook of Horatio Alger on that of Karl Marx.

85

Whether success depended upon brawn or brains was a question about which London might change his mind, but throughout his entire career he retained the firm belief that life was very much the sink-or-swim, do-or-die proposition that Alger had proclaimed it to be. Consequently, when London read the *Communist Manifesto* he responded mainly to its images of violence and upheaval, and especially to its stirring conclusion. In his personal copy of the *Manifesto* London heavily underlined its famous last words, which call for action and courage and which promise that for those who dare there is a "world to gain," while London's own socialist writings are replete with Algeresque metaphors of heroic endeavor and assertions that struggling socialist heroes are bound to win.

Yet if London admired Marx's apocalyptic and violent vocabulary, he emphatically did not conceive of the coming struggle for power in terms of class conflict. Marx's theory that the masses, in their misery, would eventually overthrow the bourgeoisie bears no relation to London's prophecy that the revolution would be conducted by a picked group of frustrated Alger heroes. In *War of the Classes* London expounded the series of propositions which had led him to such a bizarre prophecy and which more than anything else reveals how completely his socialism was dominated by the success mythology.

The book's central premise, London said in the preface, was that "first and for always . . . socialism is based, not upon the equality, but upon the inequality, of men." The proposition was basic to London — it was also basic to Alger. To the author of *Strive and Succeed,* the principle of equality obtained only at the beginning of the great race of life, and was necessarily — gloriously — absent at every point thereafter: to the victor belonged the spoils and the devil took the hindmost. Similarly, London felt that it was in the very nature of things that there should exist "a superior class and an inferior class," based on the outcome of free competition. Once the nature of things got out of joint, once competition was no longer sufficiently free to produce this class division, a revolutionary situation was bound to develop, in London's view. The period preceding the revolution would be not so much marked, as Marx had predicted, by the increasing degradation of the proletariat as by the closing down of "the outlets . . . whereby the strength and ferment of the inferior class have been permitted to escape," in short, by the denial to the potential Alger hero of his sacred right to rise in the world.

This was in fact what London was convinced had happened in the United States by the middle of the first decade of the twentieth century. Free and equal competition was a thing of the past, he felt. London nostalgically recalled the era when President Garfield had been a boy, the good old days when

> an undeveloped country with an expanding frontier gave equality of opportunity to all. In the almost lottery-like scramble for the ownership of vast unowned natural resources . . . the capable, intelligent member of the working class found a field in which to use his brains to his own advancement. Instead of being discontented in direct ratio with his intelligence and ambitions, and of radiating amongst his fellows a spirit of revolt as capable as he was capable, he left them to their fate and carved his own way to a place in the superior class.

But the turn of the century had brought the end of the frontier and the rise of the trusts, and these events, London was sure, had destroyed social mobility in America. "The gateway of opportunity after opportunity has been closed, and closed for all time," London announced with finality.

Yet, London added, and here is the crux of his Alger-hero theory of revolution, "ambitious young men continue to be born. It is they, denied the opportunity to rise from the working class, who preach revolt to the working class." The coming destruction of capitalism was not to be a triumph of the masses, but of what London called "group individualism"; the victory of socialism would likewise represent "a triumphant expression of individualism." Without the leadership of those who have been "denied room for their ambition in the capitalist ranks," the masses would be incapable of any kind of action, for in London's scornful opinion the masses generally represented the most "unfit, inefficient, and mediocre" members in all of society. "Helpless as cattle," these people certainly did not possess the ability to take over society, in fact, their tendency was not to become more revolutionary as their impoverishment worsened, but more submissive, "until, at the bottom of the social pit, they are wretched, inarticulate beasts, living like beasts, breeding like beasts, dying like beasts." Whereas London waxed indignant that the Alger heroes of the working classes had been thwarted in their drive toward the top, he felt there was a certain justice in the fact that in a "tooth-and-nail society" the weaker members of the masses were constantly being shunted toward the very bottom of the social heap, eventually to be sloughed off entirely, because by this means "the species is constantly purged of its inefficient members" and is the stronger for it as a result.

Ironically, London's contempt for the masses was so thoroughgoing that it completely undercut his vision of the socialist state of the future. Whenever London stopped talking in bold, chiliastic terms of how his socialist Alger heroes were going "to wipe out, root and branch, all capitalistic institutions of present-day society" and tried to think in a concrete fashion of what a socialist America would be like, he ran into the concept of mass welfare, a concept which at first startled him and ended by confounding him. For while under capitalism the killing off of the weak tended to keep society healthy, this salutary process would not be a feature of the socialist state. Even though it was true that socialism, as London defined it, was intended primarily "for the happiness of certain kindred races," it was also true that in the coming social order "the progeny of all, the weak as well as the strong, would have an equal chance for survival." The inevitable result, as London saw it, would be that "the average strength of each generation . . . [would] begin to diminish." To his acute distress, the deleterious effects brought on by the end of free competition and the institution of the welfare state could already be witnessed in England, where trade-unionism had already gone a long way toward annulling "the old selective law." Entirely as the consequence of greater labor solidarity, said London, the English workingman was now producing less than one half as much as his American counterpart. Thus confronted with the logical outcome of his own convictions, London could only conclude in dismay that under socialism all "progress must cease," that "deterioration would at once set in." "It is," London admitted in utter mystification, "a pregnant problem." Could it be that, like oil and water, Alger and Marx didn't mix?

Thus London's conversion to socialism was bound up with his own social and cultural advancement, while his version of socialist doctrine was interwoven with his continuing belief in

89

the mythology of success. So, too, the socialist novels and stories which poured from his pen at the incredible rate of one thousand words a day, every day for eighteen years, made London a rich man. But if this Gargantuan production enabled London to boast that he was the only man in America who was "making money out of socialism," he found it increasingly difficult — and his major novels record with what calamitous rapidity the difficulty did increase — to live with the conflicting claims made on him by socialism and success. One pregnant problem seemed to lead to another, each one a little worse than the last. Not until 1916 would he find his predicament intolerable.

iv

London's first three novels, published in three early, confident and successive years — 1902, 1903, 1904 — constitute the first wave of his attack on American capitalism; in them the young socialist vigorously set forth his indictment of a society which, as he believed, was no longer healthily fluid and competitive, but had hardened into a static, hierarchical social order, sick unto death from the fact that wealth was no longer to be earned, only inherited. Paralleling what David Graham Phillips and Robert Herrick were saying on the subject, London depicted America in *A Daughter of the Snows, The Call of the Wild* and *The Sea-Wolf* as a civilization victimized by its own success, a nation whose twentieth-century sons had gone fat and soft exactly because the ambition of their nineteenth-century fathers to make big money had been so thoroughly achieved.

In each of the novels the hero is introduced to us as an aristocrat who has been born with a silver spoon in his mouth. Buck, for example, the canine protagonist of *The Call of the Wild*, resides in "a big house in the . . . Santa Clara Valley. . . . There were great stables, where a dozen grooms and boys held forth, rows of vine-clad servants' cottages . . . long grape arbors, green pastures, orchards, and berry patches." Having lived "the life of a sated aristocrat" all of his days, Buck is no match for the man with the rope who invades the estate one night and kidnaps him. Like Vance Corliss and Humphrey Van Weyden, his flabby counterparts in the other two novels, Buck is thus abruptly yanked out of his American environment, his "lazy, sun-kissed life . . . with nothing to do but loaf and be bored," and plunged into a world where "all was confusion and action, and every moment life and limb were in peril." In point of fact, this brave new world in which Buck finds himself is the Klondike; on a symbolic level, it is the vanished American past, when fortunes were yet to be made and men were men.

Buck's indoctrination into the new (that is to say, old) order of things, with its "law of club and fang," begins with his arrival on the Dyea beach. His first experience, although a vicarious one, teaches him an unforgettable lesson. Curly, a bitch who has been brought north with Buck, decides to make friends with one of the husky dogs; the husky, however, leaps at Curly as she approaches him, ripping her face open from eye to jaw and knocking her off her feet. Seeing Curly down, a score of huskies instantly "closed in upon her, snarling and yelping, and she was buried, screaming with agony, beneath the bristling mass of bodies." In a matter of seconds, Curly is dead. Buck, who has witnessed the entire incident, thinks to himself, "So that was the way. No fair play. Once down, that was the end of you. Well, he would see to it that he never went down."

Buck at once begins to shuck off his aristocratic ways. He learns to eat fast and he learns to steal; his muscles become hard, his coat becomes thick and he grows callous to all ordinary pain. Soon he is openly challenging the leader of the dog team for his position. In the principal scene of the novel, Buck and the leader battle for supremacy and Buck is victorious. As he stands watching the other dogs tear the dying leader to pieces, Buck finds the taste of power good.

In the ensuing years, Buck becomes the king of dogs, the greatest leader the team has ever had; under his merciless, driving direction, the team makes one record run after another. But even this exhilarating life palls on Buck after a time — it is, he finds, insufficiently competitive. Basically, Buck is "a killer, a thing that preyed, living on the things that lived," and so he feels the urge growing within him to desert the team (which faintly smacks of civilization and all that that soft word connotes) in order that he may live "unaided, alone, by virtue of his own strength and prowess, surviving triumphantly in a hostile environment where only the strong survived." Finally, the night comes when Buck heeds the call of the wild and goes off into the forest, where he becomes the ruler of the wolf pack. Buck, initially a member of the false aristocracy of ease and luxury, has at last become the head of the true competitive aristocracy.

The socialist message of *A Daughter of the Snows* is exactly the same as that contained in the story of Buck: absolute wealth corrupts absolutely and competition is the health of the state. In *The Sea-Wolf* London repeated this message again, but he also added a new one. A double-barreled attack on American capitalism, *The Sea-Wolf* is not only the ac-

count of how the fainthearted Humphrey Van Weyden becomes a valid success by being forced to fight for survival in a
world where no holds are barred, but it is also the story of
Wolf Larsen, the natural-born fighting aristocrat, whose tragedy is that he has never been allowed to rise to the position
to which his abilities entitle him.

Larsen is the first of a series of heroes in London's novels
with whom the author identified himself,* for the saga of
Wolf Larsen is an imaginative account of what his creator
had once feared was happening to him, in the years between his job at the power plant and his first success as a
writer. As always with those of London's heroes who are projections of himself, Larsen is of medium height, muscular, and
intelligent. His strength is truly superlative, partaking "of the
enlarged gorilla order. . . . [a] strength we are wont to associate with things primitive, with wild animals, and the creatures we imagine our tree-dwelling prototypes to have been."
London, who was extremely narcissistic and exultantly proud
of his own medium-sized but powerful body, spared few details in his ecstatic descriptions of the physical appearance of
this man who so resembled himself. "Wolf Larsen was the
man-type, the masculine, and almost a god in his perfectness.
As he moved about or raised his arms the great muscles leapt
and moved under the satiny skin." Despite his primordial appearance, Larsen's intellect is as formidable as his body. He
has read vastly in Shakespeare, Tennyson, Poe, De Quincey,
Tyndall, Proctor and Darwin; he knows physics, astronomy
and the complete works of Browning.

But for all his magnificent mental and physical capabilities,

---

* London's nickname was Wolf — probably bestowed on him by himself. Cf. his request to his wife: "I have sometimes wished you would call
me 'Wolf' more often."

93

Larsen is nothing more than the master of an obscure schooner engaged in the seal-hunting trade. Van Weyden, who comes to admire Larsen fervently, is mystified by this anomaly. He asks Larsen:

> Why is it that you have not done great things in this world? With the power that is yours you might have risen to any height. Unpossessed of conscience or moral instinct, you might have mastered the world, broken it to your hand. And yet here you are, at the top of your life, where diminishing and dying begin, living an obscure and sordid existence. . . . Why, with all that wonderful strength, have you not done something? There was nothing to stop you, nothing that could stop you. What was wrong? Did you lack ambition? Did you fall under temptation? What was the matter? What was the matter?

With Larsen's answer we reach the heart of the novel. He begins by telling Van Weyden of his humble birth, of how he went to sea at the age of ten, of his being unable to read or write until he taught himself. "But history," Van Weyden interjects, "tells of slaves who rose to the purple." In Larsen's grim response we hear the voice of the author of *War of the Classes:* "And history tells us of opportunities that came to the slaves who rose to the purple. . . . No man makes opportunity. All the great men did was to know it when it came to them. . . . I should have known the opportunity, but it never came." Because of the blocking off of the avenue to the top, Larsen has had to content himself with his present occupation. All his great energy, ambition and talent have had no proper outlet, and he is as a result consumed "with the tremendous power that is in him and that seems never to have found adequate expression in works."

The tragic consequence of this situation has been to turn Larsen inward upon himself, causing him to dissipate his energy in meaningless torture of the members of his crew and his ambition in endless brooding about what might have been. Massive headaches are the primary symbol of his frustration — they have plagued him for years, and in the course of the action they become progressively more severe, reducing him at times to agonized helplessness.

The crisis of the novel is reached when suddenly, in mid-Pacific, a woman is introduced aboard the ship. Maud Brewster signifies everything a man could want — or so London intended. She is the daughter of wealthy, blue-blooded parents, a poetess in her own right, and as beautiful as a "bit of Dresden china." Both Van Weyden (who, thanks to the primitive life he has been leading, has been transformed from a thin-skinned dilettante into a self-reliant he-man) and Larsen fall in love with her. Maud, for her part, wastes no time in displaying her preference. Plainly, she is terrified of the brutish, uncouth Larsen, who is obviously so far beneath her own social status, and tries to avoid him whenever possible. Van Weyden, on the other hand, who is both a blue blood and a well-known writer, is very much to her taste.

One night, shortly after Maud has come aboard, Van Weyden is roused from his bed by his newly developed sixth sense, which tells him that something is wrong. In the ship's cabin he finds Maud "straining and struggling and crushed in the embrace of Wolf Larsen's arms." Van Weyden hurls himself on Larsen, but is immediately sent crashing against the wall of the room by a casual gesture of Larsen's powerful arm. It is Larsen, however, who retires from the scene in defeat, for at this moment one of his headaches sweeps over him, temporarily blinding him. Taking advantage of Larsen's incapacity, Maud and Van Weyden flee the ship in an open boat. Although they are in northern waters, hundreds of miles from land, neither the writer nor his lady poet proves unequal to the challenge. Maud had been born in Cambridge, Massachusetts (an infallible sign of weakness in London's fiction), but she rises to the occasion and does her seven-hour trick at the oar without fail, as does the now thoroughly toughened Van Weyden. Reaching a deserted island, they maintain life without any trouble, manufacturing fire, killing seals and building a hut as if they had been used to this sort of existence all their lives.

Inevitably, the day comes when Larsen's ship unerringly washes ashore on the island. On board they find only one person — the blind, maddened, paralyzed Wolf Larsen. Maud and Van Weyden decide to recondition the ship and make it seaworthy once again, but Larsen forbids them to touch the only property in the world which he has ever owned. A grim battle for control of the ship follows, climaxing in a desperate fight between the two men. When Larsen, in one last-ditch surge of energy, seizes Van Weyden by the throat, Maud enters the brawl and clubs Larsen to the floor. It is Larsen's last fight. While they are en route home in the ship, the once-mighty sea captain finally dies, and Maud and Van Weyden dump his body into the sea. A few pages more and the novel is over, as their ship is sighted by a United States revenue cutter.

Despite occasional lapses into ludicrousness, *The Sea-Wolf* is London's most fully realized novel. The detailed and often brilliant descriptions of Larsen's suffering and eventual madness, of his decline from intellectual and physical supremacy to paralysis and death, represent a memorable study in American failure and the most searching indictment of capitalism in all of London's fiction. Obviously, something was fundamentally wrong with a system nominally dedicated to success if it did not permit such a man to succeed. But never again would a London novel make such a clear-cut point. From *The Sea-Wolf* on, the fatal contradictions in London's philosophy began to corrode the power of his critique — and to destroy his personality as well.

v

Phase one of London's attack on capitalism had been forceful but negative: a society which Buck had to flee in order to realize his powers, or which blocked the rise of Wolf Larsen, deserved to be overthrown. But in projecting his next major work London proposed to tackle a more affirmative theme — to reveal how the revolution was to be accomplished and what life under socialism would be like.

The Iron Heel purports to be an eyewitness account of the bloody, revolutionary years between 1912 and 1932, an account which, after being lost for several centuries, has finally been discovered and published in the twenty-seventh century. The fact that *The Iron Heel* is a novel about the future serves to place London in the tradition of such American reform writers as Edward Bellamy and Ignatius Donnelly, who, previous to London, had discovered that the future could be employed as a way of attacking problems in the present. It also establishes London as the true, albeit illegitimate, son of his parents.

London's natural father was a certain "Professor" W. H. Chaney, a well-known astrologer and scientist of the occult. Denouncing as charlatans those astrologers who divined "through a teacup or pack of cards," Chaney insisted that his secret method was the only true way to forecast the future.

London's mother was both an astrologer (she met the man of her fate through their common interest) and an ardent spiritualist. "She held séances in which the public was invited to communicate with the dead, to send messages to former loved ones, and . . . to receive advice from them on how to conduct their business and love affairs, how to settle quarrels and control their husbands or wives." London himself was tremendously interested in such metaphysical matters throughout his life. (Indeed, if Upton Sinclair is to be believed, London's interest continued even after he was dead. In two articles which appeared in *The Occult Review* some fourteen years after London's death, Sinclair asserted that he had been in contact with London's spirit, that they had talked at length, and that London had been for some time helping him with his writing — which was why, Sinclair explained, "I was writing more fiction of late years.") From an early story of London's about a séance to a late novel like *The Star Rover* — which Sinclair affirmed was "a favourite with spiritualists and occultists" — London demonstrated many times over that he was very much in the tradition of his parents.

Given his general interest in the occult, plus the fascination with the future which socialists have always displayed, it is not surprising that London should often have turned to writing about the social and political shape of things to come. A short story called "The Unparalleled Invasion" relates how the "yellow peril" of China, which has been threatening the world by sheer weight of numbers, is reduced by germ warfare to "a howling wilderness," its billion people destroyed down to the last coolie. "The Dream of Debs" concerns a great general strike of the future which is won by labor after much suffering and violence. "The Minions of Midas" tells of how certain "members of [the] intellectual proletariat," men who have been prevented by conditions, not by lack of ability, from rising, revenge themselves on society by blackmail and murder.

In *The Iron Heel*, the mastermind of the revolutionary socialists and the hero of the novel is a man whose very name smacks of will power — Ernest Everhard. Everhard is Wolf Larsen, or rather Jack London, all over again. He stands "only five feet nine inches" in height, but he is so powerfully built that the cloth in his suit bulges "with his muscles." Although Everhard is largely self-educated, his erudition and his analytic powers are extraordinary. (This fact is made abundantly clear in the scene where we first meet Everhard. Several churchmen foolhardily attempt to take his intellectual measure at a dinner party, but Everhard's "smashing, sledgehammer manner of attack" and his command of information makes the argument distinctly no contest. "He bristled with facts. He tripped them up with facts, ambuscaded them with facts, bombarded them with broadsides of facts. . . . each fact a lash that stung and stung again. And he was merciless.") To the usual formula of medium size, muscularity and intellectuality, London added another quality which would characterize all of his heroes from Everhard on. A great point is made of the fact that even though Everhard has a working-class background he is also a "descendant of the old line of Everhards that for over two hundred years had lived in America." This detail was no less autobiographical than the other parts of the formula, for London, despite his humble origin, could remember from his childhood hearing his mother "pride herself that we were old American stock and not immigrant Irish and Italians like our neighbors," while throughout his career he was a strong advocate of an Anglo-Saxon America.

Although Everhard is directing the socialists' plot to overthrow capitalism in America, he does not trouble to hide his revolutionary designs from the capitalists. Addressing a meeting of wealthy men and women, Everhard frankly tells them, "We want all that you possess. We will be content with nothing less. . . . We want in our hands the reins of power and the destiny of mankind." Just why Everhard should have made this speech is somewhat unclear, for as the action unfolds it becomes unmistakably apparent that the forces commanded by the financial oligarchy — or Iron Heel, as it is called — considerably outnumber those of the revolutionists and that the triumph of the revolution is not foregone by any means.

One of the most gallant of the socialists' allies, a crusading publisher named William Randolph Hearst, is eliminated before the uprising even begins. Organized religion joins forces with the Iron Heel and, as Everhard predicts, the revolutionists also lose the support of the labor unions when the oligarchy agrees to subsidize them. The slum classes, it is true, remain on the side of the socialists, but the hero of *The Iron Heel* feels a vast contempt for the "brutish apathy" and "dull bestiality" of these "people of the abyss." The socialist leaders plan only a limited role in the revolution for the slum people — limited but bloody, for they are considered by Everhard and his colleagues to be nothing if not expendable. Once the revolt has begun, the people of the abyss are to be allowed to plunder the palaces and cities of the oligarchs for the purpose of diverting the attention of the police and the army away from the real revolutionists. If casualties among the poorer classes are sure to be heavy under this plan, it is, Everhard says, of no consequence.

Let the abysmal brute roar and the police and Mercenaries slay. The abysmal brute would roar anyway. It

JACK LONDON: THE BRAIN MERCHANT

would merely mean that various dangers to us were harm-
lessly destroying one another. In the meantime we would
be doing our own work, largely unhampered, and gaining
control of all the machinery of society.

Just what groups of people Everhard has in mind when he
says, "we" is, however, something of a mystery. Not only have
the labor unions and the churches gone over to the Iron Heel,
but by the eve of the revolution the oligarchy has effectively
destroyed another potential ally of the socialists, the middle
classes. This would seem to leave the farmers, but they, too,
are wiped out as an effective political group when the oligarchs forcibly prevent the Grangers from assuming office in
those states where the latter had succeeded in winning elections, while wholesale mortgage foreclosures destroy them as
a class. Thus it would seem that, like an army consisting entirely of officers, the revolution is to be undertaken and supported only by the group which is to direct it: the intellectual
Alger heroes who became revolutionary socialists when they
failed to become millionaires. A group composed of Wolf
Larsens, Ernest Everhards and various and assorted Minions
of Midas would undoubtedly be formidable, man for man, but
as a revolutionary army probably somewhat small. When arrayed against the awesome power of the Iron Heel, with its
labor castes, its one million mercenaries and its "great hordes
of secret agents and police of various sorts," undoubtedly too
small.

When the revolution does come, it is in fact a horrible,
bloody fiasco, degenerating finally into a wholesale pillaging
operation by the unleashed mob from the slums. London's account of the mob in action is well-known, but perhaps it
should be quoted again, for the sake of recording one of the
most contemptuous descriptions of a group of failures in all

the literature of success. The mob, says London's socialist narrator, was "an awful river" which

> surged past my vision in concrete waves of wrath, snarl-
> ing and growling, carnivorous, drunk with whiskey from
> pillaged warehouses, drunk with hatred, drunk with lust
> for blood — men, women, and children, in rags and tat-
> ters, dim ferocious intelligences with all the godlike
> blotted from their features and all the fiendlike stamped
> in, apes and tigers, anaemic consumptives and great hairy
> beasts of burden, wan faces from which vampire society
> had sucked the juice of life, bloated forms swollen with
> physical grossness and corruption, withered hags and
> death's heads bearded like patriarchs, festering youth and
> festering age, faces of fiends, crooked, twisted, misshapen
> monsters blasted with the ravages of disease and all the
> horrors of chronic innutrition — the refuse and scum of
> life, a raging, screaming, screeching, demoniacal horde.

On the last page of the novel, Everhard and the other leaders are hard at work attempting to reorganize their shattered forces, but it is obvious that they have lost. According to the novel's twenty-seventh-century editor, three hundred years, "all drowned in seas of blood," were to pass before the Iron Heel was finally overthrown and the Brotherhood of Man established.

The question at once arises as to why London, after building up his hero as a veritable superman, should then have permitted him and his cause to go down to defeat. Too, why should an author who was a fervent socialist write a novel depicting the downfall of the revolutionary cause? After having portrayed in his early novels how fatty and degenerate America had become since the cessation of free competition, it would seem only logical for *The Iron Heel* to show the triumph of the new order over such a pushover — and indeed, in his ideological writings London had often proclaimed that socialism was just around the corner. Why, then, does the revolution fail?

One explanation is that the unbroken series of defeats sustained by American radical movements in the last quarter of the nineteenth century — the defeat of the Greenback and Populist parties, the Supreme Court reversal of the Granger cases, the defeat of Bryan in the climactic campaign of 1896 — produced strong feelings of pessimism and even martyrdom among radicals in this country. These feelings were further reinforced "by memories of the commune of 1870, by scientific descriptions of lost worlds or of the end of this one, by the analogy with the reign of anti-Christ that was to precede the second coming, and by the figure of Christ himself." That Everhard is explicitly compared to Christ (the narrator wonders whether he is "destined for a cross") and that redemption *does* follow the three hundred years of suffering give credence to this martyrological interpretation of the novel. London's socialist hopes, strong as they were, were simply overcome by his inability to believe — and recent American history was his witness — that the financial oligarchy in this country could be overthrown by any radical group.

The bafflement which London displayed in his ideological writings about what would happen to society after socialism was established suggests another explanation to the riddle of *The Iron Heel's* ending. London, child of success as well as of socialism, believed, as we have seen, that the victory of his socialist principles would bring an end to all competition and hence lead to social decay; consequently, he found it absolutely impossible to depict in a novel the success of the socialist revolution. To show Everhard and his group in control of America would have meant that London would have been

forced (by his own convictions) to describe a society characterized by declining production, degenerating racial types and
congenital rot. Then, too, the kind of Utopia dreamed of by
his fellow American socialists only served to hamstring London's imagination even further. Solid bourgeois types, the
leaders of the socialist movement in this country at the time
of *The Iron Heel* conceived of a socialist America as a clean,
well-lighted place where graft would be eliminated from politics, prostitution would be stamped out, divorce would be re-
stricted and temperance would reign supreme. Victor Berger,
for example, the head of the Milwaukee Socialists, envisioned
that the establishment of a cooperative commonwealth would
mean public baths, municipal symphony concerts, free school-
books for children and more sleep for everyone. Other socialists entertained even more mundane dreams. The Olathe,
Kansas, Socialist platform of 1904 consisted of only one demand — "homeowners to have the option of using *either* sidewalk brick or cement." John Work of Iowa, later to become
national secretary of the Socialist Party, reported to the National Socialist Congress in 1910 that the primary task of socialism was not to organize the working class, but to uplift it.
"Under the mentally stifling pressure of capitalism," Work informed the Congress,

> millions of people are constantly poisoning themselves,
> depleting their brain power, and destroying their resisting
> power, by the use of liquor, tobacco, patent medicines,
> confectionery, soda counter abominations, unwholesome
> diet, excessive sexual intercourse, lack of ventilation, un-
> sanitary homes, ignorance of the requirements of their
> bodies, etc.

London, whose constant aim was to get less sleep, who
drank constantly and heavily, and who ran through two wives

and innumerable love affairs, naturally found the thought of such respectable, middle-class Utopias thoroughly boring. When combined with his fears of racial degeneracy under socialism, the thought of such Utopias became utterly appalling.

It is not surprising, therefore, that even though *The Iron Heel* is purportedly edited by a man living under the reign of the Brotherhood of Man some seven centuries hence, not the least hint is given as to how this heaven on earth is organized or how it operates. Indeed, only once in all of his prophetic fiction did London endeavor to describe what life in a socialist state would be like. A story entitled "Goliah," after its mysterious protagonist, relates how one man who is possessed of a dread substance called Energon comes to control the world. Once he is in power, Goliah wipes out child labor and forbids women to work in factories; Wall Street is abolished and captains of industry are installed as heads of government-owned businesses; salesmen are put "to work" and middlemen are forced into "useful occupations." With the aid of Energon, Goliah ruthlessly gets rid of all those "that sat in high places and obstructed progress."

While Goliah thus brings Marxism to the people, he maintains the benefits of Alger's competitive world by sheer force — "the extreme hereditary inefficients" are segregated from society and denied the right to marry. (Inasmuch as London's description of the rule of the oligarchy in *The Iron Heel* has often been praised as a remarkable preview of the fascist state of our time, it is odd that Goliah's combination of socialism and social health, backed up by his control of the weapons of total destruction, should never have been hailed as the literary forerunner of *Nineteen Eighty-four*.) But Energon aside, London was totally unable to imagine how competition could be maintained under socialism; the decay of Utopia seemed inevitable. Unable, or at least unwilling, to portray such a hellish paradise, London found it an easier imaginative task to depict the defeat of the effort to establish socialism in this country. To lament the tragedy of losing was infinitely more palatable than to attempt to rejoice in the tragedy of winning.

The remarkable intensity of *The Iron Heel's* cataclysmic finish is responsible for the fact that London was able to keep secret this drastic breakdown in his imaginative thought. The sheer violence of his description of the chaos following the unleashing of the mob was sufficient to conceal from view the fact that London's concomitant allegiance to Marx and to Alger indeed did not mix. So well did the book's violence do its glossary job that the novel has, over the years, deceived many a guileless reader. Thus an American socialist reviewer of the time maintained that *The Iron Heel* had set back the socialist movement in the United States by five years because its bloody climax gave the false impression that American socialists were extremists — in other words, the novel's intensity proved that London was more radical than his fellow socialists, and not that his socialism was shot through with ideas of individualism and free competition to which every businessman in the country subscribed! In more recent times, Aneurin Bevan, who read *The Iron Heel* as an adolescent in Wales, has affirmed that, like "thousands of young men and women of the working class of Britain, and, as I have learned since, of many other parts of the world," he was led to Marxism through London's novel. The fact that the man whom Bevan has referred to as "so loved an author as Jack London" considered that the men and women of the working class in Britain were a "noisome and rotten tide of humanity," makes it only somewhat more ironic that a rigidly doctrinaire man like Bevan could have found his way to Marxism via such an ambiguous document as *The Iron Heel*.

vi

Martin Eden, the most autobiographical of all the novels of an autobiographical novelist, records the fact that, as London approached the halfway mark of his career as a writer, he had begun to be disillusioned with both his allegiances. *Martin Eden* is the first of a series of books that says a plague on both socialism and success.

The novel begins familiarly enough; the stocky, muscular sailor is the traditional London hero; his rise from newsboy to sailor to fame and fortune as a successful writer parallels London's own career at every point. Thus Eden falls in love with a society girl, whom he has met by chance, and decides that he ought to attempt to better himself. With the society girl's help, he improves his grammar, pronunciation and table manners; he acquires the habits of washing his teeth and scrubbing his nails, and develops "a penchant for a cold water bath every morning." On a final voyage, the young sailor concludes that he could earn as much in three days as a writer as in three months at sea, and forthwith decides to change professions. Upon his return to San Francisco, Eden immediately sets himself the goal of writing three thousand words every day; in order to maintain such a tremendous output, he cuts his sleep down to five hours a night. So precious does he consider his writing time that Eden comes to hate "the oblivion of sleep. . . . He grudged every moment of life sleep robbed him of, and before the clock had ceased its clattering he was head and ears in the wash-basin and thrilling to the cold bite of the water."

Inevitably, Eden succeeds. With all the care that Alger had lavished on the financial details of his heroes' progress, London recorded the rising rate of pay which Eden gets for his stories. When he receives only five dollars for his first story — which is five thousand words long — Eden is ready to give up writing altogether, but then another magazine sends him a check for forty dollars for a story, and Eden knows that he has made the right choice. (The episode, down to the last penny, is based on an incident in London's career.) Cashing the check into silver, Eden is happier than he has ever been before in his life. "He was not mean, nor avaricious, but the money meant more than so many dollars and cents. It stood for success, and the eagles stamped upon the coins were to him so many winged victories."

When, however, Eden finally reaches the top of the ladder and has become both famous and wealthy, he finds that all his zest for life has inexplicably vanished. The prominent people whom he comes to know he finds disappointingly dull; like Ernest Everhard, who always won his intellectual discussions without half trying, Eden discovers that his self-taught mind is so vastly superior to those which have been college-trained that it is no fun to argue. The society girl whom he thought he loved eventually bores Eden, too. When she offers to "come to you here and now, in free love if you will, and I will be proud and glad to be with you," Eden is unmoved and casually turns her down.

Just as London thus expressed his own gathering disillusion with success through *Martin Eden,* so did he allow his fictional counterpart to announce his defection from socialism. Although London's formal break with the Socialist Party would not come until the last year of his life, by the time of *Martin Eden* he could no longer hide his doubts about Marxism either from himself or from the world. Eden's rejection of socialism occurs at precisely the point where London had always stumbled:

> As for myself [says London's hero], I am an individualist. I believe the race is to the swift, the battle to the strong. Such is the lesson I have learned from biology, or at least I think I have learned. . . . I am an individualist, and individualism is the hereditary and eternal foe of socialism.

As Eden's boredom and unhappiness increase, so does the intensity of his disillusion with socialism. Attending a meeting of socialists in Oakland one night, Eden listens to a "clever Jew" address the audience in favor of socialism, then steps to the rostrum himself and delivers a vitriolic, if repetitious, diatribe. "The old law of development," Eden shouts at the crowd,

> still holds. In the struggle for existence . . . the progeny of the strong survive while . . . the progeny of the weak are crushed and tend to perish. The result is that . . . the strength of each generation increases. . . . But you slaves dream of a society where the law of development will be annulled, where no weaklings and inefficients will perish, where every inefficient will have as much as he wants to eat as many times a day as he desires. . . . What will be the result? No longer will the strength and life-value of each generation increase. On the contrary, it will diminish. . . . Your society of slaves — of, by, and for, slaves — must inevitably weaken and go to pieces. . . .*

* As evidence that the incompatibility of Alger and Marx which hounded London into such repetitiousness did not by any means cease with *Martin Eden*, there is the letter of resignation which London sent to the Socialist Party eight years after the appearance of the novel and only eight months before his death: "My final word is that Liberty, freedom,

Hating socialism and bored by success, Martin Eden reaches the height of his fame and the end of his rope at the same moment. Having turned his back on both high life and low life, he is very much alone. In an effort to shake off his mounting depression, he decides to take a sea voyage. But on board he finds the bourgeois passengers unutterably dull, while the crew seems to be strangely lacking in the rough, colorful characters he had known long ago, in the days before he was famous. Indeed, the sailors look to Eden like so many "stolid-faced, ox-minded bestial creatures." The voyage has proved no escape; life for London's autobiographical hero has become "like strong white light that hurts the tired eyes of a sick person." One starry night, Eden squeezes out of the port-hole of his stateroom and drops into the cool, dark, eternal embrace of the sea.

In all of London's prophetic writings, there is no prophecy which came to pass more accurately than the conclusion of *Martin Eden*. Before London would reach the final moment of despair, however, there remained his equivalent of Eden's sea voyage, his one grand effort to escape.

vii

By 1908, London knew what was happening to him. The process of "making money out of socialism" slowly was killing him. Earning over sixty thousand dollars a year, London was nevertheless continually hard up; to prove that a bastard could be an aristocrat meant living on "canvasback and terra-

---

and independence are royal things that cannot be presented to, nor thrust upon, races or classes. If races and classes cannot rise up and try their strength of brain and brawn, wrest from the world liberty, freedom, and independence, they never in time can come to these royal posses-sions. . . ."

pin, with champagne," and that cost money, even more than London was making. The only way to keep on living in the style to which he had become accustomed was to write, write, write. He wrote a thousand words every morning, rain or shine, sickness or health, inspiration or no inspiration. He converted every scrap of his experience into fiction — he went around Cape Horn, and the trip became a novel; a trip to the South Seas became a travel book, a novel and three books of short stories; a trip to Hawaii was converted into two novels and several stories. He bought plot ideas from young writers from coast to coast (including a young man named Sinclair Lewis); he plagiarized from other writers so often and so flagrantly that in the last decade of his life London was scarcely ever free from a plagiarism suit; he changed the titles of stories he had already sold and resold them to different magazines. Despite such expedients, there remained the high cost of living and the consequent daily stint of one thousand words. After a time, the whole thing became murderous. Success, to London, tasted as sour as socialism.

The only way out was to make a complete break, get away entirely. Marx had referred to farming as the "idiocy of rural life," and Alger's stories had informed countless farm boys of how much more exciting life could be in the big city, so that there is an apt symbolism in the fact that when London made his escape from his career as a millionaire socialist he instinctively turned to country life.

As was so often the case with London, he embodied all of his hopes for the future in a novel. Written just before his plan to escape was put into effect,* *Burning Daylight* is a

* London had begun to purchase land in Sonoma County in 1905, but not until 1909–1910 did he definitely decide to quit city life and make his permanent home in the country.

daydream of peace and quiet, solace and serenity. The novel expresses all of London's hopes that the flight from the city would furnish him respite from the problems that seemed to bear down on him harder and harder with each passing year.

Elam Harnish, whose first name London hoped his readers would spell backwards, inevitably possesses an "almost perfect brain" and "super-strength." Even among the strong men of the Arctic, London's hero is recognized as a man out of the ordinary. He can drink titanic amounts of whisky without ill effects; he can drive a dog sled two thousand miles in sixty days, dance right through until morning the night he makes camp and hit the trail again as soon as daylight begins to burn. His business talent is nonpareil: a speculative purchase of two tons of flour which nets him a quick profit of one million dollars is the mere inauguration of a career which, by the time this Alaskan Alger hero is thirty, has made him worth eleven million dollars. Throughout the north, Harnish is known as "King of the Klondike. . . . Eldorado King, Bonanza King, the Lumber Baron, and the Prince of the Stampeders."

Returning to San Francisco — "the soft Southland" — Harnish makes an even greater success. But the pace at which he drives himself eventually begins to tell — for all its seeming softness, life in the Southland moves at a killing speed. To relax his nervous tension, he drinks increasing numbers of Martinis; like London, who had found — as he relates in *John Barleycorn* — that alcohol alone could spur his "jaded mind and spirits," Harnish discovers that without drinking life is intolerable. London, in his youthful water-front days, and Harnish in Alaska had both been capable of withstanding the punishments of dissipation, but in the years after thirty this was no longer true. London, who always had admired his own physique, was horrified to find that his teeth were beginning to go bad and that he was developing a paunch, and this horror is communicated in those pages of *Burning Daylight* which describe Harnish's physical and mental decline under the relentless pressures of excessively hard work and overindulgence in drink.

As Harnish works and drinks harder and harder, he loses his habitual geniality, his speech becomes sharp and nervous, his muscles become flabby and — worst of all — he develops "a definite paunch." But in spite of the pace he maintains, Harnish finds the days are too short for the work he has to do and he is forced to give up eating lunch. His new routine leaves him even more exhausted by evening, so that "as never before, he sought relief behind his wall of alcoholic inhibition." Each morning Harnish awakes with parched lips and mouth, but nevertheless he is at his desk by eight o'clock. Things go from bad to worse. He is terribly humiliated and upset when, at a bar, his hand is forced down by a young man in a test of strength, but the crowning blow occurs in that characteristically Londonesque situation — in front of a mirror.

> He rolled up the sleeve of his pajamas. No wonder the hammer-thrower had put his hand down. Those weren't muscles. A rising tide of fat had submerged them. He stripped off his pajama coat. Again he was shocked, this time by the bulk of his body. It wasn't pretty. The lean stomach had become a paunch. The ridged muscles of chest and shoulders and abdomen had broken down into rolls of flesh.

Terrified, Harnish at once decides to quit his job and to get away before it is too late.

One afternoon, not long before his decision to escape, Harnish had left work early and gone for a horseback ride in the Sonoma hills. Riding along, he is overwhelmed by the peaceful beauty of the scene. "No room here," he thinks, "for all the sordidness, meanness, and viciousness that filled the dirty pool of city existence." It is to the Sonoma country that Harnish goes to rebuild his life. Giving up his fortune and severing all connections with the business world, he buys a farm and settles down. Soon the outdoor life restores him to his fabled strength and throughout the valley he is known as the champion strong man. Life proceeds uneventfully until one day he accidentally discovers that his land contains many rich veins of gold ore. For an instant, Harnish is tempted, and his "old hunting instincts" are aroused. But in the next moment he realizes what the discovery of gold would do to his farm, to the region, and to himself. He laboriously covers over the traces of what he has found and hurries back to his farmhouse. In the closing sentence of the novel, Harnish is seen going down the hill from his simple house "through the fires of sunset with a milkpail on his arm."

The life of simple farmhouses and milkpails in the sunset made a nice picture, but whereas it looked appealing in dreams and novels, it seemed considerably less attractive in the cold light of day. Like the little boy who could not bear to wear homemade undershirts, London the man could not have borne to live on the scale of an ordinary farmer. When London finally decided to flee from the struggle for success, he still found it necessary to go on living like an Alger hero, to surround himself, as H. L. Mencken has sarcastically put it, with all the "trappings of a wealthy cheese-monger." London's move to the country was in the grand manner: he bought two great tracts of land in Sonoma County, rifled the nearby town of all its available talent (the local newspaper complained bitterly when London bought the town's only blacksmith shop for his personal use), and undertook to create the most lavish agricultural operation in the United States.

At its peak, London's agricultural barony produced the "biggest and best" crops of hay in the county; its livestock were "the best-bred, the sleekest and the fattest"; its vegetable garden was "a delight and a huge success." According to one awed observer, London's equipment was so modern as to be almost unique. Included among London's firsts was "the first concrete silo erected in California . . . a big one, too — forty-three feet high and eleven feet in diameter." Even the pigpens were avant-garde.

Such a barony had to have an appropriate house for the baron, and to that end London projected the fabulous "Wolf House," which was to be "the greatest castle in the United States." It would be built out of redwood and stone and would last for all time; it would have a tall stone tower for the author to work in; there were to be seven fireplaces; one of the rooms would measure eighty feet in length. In such a setting, London's insistence that his Korean valet call him "Mr. God" might not seem so incongruous. By 1913, London had thirty-five men working full time in building his dream house, in addition to the fifty-three-man crew he employed to maintain his farm. London's payroll ran to the staggering figure of three thousand dollars a month.

Thus, instead of escaping the pace that killed, London found that in the country he had to turn out fiction that would sell just as fast as ever; he had not escaped Alger's "great race" after all. Indeed, as the fancy farm went deeper and deeper into the red, he was bound ever more tightly to the daily stint of one thousand words. In a letter to an admirer, London confessed, "I go each day to my daily task as a slave would go to his task. I detest writing." Desperate to "quit pen scratching

for good" if he possibly could, London fell hard for the eucalyptus craze. Eucalyptus trees would not only provide a way
out of writing, but more money than ever before. London enthusiastically planted thousands of seedlings over hundreds of
acres. He had spent more than fifty thousand dollars and had
raised over one hundred and fifty thousand trees when the
bottom fell out of the market. Calamities mounted — his prize
pigs caught pneumonia, his prize bull broke its neck, and one
night, while London looked on with tears streaming down his
face, the almost-completed Wolf House burned to the ground.
But still the bills came, and London was forced to sell himself
into a five-year writing contract with *Cosmopolitan*. The stint
of one thousand words a day kept on inexorably.

The tone of *The Little Lady of the Big House*, another
novel about life in the country which appeared six years after
Burning Daylight, is drastically different from that of its pred-
ecessor. Dick Forrest, five feet ten, one hundred and eighty
pounds, aged forty, is no modest farmer with a milkpail on
his arm, but the master of broad California acres. Countless
agricultural specialists are employed in keeping his farm as
modern as possible. Forrest, who supervises the entire multi-
farious operation himself, begins his day at four-thirty in the
morning, when, from the bedroom of his Hispano-Mooresque
"Big House," he checks the clocks, barometers, and wind dials
which are artfully concealed in the wall behind his bed.
Happy in his work, Forrest is also happily married to a
woman who, like himself, is "compounded of sheerest democracy and equally sheer royalty."

Trouble begins when a friend of Forrest's comes to visit
them. He is Evan Graham, a handsome man of "old American stock." Paula, Forrest's wife, finds that she loves Graham
as much as she loves her husband, and that she cannot make

up her mind between them. The country idyl which Forrest had been enjoying is suddenly at an end. Admiring his friend Evan and loving Paula as much as ever, Forrest feels that the only thing for him to do is to kill himself and make it look like an accident. But before he can put his plan into effect, Paula shoots herself with a rifle. The description of her death, which ends the novel, is handled by London as if the dying Paula were simply going to sleep:

> Semi-consciously she half-turned on her side, curved her free arm on the pillow and nestled her head on it, and drew her body up in nestling curves in the way Dick knew she loved to sleep. After a long time, she sighed faintly, and began so easily to go that she was gone before they guessed.

London's dream of escape, which once had been associated with the flight from the city, was now unmistakably associated with death.

The new association was of course an old one, stretching far back to the night when the young man who had drunk too much thought to drown himself in San Francisco Bay. "To me," London once wrote, "the idea of death is sweet. Think of it — to lie down and go into the dark out of all the struggle and pain of living — to go to sleep and rest, always to be resting." On another occasion he asserted that "Man possesses but one freedom, namely, the anticipating of the day of his death. . . ." Suicide is the theme of several London short stories, just as it served as the climax for both *Martin Eden* and *The Little Lady of the Big House*. Indeed, death runs like a red thread through all of London's work.

London, in late 1916, had money, land, and international fame. But, as he expressed it in a short story called "When God Laughs," which is also an allegory of his life, to possess is to be sated. "Satiety and possession are Death's horses; they run in span." On the night of November 21, London carefully figured out on a pad of paper which lay on the night table beside his bed how much morphine sulfate constituted a lethal dose. When he had finished his calculations, he took the dose, turned out the light and went to bed. Jack London's last dream of escape did not fail him.

BOOK TWO

The Second Generation

CHAPTER III

David Graham Phillips: The Dream
Panderer

"Oh, it isn't that I mind the glittering caste system," admitted Amory. "I like having a bunch of hot cats on top, but
gosh, Kerry, I've got to be one of them."

— F. SCOTT FITZGERALD, *This Side of Paradise*

AMORY BLAINE, first of F. Scott Fitzgerald's romantic projections of himself, woke up in 1920 and looked cynically about
him. The cause of his cynicism was the realization that he belonged to

> a new generation, shouting the old cries, learning the old
> creeds, through a revery of long days and nights; destined
> finally to go out into that dirty gray turmoil to follow love
> and pride; a new generation dedicated more than the last
> to the fear of poverty and the worship of success; grown
> up to find all Gods dead, all wars fought, all faith in man
> shaken. . . .

Blaine's famous disillusionment seemed at the time to mean
that the country's memories of 1917–1918 were not nice and
that as a result the Stutz Bearcat and the pocket flask were

here to stay. Upon re-examination, however, Fitzgerald's words reveal a good deal more. They show us that World War I was actually only one of a number of experiences contributing to the process of his hero's disillusionment — indeed, perhaps only the straw that broke the camel's back — and they remind us of the validity of the historical proposition which says that in order to understand a generation in its maturity one must go back to its point of origin. The celebrated disenchantment of the American twenties did not flower out of the soil of war, but out of the bewildering and confusing times in the first decade of the twentieth century.

Bewildering and confusing for precisely those people traditionally assumed to comprise the most assured, and stable, and self-confident groups in the society of the time: the white, native-born middle classes. Despite family incomes ranging from two to fifteen thousand dollars per annum (the national average in this period was under six hundred dollars), and their proud consciousness of stemming from "old American stock," the middle classes at the turn of the century were far from content.

For one thing, it was upon these people that the "traditional American expectation of epic achievement" fell most heavily. The middle-class generation which came of age between the first election of McKinley and the re-election of Wilson was following on the heels of the most titanically successful generation in our history. The era just closed had been one of breath-taking accomplishment, which the new age admired, but dreaded to regard. For in the Alger canon success involved outdoing one's parents, yet by 1900 this was manifestly impossible. The comprehensiveness, as well as the size, of the older generation's achievement militated against a superior performance by its children. The new generation worshiped success, perhaps even more than the last, but grew up only to find all robber barons dead.*

The epic achievement of 1865–1900 had also changed the face of a continent, and this fact, too, helped to throw the new middle classes off balance. Industrialization, the dramatic and sudden growth of the cities, immigration — now increasingly from Southern and Eastern Europe — the rise of the great trust formations, the surprising entrance of the United States on the stage of world power, these things were transforming America at an incredible rate of speed. If immigrants to this country were baffled by its strangeness, the predicament of the middle classes was in a way even more acute. They fondly remembered, as the immigrants could not, the American scenes of their childhood, but now, suddenly, nothing seemed familiar; within a few years' time the America of their memory had done an inexplicable vanishing act. The Middletown of the Lynds' study had been until the mid-eighties a placid county seat of six thousand inhabitants. Industrialization doubled the population in half a decade, tripled it again in thirty years. Booth Tarkington's novels, in particular *The Turmoil* and *The Magnificent Ambersons*, catch the middle classes' bewilderment in the face of the rapid turn of events. The midland city in which the novels are set had been, just the day before yesterday, reassuringly familiar — "a pleasant big town of neighborly people," a place where "the air was clean and there was time to live"; time, indeed, and here Tarkington defined a whole world — "for everything: time to think, to talk, time to read, time to wait for a lady!"

* That the mill-boy-to-millionaire career of Andrew Carnegie could no longer be taken as the archetypal experience of the American business leader is indicated by the fact that almost half of the country's top business executives in the decade 1901–1910 had spent their entire careers on salary. They had risen, but the curve was far less steep than Carnegie's.

Then, into this peaceful, friendly place, came the turmoil. The town heaved up in the middle, incredibly, and spread, incredibly,

> and as it heaved and spread, it befouled itself and darkened its sky. Its boundary was mere shapelessness on the run; a raw, new house would appear on a country road . . . the country road would turn into an asphalt street with a brick-faced drug-store and a frame grocery at a corner.

The belching smoke and soot from the new factories covered everything, and "foreigners" poured in from everywhere, from the South, from Europe and Asia. Now there was time for nothing but getting ahead, and one's neighbors were strangers — and strange-looking. "The old, leisurely, quizzical look of the faces was lost in something harder and warier; and a cockney type began to emerge discernibly — a cynical young mongrel, barbaric of feature, muscular and cunning." The very language of the people changed: "In place of the old midland vernacular, irregular but clean, and not unwholesomely drawling, a jerky dialect of coined metaphors began to be heard."

Then, too, while the smoke of the cities cried, "Wealth!" it was not always for the same people who had in the past been accustomed to having money. The twentieth century brought with it a reduction in economic status for many middle-class families. The decline and fall of the magnificent Ambersons exemplifies the phrase current at the time: shirt sleeves to shirt sleeves in three generations. Tied up in unprofitable real estate, the Amberson fortune fades away to nothing in the short, swift years of the town's industrialization. The grandson of the Amberson who, in the eighties, had kept a stable full of the finest horses, is forced, in the early teens, to seek employment in a nitroglycerine factory.

Even for those who were more quick than the Ambersons to recognize the industrial wave of the future, the period was a trying one. The election of McKinley in 1896 had ushered in a new era of prosperity, but with the full dinner pail came steadily mounting prices, especially in rent, food and clothing. In the twenty-year period ending in 1912, prices rose exactly twice as fast as the national income. Accustomed to a comfortable standard of living and highly conscious of their status, the middle classes resented extremely the least reduction in their way of life; they could adjust to the phenomenon of increased prices perhaps more easily than a family earning six hundred dollars a year, but the frustration of many middle-class families was intense.

On top of high prices came panic, in 1907. Middle-class businessmen, already feeling the mounting pressure of competition with the big companies, took the punishment of the panic far less easily than did their more powerful rivals. Harassed, upset, the middle classes sought sublimation of their problems through the medium of entertainment. To a far greater extent than today, entertainment for middle-class Americans of fifty years ago consisted in reading books and magazines. Native-born, highly literate and lacking television, they turned to reading (mostly fiction) for solace. Constituting the largest reading audience the world had yet seen, these people afforded to those writers and editors who knew what the middle classes wanted an unparalleled opportunity.

One man who shrewdly sensed what they wanted became editor, in 1899, of a decrepit, run-down magazine which only the year before had been knocked down in a sale for one thousand dollars. Cyrus H. K. Curtis, the new owner of the *Saturday Evening Post*, gave his young editor a free hand to do with the magazine what he wanted, and sailed for Europe.

George Horace Lorimer rolled up his sleeves and went to work. Middle-class to the bone himself, Lorimer believed that what he wanted to read was exactly what his potential audience wanted as well: business fiction, articles about business leaders, political articles — preferably written by professional politicians (Lorimer had a fondness for words from the horse's mouth) — inspirational essays on getting ahead, reminiscences by famous men of their boyhoods, editorials denouncing unrestricted immigration or spanking the knuckles of the trusts, colored covers depicting George Washington, Independence Hall, the family doctor, or a man priming a frozen pump on a wintry morning. Lorimer knew what they wanted, better than they did; his only problem was recruitment of talent to do the providing. How quickly Lorimer solved the problem is indicated by the fact that in the tenth year of his editorship a new legend appeared on the cover of the *Post:* "More than a Million a Week."

Lorimer found many talented men to do the kind of work he was looking for: Norris, London and Herrick in that first decade, and, later on, Tarkington and Fitzgerald. He prospected for unknown writers by personally reading — or so Lorimer's biographer insists — all unsolicited manuscripts sent to the *Post,* and by scanning the daily press for signs of talent. It was in this latter fashion that he made one of his luckiest and earliest discoveries, a man whose writing had everything Lorimer was looking for. The writer was David Graham Phillips.

In 1900, Phillips was making eight thousand dollars a year on Pulitzer's *New York World.* Aged thirty-three, he had already been star reporter, foreign correspondent and editorial writer for the paper. In addition, he was a member of a select entourage which corresponded and conversed with the great

Pulitzer himself. Still a young man, Phillips had accomplished much, and ahead of him, if he kept on, lay the top of the *World*. Instead, in 1902, he quit. He wanted to free-lance, both in fiction and reporting.

Phillips had begun writing short stories long before he left the newspaper profession. He would work on the paper (at that time he was connected with the New York *Sun*) until midnight, then go home and write until dawn. His enormous capacity for work persisted the rest of his life. When Phillips left the *World*, he set up a schedule for writing from which he never thereafter deviated; beginning at eleven o'clock at night, he wrote until six the following morning, seven days a week. In the nine years between 1902 and his death (Phillips was murdered in Gramercy Park in 1911), he produced twenty-five books, as well as hundreds of articles and short stories. If superhuman performance were the warrant of literary fame, Phillips would be outranked only by Jack London in the national pantheon. Phillips's biographer, reverentially regarding this awesome production, has bestowed on him the ultimate American accolade — Phillips's career, he has written, was truly a "Horatio Alger story in real life."

Phillips and Lorimer must have met sometime during the first year of Lorimer's editorship. The thought of that encounter carries with it a sense of historical inevitability. Demand, that day, met, if it ever did, supply. In the ten years of their acquaintance, the two men became mutual admirers and the closest of friends, Lorimer playing the role of adviser as well as editor to Phillips even though he was the younger man. Many of Phillips's novels, including *Joshua Craig*, which would lead him eventually to his bizarre death, first appeared serially in the *Post*. In his first three years of free-lancing, over fifty articles under his name appeared in the magazine, and

THE DREAM OF SUCCESS

in this same period he wrote most of the *Post's* increasingly influential editorials.

In spite of Phillips's tremendous output, not one of his novels today gives substance to his ambitious boast that he would become the secretary of American society, that his fiction would mirror the secret history of the United States. If his name is now remembered at all, it is as the muckraking reporter whom the editor of Hearst's *Cosmopolitan* persuaded to write the sensational articles on "The Treason of the Senate." His novels, always concerned with contemporary themes, always purporting to give the "true facts" and the "inside story," are as dead as yesterday's newspaper.

Yet Phillips is an interesting figure, even an important one. For through Lorimer Phillips made contact with the great middle-class audience which was, quite literally, waiting for him. Americans read his novels with weekly devotion in the *Post,* and then bought them in hard covers, because he lent to their anticlimactic lives a sense of excitement and achievement; in the midst of a strange new world Phillips brought them back the brave old world, *redivivus;* they were unsure of themselves (Phillips numbered among his readers, so Fitzgerald has told us, the adolescent Amory Blaine) and his novels were filled with certainties. Thus — and this is what makes him important — Phillips actually did for a time become the secretary of American society, except that the "secret history of the United States" he wrote was not the Balzacian human comedy he had in mind. Phillips's novels, taken all in all, do compose a secret history — not, however, of the private lives of middle-class Americans, but of their private, innermost hopes and dreams. In pandering to those dreams, Phillips has managed to furnish us with an invaluable account of them.

ii

Phillips the novelist, like Phillips the reporter, was an inside dopester. His novels tell not only a story but the "straight story." This was a fortunate circumstance, because what the troubled middle classes were looking for in their fiction was a description of who or what was causing all the trouble. Revelation by novel began with his very first book, *The Great God Success.**

The hero, a young man with the "energy of unconquerable resolution," has come to New York to enter the newspaper profession. He soon becomes a great reporter and is regarded along Park Row as a brilliant success. In his heart, however, he knows that he is a "brilliant failure" — he does his job without half trying, he is not really interested, he listlessly lets the chances "that are always thrusting themselves" at him slip by. "Will the stimulus to ambition," he wonders, "never come?" Finally, it does, in the shape of a political campaign. "The cause aroused his passion for justice, for democratic equality and the abolition of privilege." Henceforward, he works like a demon. He becomes editor in chief of the paper; he publishes exposés of corruption and professed reformers; he attacks the best people. Under his dynamic direction, circulation soars. His income mounts right along with the circulation, enabling him in a few years to buy the paper. More steadfastly than ever "an organ of the people," the paper grows more and more influential, and profitable. Then, once more, comes a political campaign, more crucial than the last. Both

* Published in 1901 under the nom de plume of John Graham. John Graham is also the name of the hero in George Horace Lorimer's bestselling novel *Letters from a Self-Made Merchant to His Son.*

for "the people" and their journalistic champion, the escha-
tological moment has arrived:

> The great battle was on — the battle he had in his
> younger days looked forward to and longed for — the
> battle against Privilege and for a "restoration of govern-
> ment by the people." The candidates were nominated, the
> platforms put forward and the issue squarely joined.

So squarely, in fact, that the forces of Privilege are scared.
The campaign has put their control of the country in jeopardy.
They send an emissary to the hero with instructions to offer
him an ambassadorship if he will shift his editorial position.
The hero takes the bribe and political victory is once more
snatched from the hands of the people.

The childlike naïveté of Phillips's "exposé"— a New York
newspaper abruptly switches sides and a national election is
lost — was nevertheless appealing because of its very simplic-
ity. By reducing the meaning of modern America to a fight
between two great opponents — the People versus Privilege —
Phillips was using a common denominator already familiar to
his readers: this was, all over again, the Puritans' struggle
against the forces of evil for control of the world; this was the
polarized rhetoric familiar in every political campaign since
Jackson.

If the combat was familiar, however, one of the combatants
was not. There was no difficulty with "the People"— Phillips's
middle-class readers, highly conscious that they were *echte
Amerikaner,* readily defined the term as being coextensive
with themselves. But beyond telling them that the forces of
Privilege always preferred bribery and cheating to honest
combat, Phillips had not, in this first novel, given them much
more than a label. His books for the next few years were concerned with the task of further amplification.

Giving Privilege a local habitation as well as a name was easy; the address was, in the words of one of his characters, "That *damned* East!" Until the day he died Phillips blasted the East, particularly New York, with a steady stream of vituperation and abuse. Eastern businessmen were "respectable thieves" and "oily rascals," an "impudent and cowardly crowd." New York was corrupt, and corrupting, the siren city "that lures young men from the towns and the farms, and prostitutes them, teaches them to sell themselves with un-blushing cheeks for a fee, for an office, for riches, for power." New York was no place to raise a child, no place indeed for any decent person to live — anyone doing so ran the risk of becoming fouled by the "slime of sordidness" which the city dabbled "on every flower in the garden of human nature."

Determining the identity of these Eastern cowards and rascals proved to be more difficult. Phillips was sure that a conspiracy of Privilege controlled the country, controlled its finances, its political parties, its destiny. But he could never quite decide who were the conspirators. In *The Cost,* Phillips talked darkly of "the half-dozen big corporations" which, by dominating both political parties, were exploiting the country, but did not specify any further. This was still terribly vague; if Phillips was to maintain his standing as an inside dopester, it was imperative that he do better. The following year he published two novels, each purporting to be the confessions of an ex-member of the conspiracy.

The Plum Tree enlarged upon the political machinations hinted at in *The Cost.* The narrator of the novel is an expert on such machinations, inasmuch as he has been until recently the political superboss charged with dispensing "the money that maintained the political machinery of both parties," buying off legislatures and purchasing election victories.

The forces of Privilege in *The Plum Tree* controlled affairs, but as Phillips was at pains to show, the conspiracy was a house divided against itself. The narrator is a Midwesterner, which is to say in a Phillips novel, a sensible man.* His policy, albeit dishonest, is one of moderation — "to yield to the powerful few a minimum of what they could compel, to give to the prostrate but potentially powerful many at least enough to keep them quiet — a stomachful." He, and the corporations he represents, are thwarted in this plan, however, by the Eastern stockmarket crowd, which wants to milk the country dry. Thus, in *The Plum Tree*, "the half-dozen big corporations" which had played the villain in *The Cost* emerge as rather less than ruthless in the matter of exploitation and rather less than dominant within the conspiracy. Business was apt to be Midwestern and therefore could be forgiven a certain amount of judicious corruption; Wall Street was indubitably Eastern and immoderate and culpable.

The "authentic" tone of the narration and the sensationally sordid portrayal of American politics gave the book a passing notoriety — Theodore Roosevelt said the novel had been very widely read, was very popular, and gave an entirely false impression — but when all was said *The Plum Tree* only amounted to an ordinary, run-of-the-mill diatribe against Wall Street, of the sort often voiced by Roosevelt himself, and before him by Bryan and the Populists. But since Phillips desperately needed to expose the forces of evil in palpable form,

---

* A point not always recognized by modern critics. Alfred Kazin sees Harvey Sayler, the narrator, as "an incorrigible rascal." Inasmuch as Kazin misspells the narrator's name and claims that he dies "unshriven and unloved" (when, in fact, the end of the novel finds a very much alive Sayler in the arms of the woman he loves), his opinion of the novel cannot be considered reliable.

apparently even a moth-eaten scapegoat was better than none.

After *The Plum Tree* came *The Deluge*. The confession in this instance is made by a former financial agent of the Wall Street conspiracy, the "seven cliques," said Phillips, which have "the political and industrial United States at their mercy." With the country. "prostrate under their iron heels," the cliques are looting the nation at will. They have forcibly ejected "free American labor" from industry and substituted "importations of coolie Huns and Bohemians." They have for some time levied hidden taxes upon commodities all the way along the line from producer to consumer, so that the prices of "all the things for which . . . wages must be spent" are constantly being forced higher and higher. The seven cliques have also entered the business world, but not to manage, only to despoil. "They reaped only where and what others had sown; they touched industry only to plunder and blight it." While "torrents of unjust wealth" pour in upon the cliques, their systematic banditry continues to play havoc with the major industries of the country and to impoverish and demoralize the people still further. Who belonged to the seven cliques? Phillips's narrator confirmed *The Plum Tree* if not *The Cost;* the real conspirators weren't businessmen at all, they were "rascals of high finance."

But Phillips did not stick with his Wall Street story for long either. Only two years after *The Deluge* he was insisting that the insurance business was really the fount of all evil in America. As always, the new enemy was everywhere, and the cause of every wrong. The insurance trust, he claimed in *Light-Fingered Gentry,* "controlled about one half of the entire wealth of the country; not a blade was harvested, not a wheel was turned, not a pound of freight was lifted from Maine to the Pacific but that they directly or indirectly got a 'rake off.' "

Phillips's revelations did not vie merely with one another in these years; they also had to compete with those of other writers who were riding the crest of the sudden national craze over muckraking. (While, for example, Phillips was readying his insurance exposé for publication, Upton Sinclair was assuring the country that "a gigantic combination of capital" called the "Beef Trust," which had spread out from the stockyards of Chicago and now controlled "railroads and trolley lines, gas and electric franchises," was behind everything. The "incarnation of blind and insensate Greed," the Beef Trust ran the government of Chicago and dictated to that of the nation; it wiped out "thousands of businesses every year" and everywhere "drove men to madness and suicide.") The reasons for such competition were inherent in the exposé business itself; if one's revelations were not to become stale they perforce had to keep changing; and in order for the newest revelation to be considered important, omnipotent power and total depravity had to be claimed for each new villain. Eventually Phillips decided it was less hazardous to describe how the torrents of unjust wealth were spent than how they were come by, so that finally his novels became more concerned with the sociology of Privilege than with its economics or its politics.

The "reign of glitter" was also, of course, centered on New York, with outlying satrapies in Boston, Washington and the Harvard Yard. Throughout the East, said Phillips, "concentrated private wealth had been rising for a generation with amazing rapidity. Suddenly it overflowed in a waterfall of luxurious living . . . today the waterfall has become a Niagara" — and Manhattan Island was "the high-curving centre of the down-pouring, glittering stream." In New York there were more than two hundred private houses the equal of palaces in size and cost and showiness, more than five hundred imposing hotels and apartment houses built of marble or granite, hundreds of luxurious stores. In the best shops,

> you are dazzled and overwhelmed by the careless torrent of luxury . . . . twenty-five dollars for a pair of shoes, fifteen dollars for a pair of stockings, two hundred dollars for a hat, one thousand dollars for a hat-pin or parasol, fifteen hundred for a small gold bottle for a woman's dressing table, thirty or forty thousand for a tiara, a hundred thousand for a string of pearls. . . .

Phillips's official attitude toward all this extravagance was extravagantly condemnatory, in much the same way as was his attitude toward New York in general. He found particularly offensive the pharisaical caste system of the newly risen American aristocracy. A professional Anglophobe, Phillips could think of nothing worse to say of New York's "gospel of snobbishness" than to denounce it as a "disease imported into this country from England." He raged at rich Americans for allowing English servants and English fortune hunters to make fools of them. In respect to the new pretentiousness Lorimer and Phillips were particularly close, and the *Post* published three serialized books and many articles by Phillips lampooning the social ambitions of Eastern snobs. American heiresses, affected and silly, with a fatal predilection for titled Europeans, were satirized by Phillips again and again.

The "rich" American who took the brunt of his abuse, however, was Theodore Roosevelt, whom Phillips loathed. Born to the manner of snobbish New York society, Roosevelt had been educated at what Phillips called that breeding ground of idiots, Harvard College, where men were taught "to use their lips in making words as a Miss Nancy sort of man uses his fingers in doing fancy work" and were urged "to believe themselves superior in intellectual knowledge." Worse, Harvard encouraged, as did all Eastern colleges, "that most un-American thing called class and culture." T. R. in the White House was simply the product of his environment. In *The Social Secretary* (another confessional novel), Phillips had his narrator remark that Europeans in the Washington embassies "laugh all day long at the President's queer manners and mannerisms — but then, so do we, for that matter." Phillips accused Roosevelt of transforming the White House into a Continental court. "The newly evolved notion of the Presidential office," Phillips wrote,

> is that it is the centre of political, intellectual and socio-
> logical authority and also of social honor. Not only must
> the democratic — or plutocratic — overlord, anointed
> with the new kind of divine oil, be the embodiment and
> exponent of the popular will; he must also be the source
> of honor, the recognizer of merit.

These changes were astounding, and yet they were only the beginning, a crude inaugural, Phillips felt, of the Washington of the future. "But it is a beginning — a most audacious move on the part of one of the most audacious men who ever rose to first place in the republic."

Thanks to the bad example of Roosevelt and other Eastern snobs, Phillips asserted, the worship of luxury was spreading across the entire continent. Even the Midwest showed signs of succumbing to the East's crazy passion for luxury and display. Like the plutocracy of business and politics, the plutocracy of society was everywhere. "The real people," (Phillips meant his readers) "those true Americans who think, who aspire, who advance, who work and take pleasure and pride in their work, the people who have built our republic," were surrounded. They could be destroyed, he cried, if such un-American activity continued unchecked.

Yet while Phillips gave voice to the middle classes' self-pity that they were not rich, he reinforced their optimism, too, with elaborate descriptions of the luckless fate of the wealthy. The rich in his novels lead a dog's life of broken marriages, lost friends, and spiritual boredom. The greatest of all sufferings visited upon the wealthy in Phillips's fiction is their children. In describing them, Phillips raised the success mythology's traditional contempt for poor little rich boys to a memorable pitch.

The children of wealth in his books are truly fearsome. They are a "self-intoxicated, stupid and pretentious genera-tion, a polo-playing and racing and hunting, a yachting and palace-dwelling and money-scattering generation; a business-despising and business-neglecting, an old-world aristocracy-imitating generation." Phillips's rich children are ashamed of the crudity of their parents' conduct in front of the English servants; they speak to their fathers only to ask for larger al-lowances; they allow their mothers to wait on them. Not only do they not know how to think, they are so faint-hearted that the fathers must actually make their marriage proposals for them. Most important of all, they have no talent whatsoever for business, for "that is the rule — the second generation of a plutocrat inherits, with his money, the meanness that enables him to hoard it, but not the scope that enables him to make it." That the children of wealth were incapable of earning a living was a generalization which had for Phillips all the cer-tainty of a physical law.

Just as soon as one of us becomes ashamed of his birth or of his own past, becomes infected with the cheap and silly vulgarisms that Europe is always thrusting upon us,

137

just so soon does he or she begin to fall behind in the procession. Influential relatives will not long save him or her, nor inherited property. . . .

Only that part of the coming generation that was trained in "Democracy" would survive and prosper in the coming times. "The part that is bred in exclusiveness and caste feeling," he warned, "is going to be bitterly discontented and deplorably unprogressive certainly, and in all probability, except in a few rare cases, downright unprosperous."

One of Phillips's most important books, *The Second Generation*, was written to illustrate this thesis. It is the story of a father who gives away all his money for the sake of his children. If the novel is scarcely believable, it is fine fantasy. The father is a self-made man, a rich manufacturer, who in his declining years broods about the vanity and uselessness of his children. Especially is he worried about his son, a languid clotheshorse recently fired from Harvard, who is vastly insulted when his father suggests he get a job. Knowing that he will die soon, the father seeks the advice of a learned acquaintance, who tells him that wealth is a curse, that it stops the wheels of progress. A religious man, the acquaintance points to the Garden of Eden as an example of leisure-class living and reminds the father that when God saw what a bad idea Eden had turned out to be, God forthwith abandoned it. The analogy overpowers the old man; in his will he cuts off his son with five thousand dollars, leaving the bulk of his fortune to the welfare of the people. As it turns out, this plan benefits not only the public, but the son as well. Saying, "I've got to 'get busy' if I'm to pull out of this mess," the son enthusiastically pitches into his factory job. With a "thousand damn fool ideas" soon knocked out of his skull, he shows a great head for business. The end of the novel finds him happy, married, and in control of his father's old factory. The moral of the story could not have been more clear: the father's will had worked out beautifully for all concerned — therefore, would not all rich businessmen be advised to adopt it? Such a quick and painless solution to the problem of Privilege!

Time and again Phillips told the rich that work was the only way to salvation, as well as the only real earthly happiness man could know. "Remember," Phillips told them, "that working out a fixed purpose in life is just as amusing as drinking champagne and fox-hunting." Manifestly, however, they were too far gone, too stupid, to take his advice. Even the rich who enjoyed reading about the "gospel of work" still clung to their preference for the "gospel of snobbishness." James Hazen Hyde, the playboy who inherited the fortune which his father had amassed in the Equitable Life Assurance Society, was a Phillips fan — but Hyde still preferred throwing his fabulous parties to buckling down. Nor did their folly get the rich into trouble. Despite Phillips's predictions to the contrary, the plutocracy did not fall of its own weight, but obstinately continued to glitter and to control. It was all very frustrating.

From the depths of discouragement Phillips once wrote: "The Jews of ancient days are not the only people who have dreamed of a Messiah. The Messiah-dream, the Messiah-longing, has been the dream and the longing of the whole human race, toiling away in obscurity, oppressed, exploited, fooled, despised."

At the beginning of the twentieth century, there were two likely candidates for the job of Messiah of the American middle classes. Bryan could conceivably have filled the bill; certainly he stood on the side of the angels in the great battle against Privilege. But to the middle classes, Bryan's opposition to "government of, by and for plutocracy," had been, in Phil-

lips's words, "fantastic, extreme, entangled with social, economic and political lunacies." Bryan had the look of a Messiah, but free silver was not a panacea which appealed to
people who, like Phillips, had money in the bank and an income well above the national average. To some Americans,
Theodore Roosevelt had the Messianic look, too, but Phillips
was not one of them. The prince of snobs, he was sure, could
not possibly represent the self-reliant middle classes. T. R.
talked in a large way, but he was actually timid when it
came to "really acting against rich people." In addition,
Roosevelt was not the foe of bigness per se; he liked to make
distinctions between good trusts and bad ones. Phillips, convinced that some supertrust of conspirators ran the whole
show, considered distinctions between individual trusts patent
nonsense. Indeed, in his eyes such talk only rendered Roosevelt suspect of being soft toward the conspiracy. As he told his
friend Senator Albert J. Beveridge, Phillips was convinced
that "Teddy is at heart with Wall Street," a conviction which
was reinforced by the fact that the Roosevelt administration
busted very few trusts.

Thus there existed the dream of a Messiah, yet for many
Americans the dream had never materialized. In the absence
of an actual Messiah, however, there was always the solace of
Phillips's novels. For if the Saviour did not walk the earth, he
did appear in fiction. Phillips's conjuration of the hero who
would deliver middle-class America from the wilderness became the major activity of his writing career.

iii

Phillips's Lochinvars all come out of the West, that "earnest,
deeply religious" region where, although the cities might be

tainted by wealth, there were still small towns and farms with "no tendencies toward the development of caste." More specifically, they have been born and bred in Indiana. This last detail was added by Phillips not simply because he himself happened to be a native of the state. He included it quite purposefully, for all of his saviors are in reality the same character, wearing various disguises from book to book, and this archetypal Messiah is the fused and terrifically romanticized image of two famous Hoosiers of the day: Albert J. Beveridge and the politician's "oldest and best-loved friend," Phillips himself.

The two men had met when they were both undergraduates at Asbury University (later DePauw) in Indiana. Phillips was attracted to Beveridge right from the start, because "there always was a fascination for me in strength." Phillips, whose upbringing had been cushioned by a prosperous and indulgent family, was completely overawed by the ex-plowboy who was so plainly on his way toward the United States Senate. In Phillips's second year they became roommates. Beveridge was working his way through college partly by winning debates, and to this end he arose every morning at four-thirty and trudged off to the woods near the college to practice speaking. Phillips watched from the window as he went up the street and marveled.

Out in the woods where Beveridge orated in the dawn light, there was a certain tree to which, every day for four years after he graduated, Beveridge unfailingly returned and carved the letter "S," one letter above the other, standing for the word success. "I had the superstition, you remember [Beveridge wrote to Phillips], that if I did not . . . I wouldn't be successful." Phillips did remember, because in his imagination the man who had gone to the woods was in truth

141

himself. ("Men of strong energies," said Phillips, "seem to be projections of our own inner selves — of our strongest aspiration.") The Messiah of his novels acts like Beveridge, but, significantly, he looks like Phillips.

The Messiah plays two principal roles in Phillips's fiction, one political, the other economic.

The most important of the political figures is the character of Hampden Scarborough, who appears or is mentioned in several Phillips novels. Scarborough is first introduced in *The Cost* as a poor young man determined to work his way through college. He has a "look of superiority" and is yet the perfect democrat — a descendant of "men who had learned to hate kings in Holland in the sixteenth century, had learned to despise them in England." Phillips himself was six feet three, blond, and handsome, but Scarborough must be considered an instance of art improving upon nature: "The tall, powerful figure; the fair hair growing above his wide and lofty brow, with the one defiant lock; and in his aquiline nose and blue-gray eyes and almost perfect mouth and chin the stamp of one who would move forward irresistibly, moving others to his will."

Scarborough refuses to join one of the college fraternities — they are aristocratic — and he organizes a successful fight against them for control of the college literary society. The speech he makes at the height of the controversy already has the authentic ring: "It is time to rededicate our society to equality, to freedom of thought and speech. . . ." Scarborough's voice, even more than what he says, thrills the assembled throng. (He had been practicing in the woods every morning.)

From this triumph it is but an easy leap to reading law at night, and politics. Soon he is the leader of the "forces of honesty in his party," opposed to the "forces of the machine," which, like their opposite number in the other party, are controlled by the conspiracy of Privilege. Though the machine tries bribery to prevent it, Scarborough succeeds in winning his party's nomination for governor (his voice in the convention hall was "like magic, rising and falling in thrilling inflections as it wove its spell of gold and fire.") A few months later he is elected. "At last" — a phrase that longingly echoes again and again through Phillips's novels — "the people had in their service a lawyer equal in ability to the best the monopolies could buy, and one who understood human nature and political machinery to boot."

What does Scarborough do in office? How does he defeat the conspiracy — as he surely must? What happens next? The answers to these questions are strangely not to be found in *The Cost*. For, with his election, Scarborough abruptly disappears from the reader's sight, although the novel is far from concluded. After dominating the book for the first two thirds of its length, he is scarcely mentioned again in the concluding third. Nor is Scarborough allowed ever again to occupy the center of the stage of a Phillips novel for any length of time.

In *The Plum Tree* we learn that as governor Scarborough has got after "the monopolies," with the consequence that living costs are now a good 20 per cent lower in Indiana than in Ohio, but this interesting accomplishment is performed entirely offstage — we learn of it only secondhand, in a passing sentence. When Phillips finally does permit Scarborough to appear in the novel, his hero is, once again, a political candidate, this time for the Presidency. He is depicted, as always, in the process of making a speech. Scarborough's voice is inevitably musical, and as he stands up on the platform, high above the throng, he seems "a sort of embodiment of fearlessness." His platform consists of a solemn promise to obey the Constitution and enforce the laws. When the people hear this they know that at last they have found the "firebrand to light the torch of revolution back toward what the republic used to be before differences of wealth divided its people into upper, middle and lower classes, before enthroned corporate combinations made equality before the law a mockery. . . ." But he is defeated — the election is bought. Scarborough carries the farms and small towns, just as he had done when he ran for governor, but the city machines and "other purchasable organizations" are enough to beat him. As in *The Cost,* he vanishes from the story after the election without explanation, then just as abruptly turns up again four years later, again as a candidate for President. This time he is elected — and the novel ends.

The hero of *The Fashionable Adventures of Joshua Craig* is subjected to the same now-you-see-him-now-you-don't treatment as Scarborough. The scene of the novel is the nation's capital, for Craig is Attorney General of the United States. As a cabinet officer, the "strenuous young Westerner" is invited to many parties at which he cuts a wide and scornful swath through the effete ranks of Washington society. Finally, Craig becomes thoroughly disgusted with the East and returns to the West, where he is destined to become, in the name of the people, the governor of his native state. But Craig's return to the West is a vanishing act; although he is presumably just entering on the major phase of his career, the novel ends with his departure from Washington.

What distinguishes *Joshua Craig* from *The Cost* and *The Plum Tree* is that more attention is paid in it to the appearance and personality of the Messiah. The fuller portrait is instructive. There is a narcissistic concentration on the details of Craig's physical person that far surpasses anything Phillips had allowed himself before. Craig's head "suggested the rude, fierce figurehead of a Viking galley; the huge, aggressively-masculine features proclaimed ambition, energy, intelligence." But this was just the beginning — Phillips could barely take his eyes off the man: his hero has "powerful shoulders," arms and legs which are "thick and strong, like a lion's or a tiger's" and a "fine head, haughtily set." Craig's eyes "emphasized the impression of arrogance and force. He had the leader's beak-like nose, a handsome form of it, like Alexander's, not like Attila's. The mouth was the orator's — wide, full, and flexible of lips, fluent." Lest the reference to Alexander prove confusing, Phillips hastened to add that Craig's appearance was democratically perfect. That full mouth, for example, was "distinctly not an aristocratic mouth," but one which "suggested common speech and common tastes." His hero's skin, too, lacked that aristocratic "finish of surface which . . . is got only by eating the costly, rare, best and best-prepared food."

To discuss Craig's personality is to describe one of the leading boors in American literature. He habitually insults the woman who loves him, he patronizes his friends because they are, after all, "inferior," to him; his characteristic manner is a "familiar, swaggering bustling braggadocio"; he talks, as someone admiringly tells him, "like Napoleon." * What Phillips's attitude was toward all this is quite clear. Some time after the publication of the novel Phillips wrote a letter to a friend categorically denying that there was anything boorish about his hero. "Josh, it seems clear to me, is a worthy fellow. . . . I know him thoroughly. The ungentle way he acted with Margaret [the woman who loves him] was simply to impress her

* The cult of Napoleon was fashionable in these years and Phillips's Messiahs all have a dash of the Corsican.

145

with his personality, his masculinity." How anyone could have failed to admire his hero was a complete mystery to Phillips.

From his tremendous faith in political solutions, Phillips was capable at times of switching to the position that mere laws could never do the job of protecting what rightfully belonged to the people. When this latter mood was upon him, Lochinvar became an economic not a political man, a business leader not a governor.

Phillips's businessmen, like his politicians, have no desire to be rich or even to make money. What they are interested in is power, and the excitement of winning. Although humbly born, and possessing neither money nor influence, they unfailingly prove themselves more than a match for the great plutocracy in any situation. The plutocracy had, according to Phillips, choked off all competition; its sway, he said, was unchallenged; yet for men like Matthew Blacklock in *The Deluge* and Horace Armstrong in *Light-Fingered Gentry*, men who had only "a will, a brain, courage — and nothing to lose," the forces of Privilege are a pushover. Undismayed by the odds which they face, these men evince nothing but a slightly murderous contempt for their plutocratic opponents. Blacklock, who is a Wall Street financier, boasts, "I'll strew the Street with their blood and broken bones" — and he does. In Armstrong the homicidal urge is even more marked. "The will to kill! To feel that creature [an evil plutocrat] under him, under his knees and fingers; to see eyes and tongue burst out; to know that the brain that dared conceive the thought of making a slave of him was dead for its insolence!" If such tendencies seem alarming to us, they were immensely satisfying to Phillips's readers. The middle classes of the time felt themselves being stifled by overwhelming forces and therefore took vicarious pleasure in reading about what it would be

146

like to have their fingers around a plutocrat's throat. Beveridge, exclaiming over "its fierce climax of bayonet thrust and throat-clutch," called the account of Blacklock's career "mesmeric in its fascination." Phillips's business hero who slew the economic dragon embodied, even more than the politician who defeated the machines and was elected President, the most immediate kind of wish fulfillment.

In telling the story of a Blacklock or an Armstrong, Phillips was also attempting, once again, to give free advice to the rich. Just as they could make their children better people by giving away all their money when they died, so the rich could make more money while they lived if only they would run their businesses the way a Phillips hero did. The business leader of his novels refuses to indulge in "cheating and swindling, lying and pilfering and bribing"; instead of killing off competition, he encourages it; he constantly lowers prices. In the world of fiction, these policies pay off handsomely. "The Golden Rule is not a piece of visionary altruism, but a sound principle of practical self-interest" — and Blacklock and Armstrong wax fat on doing unto others as they would have others do unto them.

Phillips's confidence that the Golden Rule was the way to wealth comes out most clearly in his book of essays, *The Reign of Gilt*, wherein he devoted an entire chapter to advising a hypothetical son of John D. Rockefeller as to how he should act after his father is dead. First of all, said Phillips, Junior should immediately abandon all charitable enterprises — such benefactions were for "paupers, and panderers and parasites." Junior should then insist on selling commodities at fair prices and on paying a living wage. He should stop watering stocks and bribing legislatures. The plutocrats would denounce him for all this, Phillips predicted, but he would be "greatly cheered by the swelling, stentorian applause of the people." Next he should go into the squalid cities, tear down the tenements and erect clean houses, for which he should charge low rents. He should build "a huge department store" in every neighborhood, where, instead of shoddy clothes and "vile, poisonous, rotten meat and vegetables," he should sell decent goods and wholesome food at fair prices. The initial result of such a plan, Phillips was sure, would be that Junior would lose a great deal of money — in a sense become poor again — but he would then go on to compile an even vaster fortune than his father's. Everything he touched, said Phillips with breathless eagerness, would turn to gold. What a real opportunity big businessmen in America were missing! Why didn't they get smart?

iv

Behind all of the energy and bustle of Phillips's Messiahs, with their sensational exposés of political graft and business corruption, lay a pathetic secret. Supposedly as modern as tomorrow, his heroes were in fact hopelessly anachronistic; in terms of the twentieth century, they were programmatically barren.

Besides his friend Beveridge, the United States Senators whom Phillips most admired were men like George G. Vest, men of "ancient dress and ancient faces," whose belief in individualism and economy and principle suggested to Phillips "Cato and his little band that rose like bare, forbidding rocks in and against the swollen, splendid tide of the decaying Roman republic's prodigality." As Theodore Roosevelt was the first to point out, Phillips the novelist, like Phillips the reporter, deified the past. Hampden Scarborough was not a prophet of the future, but a remembrance of things past. His political appeal is to the small towns and farms, not to the cities. His campaign promise is that he will lead the American people *back* to the good old days of 1870 when there had been competitive equality — or at least no trusts. Since, however, the untrammeled competition of the Alger era was precisely what had produced the plutocratic world of 1900, recapturing Alger could only lead inevitably back to the troubles of the present once again. But recapturing the past was not only futile, it was impossible. Such phrases as "enforcing the Constitution" and "equality before the law" could not dispel the twentieth century, and yet, when Phillips had pronounced those words he had exhausted his political ideas. Business had to be dominant, Phillips believed, for without business in the saddle America would lose its idealism and cease to be democratic — but it must be restrained. How to interfere with business and yet not interfere was, however, completely beyond him.

It is for these reasons that Phillips always depicted his Messiah making speeches but almost never showed him in power. When he did follow his hero into the governor's or the President's office, as he did in his last political novel, *George Helm*, the Messiah's program was revealed to consist of such measures as the enforced inspection of beer production, making railroads pay taxes, and compelling merchants to give honest weight — hardly a course of action designed to crush plutocracies or to help resuscitate the dear, dead past.

When Phillips found he had not the least idea how to restrain business, he invented the Alger hero who restrained himself. Blacklock, Armstrong, the hypothetical son of Rockefeller (who qualified as an Alger hero by initially losing his

149

inherited fortune, then gaining it back tenfold) have, however, rather primitive conceptions of restraint. They strew the ground with the blood of plutocrats. Their labor policy is to fire idlers and to teach "thrift" to the workers who remain by squeezing out of them "full value for what they get." The fear of sinking to the bottom of the economic heap, said Phillips, was one of the greatest forces making for human betterment in the world, and the heroes of his novels do their best to encourage it. The abolition of poverty would be the "worst possible move" America could make, Phillips felt, and his business leaders restrain themselves admirably from making any moves in this direction. Phillips's idealized businessman, in sum, was pure robber baron out of the brave days of yore.

Phillips prided himself on the fact that his novels were up to date, hot off the press, the latest word. Yet there is nothing in them which goes beyond Alger. Even Phillips's rhetoric is, like his heroes, a relic of the past. Thus the advice he was so fond of handing out on the horrors of inheriting money and the like is not only Alger in substance, but is couched in the Alger vocabulary. His rhetorical indebtedness to the author of *Ragged Dick* can be first discerned in Phillips's newspaper days. When he worked for Pulitzer, Phillips wrote a column of "aphorisms for young men," which appeared at irregular intervals in the pages of the *World*. "Get a fixed purpose and never deviate from it." "Do not fancy that talent counts for so very much in the world. Persistence without intellect is better than an intellect without persistence." "Keep hard at it every waking hour, and when the time comes for sleep go to bed and stay there until it is time to get at it again." After he stopped writing the column, Phillips still went right on coining aphorisms, which he then sowed broadcast through his fiction. "Luck is a stone which envy flings at success," remarks the hero of *The Great God Success*. Hampden Scarborough and Victor Dorn (another of the political Messiahs) talk almost entirely in self-help maxims. Dorn, who is a socialist, affords a beautiful example of what could happen to the Communist Manifesto when it got into the mouth of an Alger hero:

> Organize! Think! Learn! Then you will rise out of the dirt where you wallow with your wives and your children. Don't blame your masters; they don't enslave you. They don't keep you in slavery. Your chains are of your own forging and only you can strike them off!

The American literary tradition of inspirational aphorisms which began with Puritan homilies was inherited by Benjamin Franklin in the eighteenth century and secularized, but it was with Alger in the post-Civil War years that the tradition reached the high point of its development; since then, there have only been variations on a theme, whether the author has been Andrew Carnegie or Dale Carnegie. Phillips's phrases are not only in the Alger vein, they are often direct steals. When a colleague of Horace Armstrong's tells him, "You're bound to win," or Joshua Craig is typified as a "hardy plotter in the arduous pathway from plowboy to President," Phillips was exploiting some of the most familiar of Alger's contributions to the American language.

The rhetoric of Phillips's novels held, as a result, a powerful appeal to a middle-class audience which had been raised on the Alger stories. Possibly the question of how any American could ever have believed in or even bothered to read the stories of Phillips's incredible heroes finds an answer here. The language of Alger, learned in childhood, exerted a hypnotic influence on Phillips's readers; they found his fantasies credible, and could will to believe in his Messiah, because of the overwhelming associations set in motion by the rhetoric. At the heart of Phillips's deification of the past lay an invocation of a childhood world.

One secret, then, behind the big modern front of Phillips's fiction was its anachronism, but there was a second secret, deeper and darker than the first. The denunciations of the American aristocracy, the abuse heaped upon the East, the celebration of small-town Indiana and "real people," were fraudulent from beginning to end.

In the world of his novels, Indiana is a country of fresh eggs, real cream and admirable men and women, but Phillips himself got out of Indiana as fast as he could. After two years at DePauw and a few months at the University of Cincinnati, Phillips transferred to Princeton, an institution which in his writing would have been excoriated as a training school for snobs. After graduation, he did a brief stint on a Cincinnati newspaper, then moved to New York. For the rest of his life he considered the "high-curving centre of the downpouring glittering stream" as his home. Friends like Lorimer often urged Phillips to accompany them on vacation trips to the West, but Phillips wasn't having any more of Indiana, even on vacations. For trips he preferred Paris and London. In New York, he occupied a sumptuous apartment off Gramercy Park where he glittered as brightly as any snob in town. Phillips was also a clotheshorse — and had been ever since the age of fifteen, when, as the youngest member of the freshman class at DePauw, he was known as "the Dude." At dressy Princeton, his classmates called him "Louis Philippe." One of his colleagues from his newspaper days remembered Phillips as "the most perfect dandy on Manhattan Island, wearing individual clothes with a distinction that much-advertised beau, E. Berry Wall, never approached." (As Phillips himself once said, the worst snobs of all were Western "perverts to New

York's gospel of snobbishness.") There was a fresh chrysanthe-
mum in the buttonhole of his coat every morning — but perhaps the most extreme mark of his fastidiousness was that he
took three or four baths a day, at a time when baths were not
considered healthful. There is a sartorial story about a meeting in New York between Phillips and Jack London which
sheds light on both men. Phillips, whose masterful heroes were
a kind of domesticated version of London's supermen, and
who was fond of flirting with socialism, expressed a desire to
meet London. Finally, the opportunity arose when London
paid a visit to New York, and they were brought together for
lunch. The encounter was a fiasco, each being put off by the
other's appearance, Phillips by London's open-throat flannel
shirt, London by Phillips's finery.

That Jack London or anyone else should suspect him of being an aristocrat annoyed Phillips terribly. He thought of himself as the perfect democrat and always considered that his
actions bore him out in this opinion. "It has been my lot," he
complained in a letter to a friend,

> to be misunderstood both as a writer and as a man. I have
> even been accused of being aristocratic — me, the soul of
> democracy. Why, I have even avoided riding in a carriage
> or an auto, for I know that the man or woman who does it
> gets out of sympathy with the masses.

But in spite of such gestures, Phillips kept giving himself
away, and nowhere more than in his novels. His Messiahs are
men of the people, but they all want to become gentlemen.
They hire instructors to train them in good form, good clothes
and good grammar, and dancing masters to teach them how to
walk. With their usual superiority, they quickly master all the
details of aristocratic living; they are still scornful, but are
henceforth better dressed and better housed than the pluto-

crats, who have money but no taste. Phillips's heroes have an instinct for the best in women as well as in clothes. Although contemptuous of society snobs and fortune hunters, they nevertheless all marry heiresses.

Having to cloak his interest in expensive things behind the excuse that he was merely demonstrating that an Alger hero could beat an aristocrat even at his own game eventually proved unsatisfying to Phillips. Posing as the perfect democrat with a distaste for what fascinated him grew as wearisome as always walking instead of riding must have. To fulfill himself, Phillips wrote a secret novel. He did not publish it, but kept it by him in his Gramercy Park apartment, writing it over and over and over again. Not until after he was dead did *Susan Lenox. Her Fall and Rise* see the light of day. Almost one thousand pages long, published in two volumes, *Susan Lenox* was Phillips's last will and testament.

The novel is the story of a prostitute. Susan is, however, not just another girl of the streets, but a special, demo-aristocratic kind of trollop. Born, inevitably, in a small Indiana city, she is raised by one of the more socially prominent families in town. The family, however, is not her own — Susan's origin was in democratic bastardy. Despite this, or rather because of it, Susan is superior to her contemporaries among the better families. Even as a small child she likes to walk by herself with no help from anyone; she is better-looking, has more fastidious taste in clothes and reads more difficult books than the other boys and girls in town. This combination of superiority and bastardy is too much for the other families and they jealously ostracize Susan from local society. Realizing she has no future in Indiana, Susan sets out "into the fascinating golden unknown."

At this point, Susan's endless series of falls and rises is set in motion. She becomes a successful riverboat singer, but her career is terminated when the boat burns. She finds work in a factory, then is finally reduced to streetwalking, whence the long climb back to the top is resumed. After a brief period of affluence, events drive her down to the bottom again. By this continuous sine wave of the plot action, Phillips's heroine is able to avoid the dilemma which plagued Sister Carrie. Carrie yearns for material things, but possession of them eventually bores her. Susan never has her desires fulfilled long enough to reach the point of satiation, and so she goes on and on and on, alternately yearning for and delighting in the jewelry and clothes and splendid apartment suites which Phillips never tired of describing.

Whereas Phillips's heroes had had to temper their rampant individualism with lip service to the public welfare, his secret heroine has only herself in mind. Susan has the "self-reliance and . . . the hardiness — so near akin to hardness" which "must come into the character before a man or a woman is fit to give and take in the combat of life." Abolishing inequality either by law or by Golden Rule Susan finds "fantastically false." Her tough philosophy of life is embodied in the advice she receives from one of the earliest of her men friends. "You're going to fight your way up to what's called the triumphant class — the people on top," he tells her,

> they have all the success, all the money, all the good times. Well, the things you've been taught — at church — in the Sunday School — in the nice story books you've read . . . they don't apply to people like you. . . . Once you've climbed up among the successful people you can afford to indulge — in moderation — in practicing the good old moralities. . . . But while you're climbing, no Golden Rule and no turning of the cheek. Tooth and claw

then — not sheathed but naked — not by proxy, but in your own person.

Even as Susan falls for the first of so many times, she never takes her eye off the ball. In the factory she holds herself apart from the workers with the same aloofness that had characterized her among the better families in her home town. To Susan, they are not comrades, but people who smell bad. Although employed only a brief time, she becomes so skilled at her job that she turns out 25 per cent more work than the best hands in the plant. When someone tells her she is superior to "the rest of them dirty, shiftless mutton-heads," Susan blushes, but has to agree. Her descent to the streets does not in the least alter her consciousness of being a superior individual, for her decision to become a prostitute is not a mark of degradation, but a sign of her enormous self-reliance.

Susan's arduous career, extending over a period of years, has no deleterious effect whatsoever on Phillips's master-spirited girl. Her "iron strength" and "almost exhaustless endurance" are proof against all hazards. Fighting and clawing her way along, Susan at the end reaches the triumphant class. Like Carrie, she has become a famous actress. As lovely and unspoiled as the day she left Indiana, Susan is supremely happy, for at last she has reached "the world worth living in, the world from which all but a few are shut out."

By 1911, Phillips had been working on *Susan Lenox* for seven years. One morning in January of that year, he emerged from his Gramercy Park apartment to take a walk and to pick up his mail at the Princeton Club. Outside the club he encountered a man named Fitzhugh Coyle Goldsborough. Phillips did not know the man, but Goldsborough knew Phillips — he had been shadowing him for days.

Goldsborough was a member of an old Washington family.

He had read Phillips's novels, which made such a show of denouncing American aristocrats, and felt insulted by them. Slowly, but with paranoid certainty, Goldsborough became convinced that these novels were malicious attacks on his family. When he came upon *The Fashionable Adventures of Joshua Craig*, with its scornful descriptions of Washington society, Goldsborough was finally sure. He secured a revolver, took a train to New York, found Phillips and murdered him. No man could attack America's glittering caste system and get away with it.

CHAPTER IV

Frank Norris: Mama's Boy

As a rule, there is more genuine satisfaction, a truer life, and more obtained from life in the humble cottages of the poor than in the palaces of the rich. I always pity the sons and daughters of rich men.

— ANDREW CARNEGIE

D**AVID** G**RAHAM** P**HILLIPS**'s scorn for the sons and daughters of the rich — the so-called "second generation" — constituted no mere personal prejudice, but was, and indeed still is, representative of a widespread American attitude, one which lies at the very heart of the success mythology. Thus Frank Norris, who was the scion of a wealthy family, would have been publicly pitied not only by Phillips, but also by such well-known success writers as Andrew Carnegie, Edward Bok and William Makepeace Thayer. There is no doubt that the view of Norris's financial background taken by Orison Swett Marden, the editor of the magazine *Success*, would have been dim indeed: "It is as easy to distinguish the sturdy, self-made man from the one who has been propped up all his life by wealth, position, and family influence [Marden once wrote] as it is for the shipbuilder to tell the difference between the plank from the rugged mountain oak and one from the sapling of the forest."

And there is, of course, no mistaking how Horatio Alger would have felt. For three decades and in more than a hundred novels Alger heaped contempt, sarcasm and condescension on the second generation. His first group of novels, the *Ragged Dick* series, is both a paradigm of all that he would ever say about the rich as well as a classic statement of the general American prejudice against the well-born.

While Alger's impoverished hero, Ragged Dick, is quick-witted, energetic and overpoweringly self-confident that he will triumph in "the great race" of life, Roswell Crawford, who has had the ill luck to have been born a gentleman's son and who has never blacked a boot or sold a newspaper in his life, is supercilious, lazy and unpopular. Having been born to wealth, Roswell has ostensibly won the race before he ever entered it, which is to say, paradoxically, that he has in fact lost. Inheritance has cheated him of his chance to get to the top the hard way, which, by the rules of the myth, is the only way that counts. (As Marden observed, success in America is not simply "measured by what a man accomplishes, but by the opposition he has encountered, and the courage with which he has maintained the struggle against overwhelming odds.") In front of Ragged Dick, "the future expands . . . a bright vista of merited success," but there is no corresponding allure in Roswell's anticlimactic life.

Clearly disturbed by all this, Roswell takes out his frustrations in surliness and snobbery. These, however, are make-shift comforts, hardly compensation for the overwhelming fact of his disqualification from the race. Poor little rich Roswell has nowhere to go except to pieces, which he soon does. In the kind of whirlwind reversal of which Alger was master, Roswell's father dies, the Crawford fortune vanishes in thin air, and he is compelled to seek employment. Abruptly plunged into the competitive struggle, Roswell proves totally unequal to the challenge. Instead of working diligently, he takes to gambling in a club, a habit which quickly leads him to "moral shipwreck and ruin." Needing money in a hurry, he steals some from the store where he works, tries to pin the theft on another boy, and is caught. The last we see of Roswell he is forsaking his unhappy life in New York City for adventure in the Great West. "Let us hope," Alger wrote, "that, away from the influences of the city, his character may be improved, and become more manly and self-reliant. . . . If he can ever forget that he is 'the son of a gentleman,' I shall have some hopes for him."

Whatever the general validity of Alger's portrayal of the second generation, there is, in the case of Frank Norris, a remarkable congruence between reality and myth. Like Roswell Crawford, Norris suffered all his days from having been born with a silver spoon in his mouth. If any American ever did, Norris knew that it was quite as difficult as Alger had said it was to escape the consequences of such a handicap.

ii

Norris's father was a tall, broad-shouldered, indomitable man. A lifelong victim of a chronic disease of the hip, he never allowed his physical handicap to interfere with anything he did. Growing up on a small farm in Michigan, he unfailingly performed his full share of the chores, "getting up during the cold winter before daybreak to attend to the stock and running into the stable to warm his feet in the cow fodder." When he was fourteen, it was decided to send him

off to a boarding school, but, as he always would, the boy felt
that making money was more important than education.
While supposedly en route to the school, he instead sought
out a jeweler's shop and apprenticed himself. As soon as he
had learned the rudiments of the craft, he set out on the road
repairing jewelry and clocks; upon reaching New York he
abandoned his trade in favor of a more lucrative job as a
salesman with a large jewelry firm. Within the space of the
next few years he had saved sufficient money to open his own
jewelry business in Chicago.

Norris's mother, at the time she met her future husband,
was a struggling young actress, filled with romantic ambitions of becoming the leading lady of the stage. She had originally come to Chicago from New England at the age of six-
teen to teach in a private school, a job in which, because of
"her vivid imagination and talent for reading and story-tell-
ing," she had enjoyed considerable success. Transferring her
histrionic abilities to the stage, she made her theatrical debut
in the part of Emilia in a Chicago production of *Othello,* and
thereafter traveled with a stock company, playing important
roles in "the grand manner of the old school." She at first refused the marriage proposals of the rising young jewelry
salesman who was pursuing her, but by applying to courtship
"the persistent tactics which had brought him success in business," Norris's father eventually wore her down. The sales
talk by which he finally won her consent was his assurance
that she could continue her dramatic career after marriage.
This, however, was only campaign oratory; following her wed-
ding Norris's mother never again appeared on the stage.

Their first son was named for his father: Benjamin Franklin
Norris, Junior. It was the greatest point of similarity between
father and son, for Junior turned out to be bookish and shy,

neither of which qualities characterized Senior in the slightest. Even if they had not been profoundly divided in temperament and interest, father and son would have been kept apart by the former's fanatical absorption in his business. While Junior occupied himself with his books at home, Senior was busy downtown making money, so much, indeed, that by the time Norris was twelve years old his father could afford to move the family into a spacious Michigan Avenue mansion, keep a handsome stable (complete with fine horses, monogrammed carriages and a coachman with varnished boots and a cockade), and give his wife the means to travel in the same social circles as Mrs. Potter Palmer.

Norris's relationship with his mother was, by contrast, quite close. She took out her dramatic frustrations in reading Scott and Dickens to him by the hour, and she found that although her husband had no use for literary criticism she could always discuss poetry and fiction with her son. The same fellow feeling, between mother and son obtained in religion. Norris's father was an enthusiastic admirer of Dwight L. Moody and his philosophy that business principles should be applied to Christianity; Norris's mother, despite the long line of Unitarian ministers in her New England ancestry, was not nearly as religious as her husband, but she did like the form and ritual of High Church Episcopalianism. Junior became an Episcopalian, too.

The pattern of this relationship to his parents intensified as Norris grew older. In 1884, the family moved to San Francisco, where Norris's father went into the business of building cheap apartments, at the same time continuing to direct the affairs of his jewelry firm in Chicago. While his father thus became busier than ever, Norris, now in his teens, stayed at home and acted out *Ivanhoe*, using lead soldiers as characters, for the benefit of his two small brothers, while his mother looked on benevolently. When Norris began to make up chivalric stories of his own to tell his brothers, she encouraged him to write them down; when he began to illustrate his stories with sketches of knights in armor and to make costumes for the toy soldiers, his mother "began to dream that her eldest boy might become an artist instead of a businessman."

The first serious battle his parents fought over Norris was on the issue of his education. His father won the first skirmish, but he lost the war. Insisting that Norris be prepared for a business career, he succeeded in compelling his wife, who wanted her son to be enrolled in an art school, to agree to send him to the Boys' High School in San Francisco. But the crude manners of the other boys in the school deeply offended Norris, nor did they care for him. Sizing him up as a pampered weakling, they neatly dubbed him "Skinny-well-fed." His teachers were no more sympathetic, objecting when he covered his books with drawings and seemingly interested only in such hated subjects as commercial arithmetic. Norris's patent misery, when added to his mother's pressure, was too much for his father; a scant few weeks after his victory, Senior threw in the sponge. Junior was withdrawn from Boys' High and sent to an art school. The projection through Norris's life of his mother's thwarted artistic career now commenced in earnest.

Because of his mother's insistence that he must have the best training that money could buy, the entire Norris household removed to Paris in the summer of 1887 so that he could study painting in the Atelier Julien. If, however, the training was good, Norris was a bad student, or rather, a lazy one. Even at the beginning, he worked only half-heartedly at his painting, and after his father returned to the United States (he was homesick for American cooking), Norris became even more of a dilettante. There were, he found, so many other things which engaged him. He loved listening to his mother read French poetry aloud; he discovered "his favorite book," Froissart's *Chronicles*, and developed a passionate interest in medieval armor; ostensibly to amuse his six-year-old brother, Norris revived the lead-soldier game, spending hours in making proper medieval cannon out of his paint-brush handles and in concocting the intricate adventures of a bold fourteenth-century fellow whom Norris named Gaston le Fox. He bought foils, a mask and long black tights and learned to fence. When his mother left him on his own in Paris, he acquired a French girl friend. Briefly remembering his initial purpose in coming to Europe, he began a huge canvas depicting the Battle of Crécy as it was described in Froissart, but never finished it. Somehow, Norris decided, he didn't especially want to be a painter any more.

That made it his father's turn once again. Discovering that his son was thinking more about Gaston le Fox than he was about painting, he angrily ordered him to return home at once. If Norris was not going to be a painter, as his mother wanted, then he must do what his father desired, and Senior's fondest dream was that his oldest son and namesake would enroll at the University of California, take a bachelor's degree, and then assume direction of his jewelry business.

Complete with long sideburns, a walking stick and a Continental air, Norris entered Berkeley in the fall of 1890. Once again, however, his father's victory quickly proved more seeming than real. Instead of working at his courses, Norris wrote *Yvernelle*, a long narrative poem in the style of Scott, full of horses and armor and derring-do. His mother, whose readings of Browning were currently famous in the Bay Area, was thrilled by her son's poem and paid Lippincott to publish it. Norris also managed to evade studying by being very collegiate. He joined a fraternity, strummed a banjo, played poker — at which he always lost — went on binges with the other brothers of Phi Gamma Delta (in the back room of Hagearty's Saloon the walls were covered with Norris's drawings of seminude girls), and went dancing with the coeds.

Furious at having been defeated once again, his father stormed off by himself on a trip around the world; upon his return to America, he took up residence in Chicago and filed suit for divorce. In the year that Norris finished his fourth year as an undergraduate but without fulfilling the requirements for a degree, the divorce was made final. Norris never thereafter saw his father.

As soon as Senior had gone from the house, Norris's mother signalized her final triumph by converting the attic into a studio where Junior could write. Deciding in the next breath that her son had to have another dose of the best training possible, she sent him to Harvard for a year to study creative writing. She, of course, went along with him, and although Norris lived in a college dormitory throughout his stay in Cambridge, she rented rooms for herself in a boardinghouse that was quite close by. The man who had tricked her out of the life she should have had would never again be allowed to tamper with her son's career. Quite definitely, Junior was going to be a writer, not a businessman.

Norris, however, did not recover from his father's departure as easily as his mother had. As a boy, Norris had been very much his mother's son, but always in his mind there had been the exalted image of the powerful, limping, intensely moral man who was his father. Senior moved with swiftness and assurance through the world, for, in his son's eyes, he could do everything and do it well. He had risen from rags to riches, he drove fast horses, he was a singularly expert fisherman, he ran a Sunday school which was the envy of Dwight L. Moody himself. Even as an old man his energy and drive were awesome — when he was well past sixty, he became so impatient with a delay in the delivery of a heavy cornice for a house he was building that he went to fetch it himself, returning with it on his shoulder.

Norris, despite his dilettantism, yearned to prove himself to this great man, to show him he was not the inadequate weakling he was sure his father considered him to be. But as the aggressive father moved from one success to the next, the slender, indecisive son went from defeat to defeat. One of Norris's key failures occurred during his brief sojourn as a student at a fashionable preparatory school near San Francisco.* Passionately fond of football, Norris decided to go out for the team; perhaps this would show he was a chip off the old block. They brought him home with his arm broken in two places. It is just possible, as has been remarked, that F. Scott Fitzgerald's career as a writer stemmed from the day he failed to make the freshman football team at Princeton, but there is no doubt that Norris's failure to prove himself to his father on the playing field was a crucial event in his life.

Until the day of his death, football exercised a special hold over Norris. He never missed seeing a game while he was a student at Berkeley; football, he confessed in a pathetically admiring statement, was as dramatically exciting as warfare, wherein "two teams, like armies, faced each other and shed blood in noble strife, and captains constantly met situations demanding quick decisions and shrewd thinking." Two years

* Belmont Academy, where Jack London was for a time employed in the laundry.

after he left the University of California, Norris went to work
for a West Coast magazine called *The Wave,* for which he conducted a department called "The Week's Football." So abject
was his worship of the players, who could do what he could
not, that shaking hands with one of the stars after the game
became an event of the first magnitude for Norris: "He is so
big that he ceases to be broad and tall — you feel like speaking of him as wide and high, as though he were the steeple of
a clock tower — and he has an enormous bell-toned voice and
a fist that your hand loses itself inside." The great irony of
Norris's passion for football was, of course, that his father was
disgusted with his son's rah-rah antics, not realizing that wor-
shipful descriptions of football players sprang from Norris's
desolate awareness that he did not have the physical vigor of
a man who at sixty-plus could carry a heavy cornice on his
shoulder.

Nor did his father grasp the true significance of Norris's
devotion to Froissart. This was not merely a dilettante's interest in something useless, as he thought, but rather another
way his son took to hide his naked hero worship of his father.
For in Norris's mind the worlds of medieval chivalry and modern business were one and the same. Thus Norris believed
that Richard the Lion Hearted, if he had lived today, would
probably have been a steel executive; conversely, Andrew
Carnegie, had he "been alive at the time of the preachings of
Peter the Hermit . . . would have raised a company of *gens
d'armes* sooner than all of his brothers-in-arms, would have
equipped his men better and more effectively, would have
been the first on the ground before Jerusalem, would have built
the most ingenious siege engine and have hurled the first cask
of Greek fire over the walls." And Gaston le Fox, the fourteenth-
century nobleman whom Norris himself had dreamed up, and

whose stirring deeds he never tired of inventing, was but the medieval counterpart of his dynamic parent.

None of this his father understood — as far as Senior was concerned, Junior had failed to become either a football player or a painter, had failed in college, had even failed as a poker player. According to Norris's brother Charles, even if Junior had attempted the business career his father wished him to have, he would almost surely have been a "conspicuous failure in the wholesale jewelry business." When he entered Harvard in September of 1894, Norris had eight years of his life remaining in which to become a success in the eyes of a man who had already turned his back on him forever.

iii

Norris's first novel, *Vandover and the Brute,* is, just as his last novel would be, a reflection of what concerned him most, his relationship with his father. Written during the period immediately following his parents' divorce, *Vandover* reeks of guilt, unhappiness and insecurity. Into it Norris poured all his miserable memories of the past and all his fears of what the future held in store.

Norris's mother was right beside her son when he wrote his first novel, but — significantly — in the world of Norris's imagination artistic women were destined always to be depicted in an unfortunate light, and *Vandover* is no exception. As the novel opens, a father and mother and their eight-year-old son, Vandover, are on a train bound for San Francisco, where they have decided to live. En route across the Continent, the mother falls deathly ill.

By and by she drew a long sigh, her face became the face of an imbecile, stupid, without expression, her eyes half-closed, her mouth half-open. Her head rolled forward as though she were nodding in her sleep, while a long drip of saliva trailed down from her lower lip.

This scene of her death, Norris added, "was the only thing Vandover could remember of his mother."

Vandover's father is utterly unlike the sickly woman he had married. Although he has moved to California with the intention of retiring, his restless, driving nature will not allow him to remain idle for long.

He had given his entire life to his business to the exclusion of everything else, and now when his fortune had been made and when he could afford to enjoy it, discovered that he had lost the capacity for enjoying anything but the business itself. Nothing else could interest him.

To escape the "mortal *ennui*" of leisure, he begins, most successfully, to build and rent apartment houses.

In sharp contrast to his father, Vandover is shy, awkward and physically weak. In high school, "the boys called him 'Skinny-seldom-fed,' to his infinite humiliation." Never a good student, Vandover does have considerable talent in art and writing, and his father tolerantly allows him to have a drawing teacher. When, however, Vandover expresses the desire to study in Paris, his father refuses, and sends him off to Harvard instead, sweetening the pill by giving Vandover money for art lessons in Boston.

At Harvard, Vandover discovers that the real enemy of his artistic career is not so much his father, but himself. He is incorrigibly lazy — and something worse. Despite the moral training he has received from his religious father, Vandover is inordinately susceptible to the lure of vice in its various manifestations. He had first noticed this about himself when he was in high school. Through "the abominable talk of the . . . boys," and the horrifying article in the *Encyclopaedia Britannica* on "Obstetrics," Vandover had "acquired the knowledge of good and evil." The revelation "was very cruel, the whole thing was a grief to him, a blow, a great shock; he hated to think of it." Then, as the shock wore off, "little by little the first taint crept in, the innate vice stirred in him, the brute began to make itself felt, and a multitude of perverse and vicious ideas commenced to buzz about him like a swarm of nasty flies." At college, away from his father's moral influence, Vandover begins to contract "irresponsible habits." He takes up smoking, learns to drink beer and plays cards for money. One evening, "moved by an unreasoned instinct," he seeks out a vulgar, tawdry girl ι. d stays with her all night. "He passed the next few days in a veritable agony of repentance, overwhelmed by a sense of shame and dishonour that were almost feminine in their bitterness and intensity." Inexorably, his guilt feelings compel him to "send a long letter to his father acknowledging and deploring what he had done, asking for his forgiveness and reiterating his resolve to shun such a thing forever after." The relief of confessing himself to his father is sufficient to rid him of his interest in any kind of vice for the rest of his college career.

Returning to San Francisco after Harvard, Vandover decides not to live in his father's capacious house, but to establish himself and his paints in a studio downtown, for which his father pays the rent. But instead of working at his painting, Vandover once more falls into evil ways. He comes to know the life "that began after midnight in the private rooms of fast cafés and that was continued in the heavy musk-laden air of

certain parlours among the rustle of heavy silks." It is in this
fashion that Vandover encounters "a girl called Flossie." She is
an obsessive type in Norris's fiction, so it will be well to take a
closer look at her: "She was an immense girl, quite six feet
tall, broad and well-made in proportion. She was very handsome, full-throated, heavy-eyed, and slow in her movements.
Her eyes and mouth, like everything about her, were large."
Although she is a prostitute, "Flossie radiated health; her eyes
were clear, her nerves steady, her flesh hard and even as a
child's." In Norris's description of this woman's abnormal size
and superlative health we catch a first glimpse of an aberra-
tion which would only be fully revealed in his later work.

After a night of riotous drinking with Flossie and her
friends, Vandover goes to communion while still drunk. "It
was perhaps the worst thing he had ever done," he tells himself, "now he had reached the lowest point." But he is wrong.
There was, in Norris's lexicon, an act even lower; not until
Vandover seduces a girl of his own social class does he plumb
the moral depths. When, a short time later, he learns that the
girl has committed suicide, he is so overcome with remorse
that he again succumbs to "an overwhelming childish desire
to tell his father all about it." Going before his father, Vandover confesses everything. Realizing what a blow such a sordid story must be to him, Vandover breaks down and sobs.
"'Oh, governor!' he cried. It was as if it had been a mother or
a dead sister. The prodigal son put his arms about his father's
neck for the first time since he had been a little boy, and
clung to him and wept as though his heart were breaking."

Purged of his guilt by his confession, Vandover resumes his
career as a painter and works harder than ever before in his
life. Just as he is beginning to believe that he has rid himself
of his evil habits, his father dies. Wild with grief, Vandover

wanders about the house whispering to himself: "Oh, my poor, dear old dad — I'm never going to see you again, never, never! Oh, my dear, kind old governor!"

Without his father to turn to, Vandover goes to pieces with a greater vengeance than Roswell Crawford. Recklessly squandering the money from his father's estate, Vandover for a time leads "a life of luxury and aimlessness which he found charming." He gives up art entirely and fritters away his time; for a brief period, he takes up banjo-playing "seriously," but his only constant interest is gambling. In nine months he goes through fifteen thousand dollars. As Vandover dissipates his inheritance, his talent for painting disappears and his health collapses; his hands swell, his nerves bother him, he feels a "strange numb feeling at the base of his skull." Vandover does not know as yet what is wrong with him, but he is aware that "it was the punishment that he had brought upon himself . . . [as] the result of his long indulgence in vice." Only by degrees does he realize that he is a victim of lycanthropy, but one night as he is going to bed the evidence becomes horrifyingly unmistakable. Stripping off his pajamas, he

> began to walk the floor . . . with great strides, fighting with all his pitiful, shattered mind against the increasing hysteria, trying to keep out of his brain the strange hallucination that assailed it. . . . Suddenly and without the slightest warning Vandover's hands came slowly above his head and he dropped forward, landing upon his palms. . . . Now without a moment's stop he ran back and forth along the wall of the room, upon the palms of his hands and toes, a ludicrous figure, like that of certain clowns one sees at the circus, contortionists walking about the sawdust, imitating some kind of enormous dog. Still he swung his head from side to side with the motion of his shuffling gait, his eyes dull and fixed. At long intervals he

uttered a sound, half word, half cry, "Wolf — wolf!" but it was muffled, indistinct, raucous, coming more from his throat than from his lips. It might easily have been the growl of an animal. A long time passed. Naked, four-footed, Vandover ran back and forth the length of the room.

Incurably sick, penniless, ostracized by society and deserted by his friends, Vandover at the end of the novel is reduced to the horrid task of cleaning out filthy sinks and basements in a group of run-down houses. The job pays just enough to keep him alive. Thus Norris's nightmare concludes.

The companion volume to *Vandover* is *McTeague,* which was also a product of the year Norris spent at Harvard. Writing a second novel more or less simultaneously with the first was necessary for Norris in order to round out his dark parable on the wages of self-indulgence and sexual dalliance. It took *McTeague* to prove that what had been true of high life in *Vandover* was equally true of low life, that succumbing to the temptations of the flesh could wreck the career of a strong, healthy, self-made man as easily as it could that of a pampered, wealthy Harvard boy. Because *McTeague* is a novel of how the other half of San Francisco lives, it stands at a greater distance from the center of Norris's imagination than did *Vandover* — there are no fictional projections of the author or of his father to be found in it. Nonetheless, all the guilt and horror of Norris's first novel are present in his second as well.

McTeague is a dentist on Polk Street in San Francisco. Lower-middle-class himself, his clientele is composed of "butcher boys, shop girls, drug clerks and car conductors." But if he is not rich, McTeague's wants are modest; on Sundays he sits in his dentist's chair, drinks a pitcher of steam beer, plays his concertina, and is content. He is not overly ambitious and none too bright, but on the other hand McTeague has come a long way. His father had been a drunkard, his mother had worked as a cook in a mining camp, and McTeague himself had gone to work in the mines while still a child, but by dint of reading a few textbooks on dentistry, he has succeeded in lifting himself up from being a manual laborer to his present professional status. What he lacks in erudition as a dentist he makes up for in strength, for he is as physically impressive as a football star:

> McTeague was a young giant, carrying his huge shock of blond hair six feet three inches from the ground; moving his immense limbs, heavy with ropes of muscle, slowly, ponderously. His hands were enormous, red, and covered with a fell of stiff yellow hair. . . . His head was square-cut, angular; the jaw salient, like that of the carnivora.

As the novel begins, McTeague is a happy and satisfied man. Then one day Trina Sieppe walks into his office. Quite a pretty girl, Trina's most striking feature is her hair — "heaps and heaps of blue-black coils and braids, a royal crown of swarthy bands, a veritable sable tiara, heavy, abundant, odorous." Looking at her, McTeague realizes "that there was something else in life besides concertinas and steam beer. . . . The male virile desire in him tardily awakened, aroused itself, strong and brutal. It was resistless, untrained, a thing not to be held in leash an instant." As Trina lies in the dentist's chair, unconscious from the ether he has given her, McTeague becomes more and more excited — "the blood sang in his ears; his face flushed scarlet; his hands twisted themselves together like the knotting of cables." Leaning over her, he kisses her "grossly, full on the mouth." Instantly he is ashamed. "Ah, the pity of it! Why could he not . . . love her purely, cleanly? What was the perverse, vicious thing that lived within him,

knitted to his flesh?" By this gross act, McTeague reveals the
fatal weakness in his character: "Below the fine fabric of all
that was good in him ran the foul stream of hereditary evil,
like a sewer."

Unashamedly attracted to her ("I can't help it. It ain't my
fault, is it?"), McTeague pays court to Trina. She, in turn, is
attracted to McTeague because of his brute strength, although
she is not aware of the reason behind her fondness. "Why,"
she wonders, "did she feel the desire, the necessity of being
conquered by a superior strength? Why did it please her?
Why had it suddenly thrilled her from head to foot with a
quick, terrifying gust of passion, the like of which she had
never known?" Eventually, their awful attraction for one another leads them to the altar.

Just as Vandover had enjoyed several months of high living
before his final downfall, so McTeague and Trina prosper for
a time. Trina wins five thousand gold dollars in a lottery,
while McTeague learns to wear clean linen and a silk hat and
"to have ambitions." But their punishment is not long in coming. The authorities learn that McTeague has no diploma and
he is barred from practicing dentistry. Selling their furniture
and his equipment, they move to a cheap room; Trina makes
McTeague part with his Prince Albert coat and his silk hat, although she herself refuses, even after a bitter quarrel, to give
up any of her hoard of gold pieces. McTeague finds a job for a
time with a surgical-instrument house, but is soon fired. Ordered out of the house by Trina, he finds comfort in alcohol.

The deterioration of their economic situation is accompanied, as it had been in Vandover's case, by an acceleration
of their moral degradation. In the sixty-five pages between
McTeague's first bout of drunkenness and his murder of
Trina, Norris's vision of the loathsomeness of sex reaches an

intensity unmatched by anything even in his first novel. Trina discovers that she derives pleasure from polishing her gold pieces. Burying her face in the heap of coins, she is "delighted at the smell . . . and the feel of the smooth, cold metal on her cheeks. She even put the smaller gold pieces in her mouth, and jingled them there." In the course of a particularly violent quarrel with McTeague, during which he strikes her and bites her fingers, "crunching and grinding them with his immense teeth," she makes an even pleasanter discovery: she likes to be hurt. "In some strange, inexplicable way this brutality made Trina all the more affectionate; aroused in her a morbid, unwholesome love of submission, a strange, unnatural pleasure in yielding, in surrendering herself to the will of an irresistible, virile power." Pretty little Trina, with her white face and her enormous pile of hair, knows at last what had interested her about this man with the enormous red hands. From this moment on, her whole life becomes focused on "her passion for her money and her perverted love for her husband when he was brutal."

Thus Trina and a Mexican woman who lives in the neighborhood, and who has recently married a Jewish junk dealer named Zerkow, sit together by the hour and critically compare the bruises given them by their husbands, "each one glad when she could exhibit the worst." They engage in "long and excited arguments as to which were the most effective means of punishment, the rope's ends and cart whips such as Zerkow used, or the fists and backs of hairbrushes affected by McTeague." (Their conversations are finally terminated by Zerkow, who cuts his wife's throat one night.) When McTeague deserts Trina, she is reduced to her hoard of gold and her own compensatory devices. "One evening she . . . spread all the gold pieces between the sheets, and . . . went to bed, stripping herself, and . . . slept all night upon the money, taking a strange and ecstatic pleasure in the touch of the smooth flat pieces the length of her entire body."

The climax of her fondness for McTeague's brutality occurs the night he returns and beats her to death.

> Trina lay unconscious, just as she had fallen under the last of McTeague's blows, her body twitching with an occasional hiccough that stirred the pool of blood in which she lay face downward. Towards morning she died with a rapid series of hiccoughs that sounded like a piece of clockwork running down.

The morning after Zerkow murdered his wife he was found drowned; at the end of the novel McTeague is still alive, but his doom, too, has been implacably sealed. Norris leaves no doubt that McTeague will die, horribly, of thirst in the middle of Death Valley.

The tale was told, but Norris could not let go of McTeague and Trina. Their sado-masochistic love exercised such a fearful fascination over him that after he had finished the novel he retold the events of the latter phase of their marriage in a short story called *"Fantaisie Printanière."* With the exception that Zerkow's wife is called Mrs. Ryer, there is no difference from what he had already described in the novel. In another short story, "A Case for Lombroso," Norris once again reverted to the same theme, only this time he set the McTeague-Trina relationship in the milieu of Vandover. The story tells of a young Harvard graduate by the name of Stayne, a member of the Porcellian Club and a man of "fine male strength and honesty and courage," who enters into an affair with a proud, aristocratic girl who, despite her Spanish origins, is as fair as a Viking. (She is also six feet tall.) Even though both of them soon discover that the affair is destroying them, they are powerless to terminate their perverted relationship. For Stayne it had become

> a pleasure — a morbid, unnatural pleasure . . . to hurt and humiliate her. He hurt her while he sickened at the thought of his own baseness, and she submitted to it while she loathed herself for her own degradation. They were a strange couple.

At the conclusion of the story, Stayne's name has been erased from the rolls of his club and the girl is "thoroughly *declassée*."

With *Vandover* and almost all of *McTeague* completed, Norris's year at Harvard came to an end. Whether or not his father was impressed, or even aware, that his son had written two unpublished novels is unrecorded, but it is certain in any event that Norris did not consider that his literary efforts constituted vindication of himself to his father. Twenty-five years old, Norris had, after all, never been anything but a student. As for the future, was there not always the fearful possibility that because he had become involved with a girl in Paris instead of learning to paint, and had drawn suggestive pictures of women on the walls of a saloon instead of preparing himself for the jewelry business, he would be punished in the way McTeague and Vandover had? Never having been anything but a failure, was it not unlikely he would ever become a success? As he left the sheltering groves of the academy and launched out into the great world, Norris was desperately unsure of the answer to these questions.

iv

As men like Theodore Roosevelt and Jack London had begun to demonstrate, there were other ways than business suc-

cess in which an American in the nineties could show he
was worth his salt. A man could travel to the ends of the earth,
for instance, or he could become a soldier. Norris surprised his
mother when they arrived back in San Francisco with the an-
nouncement that he was leaving immediately for South Africa.
What he did not tell her was that he planned to traverse the
Dark Continent from Cape Town to Cairo — he would go by
train as far as Johannesburg, take a wagon across the wilderness of Matabeleland to Bulawayo, then trek northward to the
headwaters of the Nile and go down the river to the Mediter-
ranean. Such a trip ought certainly to prove he was as bold
and determined as anyone.

Norris never got any farther than Johannesburg. Reaching
the city on the eve of its uprising against the Boer government, Norris made several comic attempts to enlist as a soldier
on the British side, but no one seemed interested in his military talents. Instead of a gun, he was given the inglorious job
of helping to close down miners' canteens, so that the natives
could not gain access to strong drink for the duration of the
crisis. One evening, while doing his duty, Norris was caught
in a rainstorm, and woke up the next morning delirious with
an attack of African fever. For a week he lay near death. Although he eventually recovered, his constitution was permanently weakened; thanks to African fever, the illness which he
was destined to contract six years later would prove fatal. His
mother, "sick with fear," at once wired him money to come
home. Broken in health, Norris sailed for home and mother.
Africa had been an enormous fiasco.

When his mother had nursed him back to health, Norris
seemed to become once again the same dear son he had been
to her in his undergraduate days at Berkeley. He contributed,
when the mood was upon him, book reviews, football write-

ups, short stories and the like to *The Wave,* and for a time acted as assistant editor of that magazine — at a maximum salary of one hundred dollars a month. Mostly, though, he played. The Phi Gam house saw him often, as did the Bohemian Club, where he liked either to sit in the window with his cronies and comment on the girls walking by, or to play poker all night in the back room. Socially, he ranged far and wide, from his mother's musicales to the cocktail bars on Kearney Street to the kind of Barbary Coast joints that Vandover had frequented.

The life of a dilettante had ended calamitously for the hero of Norris's first novel; in the spring of 1897 Mrs. Norris's playboy son suffered some sort of nervous collapse. He stopped writing entirely and relinquished his duties on *The Wave.* Convinced that his creative talent was permanently gone, Norris alternated between periods of listless indifference and deep depression. During the following summer he frantically wrote a dozen or so stories, among them "A Case for Lombroso" — which suggests the kind of psychological pressure that lashed him into such compulsive productivity.

In the fall he went to the Sierras. Leading the strenuous life in the great outdoors, Norris relaxed and recovered from his depression. His fear of and attraction toward the vices offered by city life shifted slightly and became contempt. After a time, of course, he gave up mountain climbing and horseback riding and returned to San Francisco, for Norris was an incorrigible metropolitan type, but the Sierras definitely had had an effect on him. In the ensuing year and a half Norris wrote three self-consciously muscular novels in which "everything," as he said of one of them, was "healthy and clean and natural."

The first two of the series, *Blix* and *Moran of the Lady*

Letty, tell basically the same story: how a young society dilettante is made into a man through the influence of a muscular,
sex-abhorring girl friend. Of the two, *Moran* is clearly the more
"healthy" and therefore deserves more attention.

Ross Wilbur, the hero of *Moran*, is tall and athletic and has
"plenty of jaw in the lower part of his face," but as a member
of the wealthy younger set in San Francisco he wastes his
time going to dances, teas and yachting parties. One day as
Wilbur is lounging along the water front killing time, he is
shanghaied by a shark fisherman named Kitchell.

After a few days at sea, Kitchell's ship encounters a derelict
vessel, the *Lady Letty*. On board, Wilbur and Kitchell discover Moran, the daughter of the ship's captain and the sole
survivor of the disaster which had struck it. Her appearance is
arresting:

> She was not pretty — she was too tall for that — quite as
> tall as Wilbur himself, and her skeleton was too massive.
> . . . What beauty she had was of the fine, hardy, Norse
> type. Her hands were red and hard, and even beneath the
> coarse sleeve of the oilskin coat, one could infer that the
> biceps and deltoids were large and powerful.

So that Wilbur can be left alone to admire Moran's muscles,
Norris introduces a convenient squall in which Kitchell is
drowned, the *Lady Letty* is sunk and the hero and Moran are
left with Kitchell's ship and its Chinese crew.

Moran immediately begins to demonstrate to Wilbur what a
real woman is like. She, not Wilbur, takes command of the
ship, for "her fine animal strength of bone and muscle" is "ad-
mittedly greater than his own." She eats food with her knife,
drinks whisky by the tumbler, and can fight like fury. Although she has spent her entire life among the toughest sailors

on the seas, she is "without sex," a "virgin unconquered." The effect of her personality on Wilbur is profound. "You swear like a man, and you dress like a man," he says to her in an awestruck voice. "I love you more than I imagined I ever could love a girl." Moran, however, keeps her relations with him on a didactic level. She prefers lecturing him to love-making: "I've lived by doing things, not by thinking things, or reading about what other people have done or thought; and I guess it's what you do that counts, rather than what you think or read about."

Anchoring in Magdalena Bay on the coast of Lower California, they discover ambergris worth one hundred and fifty thousand dollars in the carcass of a dead whale, but it is stolen from them by some Chinese beachcombers. Wilbur is still enough the unaggressive son of a rich man to point out that the ambergris does belong at least in part to the beach-combers, inasmuch as they had first found the whale, but Moran has the spirit of a true Alger hero, or of Frank Norris, Senior. In a blaze of fury, she yells at Wilbur,

the stuff belongs to the strongest of us. . . . We're dumped down here on this God-forsaken sand, and there's no law and no policeman. The strongest of us are going to live and the weakest are going to die. I'm going to live and I'm going to have my loot, too, and I'm not going to split fine hairs with these robbers. . . . I'm going to have it all. . . .

Wilbur finally shakes off the weakness of his class when, in the course of the ensuing battle with the beachcombers, he stabs one of the Chinese to death. "He felt his muscles thrill-ing with a strength they had not known before. . . . Never had he conceived of such savage exultation as that which mastered him at that instant. The knowledge that he could kill filled him with a sense of power that was veritably royal."

Such a sense of power, indeed, that when Moran mistakenly attacks Wilbur during the fight, he defeats her. For yet one more time in his fiction, Norris reveled in the description of a man beating a woman to a pulp. (He "planted his knuckles squarely between her eyes," et cetera.) When it is all over, and Moran acknowledges that she has been beaten, the discovery is made that physical contact with the opposite sex has robbed Moran of her strength. Henceforward, she becomes all weak and womanly; she unashamedly admits she loves Wilbur. Upon their return to San Francisco, she is easily overpowered and murdered by one of the Chinese beachcombers, who has slipped on board ship to steal back the ambergris which Moran had once sworn would be hers alone.

As for Wilbur, the beating he gave Moran has completed his transformation. Strong, hard and self-reliant, he finds that "city life, his old life, had no charm for him now." To escape boredom, Wilbur decides, at the close of the novel, to try filibustering in Cuba for a while. It may be a crazy idea," he concedes, "but it's better than dancing."

As for Norris, he decided he felt the same way. A few weeks before he finished *Moran*, the *Maine* was sunk in Havana Harbor, an event which furnished both Norris and the country with an excuse for muscularity. War was declared in April and a month later Norris was at Key West, waiting to go to Cuba as a war correspondent for *McClure's*. Unlike many of his journalistic colleagues, Norris was actually permitted to follow the army through the El Caney and Santiago fighting, but as one of his military friends remarked, "Frank Norris never knew how to rough it." Malarial fever hit him hard, and once more Norris went home from a war in shattered health.

As he again recuperated under his mother's care, Norris wrote the third of his "healthy and clean and natural" novels, *A Man's Woman*.

It is, by all odds, the "healthiest," for *A Man's Woman* is the story of a brave explorer who falls desperately ill with a virulent fever and who then, in the antiseptic atmosphere of a hospital, falls in love with his six-foot nurse. That the relationship between patient and nurse should become a love affair is of course extremely interesting when viewed against the background of Norris's own two convalescences. In addition to throwing into relief, as we shall see, certain significant aspects of Norris's last novel, *The Pit*, the idea that the romance between the hero and heroine of *A Man's Woman* was somehow a refraction of Norris's relationship with his mother furnishes the key to the mystery of why the heroines of his fiction are so tall and powerful: it is not so much that they are of abnormal size, but that the viewpoint from which they are described is that of a small boy looking at his mother. This idea is also helpful in understanding why Norris's women play the role of teacher and guide in the lives of the men they love and why physical contact between hero and heroine should be regarded as abhorrent, if not utterly unthinkable. And finally, it helps to relate Norris's fiction to one of the most widely and fiercely believed tenets of the success mythology, namely, "Everything I have I owe to my mother." However salient their jaws and broad their shoulders, Norris's fictional protagonists eventually find the effort to be a success in the world almost as harrowing as their creator had discovered it to be; in endeavoring to carve out a place in the sun for themselves, Norris's heroes thankfully draw aid and comfort and renewed strength from their surrogate mothers, their gigantic female pals.

v

In the course of Norris's second convalescence, a momentous event in his life took place; one of his novels — it was *Moran* — was finally published. Within the next twelve months, both *Blix* and *McTeague* also appeared. At long last, Norris had finally accomplished something tangible, something his father could understand. He was no longer simply a hack journalist or an assistant editor of a third-rate magazine, he was a novelist, three times over. The effect on his art was immediate and apparent.

In a series of essays (later collected in a book called *The Responsibilities of the Novelist*), Norris set forth his new and bold conception of the function of the literary artist in society. Having become something of a success himself, Norris promulgated a theory of the novel which can best be described as the aesthetic counterpart of the Alger ethic and which reads like a self-justificatory apology to his father.

To begin with, Norris wrote, "literature is of all the arts the most democratic; it is of, by and for the people." Yet literature, like Alger's bootblack, is elitist as well as democratic. "The survival of the fittest is as good in the evolution of our literature as of our bodies." Having accommodated his view of literature to the basic image of the success society, Norris then asserted that the literary artist, particularly the novelist, had moral responsibilities to that society which exceeded in importance even those of the minister and the Sunday-school teacher, "for the novel is the great influence of modern life." The son of a man who admired Dwight L. Moody, Norris proclaimed that inasmuch as the novel had superseded the minister in American life, the highest kind of novel was the "preaching novel."

THE DREAM OF SUCCESS

Perhaps the strongest index that in these essays Norris was attempting to please his father was his flat contention that the preaching novel must deal with modern capitalism, that the growth of business enterprise was the proper subject of modern fiction. Within the general context of entrepreneurial activity, the novelistic sermon of the turn of the century should celebrate the conquest of the world's frontiers and show "that the course of Empire is not yet finished." War, said Norris, has become Trade with our race, "competition and conquest are words easily interchangeable"; and the Alger hero with his eyes set on the markets of the East is the truest modern-day equivalent of the medieval knight.

As he was finishing *A Man's Woman* in March of 1899, Norris wrote to William Dean Howells that he had finally found a theme worthy of the preaching novel — a "big epic trilogy" on the production, distribution and consumption of wheat. Such a gigantic panorama of the capitalist process must have seemed to Norris to possess the same sort of amplitude he had sought long ago in Paris in his canvas on the battle of Crécy. If, like the Crécy picture, the trilogy of the wheat was destined never to be completed, nevertheless the two volumes which he did finish represent Norris's major effort to grow up, to act like a man, to deal directly and boldly with the great world in which his father worked and lived.

According to Norris's grand plan, *The Octopus* was to be the novel of production, but actually its main action is a fictionalized version of an event only tangentially related to the raising of wheat: a historical incident called the Battle of Mussel Slough, which was fought in 1880 between certain farmers in the San Joaquin Valley and the Southern Pacific Railroad.

The trouble between the farmers and the railroad had begun in the 1870's when the Southern Pacific commenced to extend its lines through the San Joaquin and encouraged settlers to occupy lands that the railroad owned, with the implication that at some future date the land would be sold to its occupants at moderate prices. When the railroad subsequently placed the lands on sale in the open market for five to eight times the price the farmers had been led to expect, they were outraged. They refused to leave "their" land, and, when eviction orders were issued, decided to resist the authorities by force of arms. In the ensuing battle, five farmers were killed and many more were arrested.

In adapting the Mussel Slough affair for the first volume of his trilogy, Norris made several important alterations, the most significant being a change in the farmers' economic status. The Mussel Slough farmers had occupied third-rate land, at best, and would have been economically depressed whatever the policy of the Southern Pacific; among the other San Joaquin farmers, they were derogatorily referred to as "sand-lappers." Literature, Norris proclaimed, ought to be "of, by, and for the people," but literary populism apparently had its limits, which not even considerations of historical accuracy could extend. Far from being lowly sand-lappers, the farmers in *The Octopus* are veritable robber barons of agriculture. Los Muertos, the ranch operated by Magnus Derrick and his son, Harran, is a feudal empire of ten thousand acres, yielding three hundred and fifty thousand bushels of wheat per year; it is equipped with grain drills, seeders and harvesters, and is directed from a central office outfitted with typewriters, telephones, maps and a ticker connecting Los Muertos with all the grain-trading centers in the United States, plus Liverpool. Although tenant farmers work some of Derrick's land, only one of them, Hooven, gets into the novel at all, and he is a very minor figure. As for farm workers, only two are of any importance in the story; however, neither of these men makes the list of "Principal Characters in the Novel" with which Norris prefaced his book, although — significantly — he did list several ranchers who figure less importantly in the action. Presley, the Eastern-college graduate and dilettante poet whose physical description corresponds so closely to his creator's — thirty years old, high forehead, dark complexion, delicate and sensitive mouth and chin — and from whose point of view the bulk of the novel is seen, admires the important ranchers, but "these uncouth brutes of farmhands and petty ranchers, grimed with the soil they worked upon, were odious to him beyond words. Never could he feel in sympathy with them, nor with their lives, their ways . . . and all the monotonous round of their sordid existence." Presley overcomes some of his disdain in the course of the novel, but he displays a sustained interest only in the agricultural entrepreneurs, never in the farm proletariat.

The story begins shortly after the arrival in the San Joaquin of Presley, who has sought out the warm, dry climate of Tulare County because of his bad health. Presley's great ambition is to be a famous poet, but thus far his work has been quite slight and unimportant. "He was in search of a subject; something magnificent . . . some vast, tremendous theme, heroic, terrible." After he has lived at Los Muertos a few weeks, he realizes that the epic of the wheat, "the nourisher of nations, the feeder of an entire world," is the theme for which he has been looking. As it turns out, however, Presley, or rather, Norris, is sidetracked from his paean of production for the better part of the novel by the developing conflict between Derrick and the other great wheat ranchers and the Pacific and Southwestern Railroad.

In the struggle, Presley's allegiance is with the ranchers, or,

as he often calls them — in spite of their baronial status —
"the People." Arrayed against the ranchers is the railroad,
"a vast power, huge, terrible . . . the leviathan, with tentacles
of steel clutching into the soil, the soulless Force, the iron-
hearted Power, the monster, the Colossus, the Octopus." The
conflict arises out of the fact that each side is endeavoring to
squeeze every last dollar out of the San Joaquin. Derrick and
the other ranchers have, for their part, "no love for their land.
They were not attached to the soil." To Magnus Derrick, "the
idea of manuring Los Muertos, of husbanding his great re-
sources, [was] niggardly, Hebraic, ungenerous." The ranchers
also exploit the men who work for them and are bitterly
against the labor organizations with which from time to time
they have to deal. The tenant farmers on their land fare
scarcely any better at the hands of the ranchers; Hooven has
worked for Magnus Derrick for seven years, but in the early
part of the novel he is in danger of being summarily dispossessed because Derrick wants to bring more land under his direct control.

Exploitation has paid off handsomely for the ranchers, too.
Magnus Derrick, for example, lives in a house of "much ele-
gance," and Mrs. Derrick, a most uncommon farmer's wife, is a
lady of leisure who spends her days on the spacious porch of
their house drinking coffee and reading Walter Pater. But despite their affluence, the ranchers want more, and are not particular how they get it. Thus they hope to influence the state
railroad commission to lower freight rates by 10 per cent, and
thereby make a killing; when Magnus Derrick is asked to consider what would happen if the commission, after having low-
ered the rates one year, were to up them the next, he replies
that he is willing to gamble, "to hazard a fortune on the chance
of winning a million." The ranchers also count on purchasing

THE DREAM OF SUCCESS

the extremely valuable land which they hold on lease from
the railroad at the initial government price.

The ranchers' ambitions, however, are frustrated by the all-
powerful railroad, which is also out for all the money the traf-
fic will bear. Presley first learns of its opposition to ".the People" when Harran Derrick reads him a letter from his father
which announces that a judge, by the name of Ulsteen, has
reversed the railroad commission's decision to lower grain
rates and restored the previous high tariff. Harran Derrick is
sure that it is the railroad's hatchetman who is beihnd Ulsteen's
decision: "That's our friend S. Behrman again," he exclaims
bitterly:

> He's the man that does us every time. . . . If there's dirty
> work to be done in which the railroad doesn't wish to ap-
> pear, it is S. Behrman who does it. If the freight rates are
> to be adjusted to squeeze us a little harder, it is S. Behr-
> man who regulates what we can stand. If there's a judge
> to be bought, it is S. Behrman who does the bargaining.
> If there is a jury to be bribed, it is S. Behrman who
> handles the money. If there is an election to be jobbed,
> it is S. Behrman who manipulates it. It's Behrman here
> and Behrman there. It is Behrman we come against every
> time we make a move. It is Behrman who has the grip on
> us and will never let go till he has squeezed us bone dry.

Banker, real-estate agent, grain buyer, political boss, representative in Tulare County of the Pacific and Southwestern
Railroad, Behrman is, indeed, seemingly everywhere. In appearance, he is an ugly and sinister figure:

> A large, fat man, with a great stomach, his cheek and the
> upper part of his thick neck ran together to form a great
> tremulous jowl, shaven and blue-grey in colour; a roll of

fat, sprinkled with sparse hair, moist with perspiration, protruded over the back of his collar. He wore a heavy black moustache.

A sinister figure and a familiar one, for this dark, paunchy man is the stock character of the avaricious Jew who haunted the imagination of so many rural Americans in the years after 1890. Thwarted by low prices and high production costs, farmers of the period found it easy to fasten the blame for their inexplicably deteriorating circumstances on some invisible empire of financial oligarchs. They became convinced, in their frustration, that the Jews, who "controlled the great fortunes of the world," were victimizing them. The international prominence of such bankers as the Rothschilds and Lazard Frères, and the fact that an American Jew like Perry Belmont actively opposed the Western agitation for free silver, were sufficient evidence for many farmers that Jewish lust for gold was responsible for all their misfortunes.

In describing Harran Derrick's suspicions that behind the railroad's greed was a greedy man named Behrman directing a greedy man named Ulsteen, Norris was not simply being the objective reporter. He himself was thoroughly anti-Semitic, thoroughly convinced that the Shylock image was a valid one. The Jews in his novels are invariably depicted as avaricious. Zerkow, the Jew in *McTeague*, is described as a man dominated by "greed — inordinate, insatiable greed. . . . He was the Man with the Rake, groping hourly in the muckheap of the city for gold, for gold, for gold." Vandover is approached at one point by a nameless Jew who "wore a plush skull-cap with ear-laps" and who tries to sell him "two flawed and yellow diamonds." Along with Norris's conviction of the Jew's appetite for financial gain went a disdain for him as an individual. In *The Pit,* one of the speculators on the Chicago

Board of Trade is a character named "Grossman, a Jew," a sweaty, slimy man who wears "a grimy flannel shirt," while an art dealer in the same novel is referred to as a "greasy old Russian Jew." In *The Octopus*, Norris glorified Magnus Derrick's refusal to shake S. Behrman's hand.*

Besides anti-Semitism, *The Octopus* displays other signs of xenophobia. For as long as Norris had lived in California, farm and labor groups had been discharging their economic dissatisfactions through racist attacks on "foreign" racial and ethnic groups within the state — Portuguese, Mexicans and especially Orientals. At the end of the seventies, the Workingmen's Party in California, under the leadership of Denis Kearney, had fastened the blame for low wages on Oriental competition and had raised the cry that "the Chinese Must Go!" Political radicals who became prominent in California in the decades after Kearney, men like James T. Phelan, V. S. McClatchy and Hiram Johnson, were all racists.

The appeal of these men to the native-American farmer of California sprang from a combination of factors, of which by

---

* With the exception of David Graham Phillips, all of the novelists under discussion in this study were anti-Semitic. London was forever asserting the superiority of the "blond Anglo-Saxon" to the Jew. Thus to Martin Eden Jews were "a symbol . . . of the whole miserable mass of weaklings and inefficients who perished according to biological law on the ragged confines of life. They were the unfit. . . . Nature rejected them. . . . Out of the plentiful spawn of life she flung from her prolific hand only the best. It was by the same method that men, aping her, bred race-horses and cucumbers." The Jew in Dreiser's novels is characteristically cast in the role of blocking the protagonist's attempts to get a job or to advance financially. Sister Carrie upon her arrival in Chicago seeks employment from a sharp, quick-mannered Jew in a store, but he coldly turns her down; Eugene Witla tries to make a comeback in the art world by selling one of his pictures, but the proprietor, "a small, dark individual of Semitic extraction," offers him only ten dollars. It was Dreiser's firm opinion that Jews were "money-minded, very pagan, very sharp in practice." For a discussion of Robert Herrick's anti-Semitism, see Chapter V.

all odds the most important was the latter's fear that the immigrant was a better farmer than he was. The most galling thing about this fear was that it was well-grounded. In contrast to the elaborately mechanized operations of the native-American farmer such as Norris described in *The Octopus,* the Portuguese, the Italian and the Oriental farmer relied on a far simpler and cheaper method of working his land: the bent backs of himself, his wife and his children. And just as a native-American farmer like Magnus Derrick recklessly "mined" his ranch for all it was worth and was heedless of the future, so the immigrant farmer carefully husbanded his land, remembering always that someday it would belong to his children. The inevitable result of the immigrant farmer's low overhead, hard work and long-range view was that he became increasingly prosperous, and as he prospered, he bought more land.

The American farmers saw the result, but did not understand the reasons behind it. Something of their baffled resentment is caught by Jack London in his novel of California agriculture, *The Valley of the Moon,* wherein a dispossessed American-born farmer, who knows that his farm has been taken over by a Portuguese family, angrily demands to know why people like himself have lost out in the race for the top to "inferior" peoples: "I can lick any Dago that ever hatched in the Azores . . . [yet] how in thunder do they put it all over us, get our land, an' start accounts in the banks?" Unable to face up to the right answers to these questions, and finding it intolerable that they should be less successful in their own country than the immigrant, the farmers of California took out their fears and frustrations in xenophobic contempt of the "foreigner."

In detailing the ethnic prejudices of the ranchers in *The*

Octopus Norris was once again not merely reporting; his own antiforeign bias had been on the record since his college days, when he had defended the institution of fraternity hazing as proof of the superior qualities of the Anglo-Saxon over the decadent races.

If the boys of our universities want to fight, let them fight, and consider it a thing to be thankful for. They are only true to the instincts of their race. We Anglo-Saxons are a fighting race; have fought our way from the swamps of Holland to the shores of the Pacific coast at the expense of worse things than smashed faces and twisted knees. One good fight will do more for a boy than a year of schooling. If he loses, he has at least had an experience which can be made profitable; if he wins . . . it wakes in him that fine, reckless arrogance, that splendid, brutal, bullying spirit that is the Anglo-Saxon's birthright; that got for us this whole mid-ocean country from under the guns of England; that got Texas and New Mexico, and the whole Southwest for us, and California and the northern boundary.

Several of Norris's short stories make reference to the "degeneracy" of people of Spanish blood in California, while others revolve around the inferior courage of the Irish vis-à-vis the "one hundred percent" American. In *Moran of the Lady Letty* Norris demonstrated that he was very much in the Kearney tradition on the Chinese question. Speaking in his own voice, Norris described the Chinese beachcombers in the following fashion:

The faces were those of a higher order of anthropoid apes: the lower portion — jaws, lips, and teeth — salient; the nostrils opening at almost right angles, the eyes tiny and bright, the forehead seamed and wrinkled — unnaturally old. Their general expression was one of simian cunning and a ferocity that was utterly devoid of courage.

The physical contrast between Moran and the leader of the beachcombers is a moral contrast as well. "The man, the Mongolian, small, wizened, leather-coloured, secretive — a strange, complex creature, steeped in all the obscure mystery of the East, nervous, ill at ease; and the girl, the Anglo-Saxon, daughter of the Northman, huge, blonde, big-boned, frank, outspoken, simple of composition, open as the day, bare-headed, her great ropes of sandy hair falling over her breast and almost to the top of her knee-boots." As the hero of the novel regards them, he asks himself, "Where else but in California could such abrupt contrasts occur?" But perhaps the most overwhelming expression in the novel of Norris's contempt for the Chinese is contained in the hero's patronizing advice to the leader of the beachcombers — "Don't try to fight white people. Other coolies, I don't say. But when you try to get the better of white people you are out of your class."

In *The Octopus*, Norris developed his view of the difference between superior and inferior races most tellingly in the scene of the great jack-rabbit drive. All the countryside takes part in driving thousands of rabbits toward a central corral, where they will be slaughtered. The actual killing of the rabbits is done by boys armed with clubs. "They walked unsteadily upon the myriad of crowding bodies underfoot, or, as space was cleared, sank almost waist deep into the mass that leaped and squirmed about them. Blindly, furiously, they struck and struck." Confronted with this horrid sight, the spectators react according to their ethnic background. "The Anglo-Saxon spectators roundabout drew back in disgust, but the hot, degenerated blood of Portuguese, Mexican, and mixed Spaniard boiled up in excitement at this wholesale slaughter." There is of course no mention made of the taste for wholesale slaughter possessed by the author of the novel.

In the climactic chapters of *The Octopus,* however, the hatred for "the Dago" pales into insignificance beside the virulence of feeling expended on the man with the paunch, S. Behrman. The ranchers' fury at Behrman mounts across the length of the novel, exactly in proportion to their realization that they are unable to defeat him. Harran Derrick expresses the explosive frustration of all of them when he mutters, "Why, when I think of it all sometimes, I wonder I keep my hands off the man." However secret and desperate the ranchers' plans become, Behrman is there beforehand to thwart them. They try bribery to insure that their representatives will be elected to the railroad commission, but even though they are elected, Behrman buys them away from the ranchers, with the result that freight rates are not reduced. It is Behrman, too, who announces to the ranchers that their land will be offered for sale at twenty-seven dollars an acre, instead of the low price they had been counting on. When they learn that Behrman, accompanied by a United States marshal and his posse, has come to evict them from their ranches, they get out their guns.

Why Norris had allowed himself to be diverted from the epic of the wheat to a story of freight rates and land prices becomes apparent at this moment in the novel. For a man who reveled in bloodshed, writing about wheat production did not compare with describing "the direct, brutal grapple of armed men." With Presley looking on in pleasurable horror, the bloody battle between the railroad and the ranchers, between the Octopus and "the People," between Jew and American, begins. The carnage is terrific. Harran Derrick, Hooven and three other ranchers are killed, and others are wounded. Presley, "sick with horror, trembling from head to foot," and the women do what they can to aid the wounded, but some of them are beyond help:

> Harran lay straight and rigid upon the floor, his head propped by a pillow, his coat that had been taken off was spread over his chest. One leg of his trousers was soaked through and through with blood. His eyes were half-closed, and with the regularity of a machine, the eyeballs twitched and twitched. His face was so white that it made his yellow hair look brown, while from his opened mouth, there issued that loud and terrible sound of guttering, rasping, laboured breathing that gagged and choked and gurgled with every inhalation.

S. Behrman, needless to say, has come through the battle without a scratch and proceeds with his eviction of the ranchers. The thought that evil has triumphed drives Presley wild with rage. "Was S. Behrman to swallow Los Muertos? S. Behrman! Presley saw him plainly, huge, rotund . . . his jowl tremulous and obese. . . ." The grief-stricken young poet resolves to kill the fat man himself.

Whenever Norris himself had moved out of the grandstands onto the football field or the battleground, he had managed to look ridiculous, and Presley in action is just as ineffectual. At a mass meeting immediately following the massacre, Presley makes an inflammatory speech urging "the People" to revolt against their tyrannical rulers, but his tone is unconvincingly shrill and he is applauded only perfunctorily. Afterwards, even Presley agrees that his speech had been dreadfully literary. His effort to kill Behrman is even more ludicrous. Procuring a bomb from an anarchist in the neighborhood, he rides to Behrman's house and hastily throws it through the dining-room window, just as Behrman is sitting down to supper. The explosion wrecks the room, but Behrman is completely untouched. Indeed, the only casualty of Presley's action is Presley himself. The whole experience unnerves him and he suffers a "general collapse all along the line"; a doctor diagnoses his ailment as a case of "over-cerebration" and recommends he take a long ocean voyage.

But in spite of the utter rout of "the People" and the collapse of the poet, the world is far from lost. On a visit to San Francisco earlier in the novel, Presley had encountered a well-known capitalist named Cedarquist, "one of our representative men." Cedarquist, too, has felt the pressure of the Octopus; he has had to close the iron-and-steel enterprise which he had begun on the West Coast as a result of its high tariff policy. Yet he is still optimistic about the future, for he believes he has discovered a way out of the viselike grip of the Octopus. Cedarquist is certain that the solution to the problems of high railroad rates, low prices and overproduction — indeed, to all problems — is to find new customers for American goods in the Orient. "The remedy," he tells Presley and Magnus Derrick, "is . . . this, *we must have new markets, greater markets.* . . . We must march with the course of empire, not against it. I mean, we must look to China."

The new-markets argument was a familiar one in the United States at the time Norris was writing *The Octopus;* Cedarquist's words echo the line taken by all imperialists of the period. Imperialism was popular at the turn of the century because, like racism, it offered "the People" another explanation of their difficulties — plus an exciting and superficially plausible escape from them. Theodore Roosevelt, like many another anti-Octopus politician, battened on the imperialist theme; Senator Albert J. Beveridge of Indiana became famous almost overnight because of the alluring picture he painted of the fabulous market potential of the East. And on top of their appeal to American pocketbooks, the imperialists invoked the more enthralling argument of Manifest Destiny and the white man's burden. Imperialism was "a part of the Almighty's infinite plan," which called for "the disappearance of debased civilization and decaying races before the higher civilization of the nobler and more virile types of men."

At the conclusion of *The Octopus*, Presley encounters Cedarquist again, as the poet is about to embark on an ocean voyage aboard one of the wheat ships which Cedarquist has built for the Oriental trade. The imperialist tells Presley that the new destiny of American success is in the East:

> You are up with the procession, Pres, going to India this way in a wheat ship that flies American colours. . . . Write to me from Honolulu, and *bon voyage*. Give my respects to the hungry Hindoo. Tell him "we're coming, Father Abraham, a hundred thousand more." Tell the men of the East to look out for the men of the West. The irrepressible Yank is knocking at the doors of their temples and he will want to sell 'em carpet-sweepers for their harems and electric light plants for their temple shrines. Good-bye to you.

Unbeknownst to both Presley and Cedarquist, the ship contains not only American wheat, but the dead body of S. Behrman. Impervious to the vengeance of the ranchers and Presley, he is destroyed by the wheat itself; in the course of watching grain from Los Muertos, which Behrman had taken over after the dispossession of Magnus Derrick, being chuted into the ship, he slips and falls into the hold. Terrified, screaming, he tries to escape, but the ocean of wheat inexorably pours in upon him through the chute. "It filled the pockets of the coat, it crept up the sleeves and trouser legs, it covered the face." * The archenemy of "the People" is swallowed up by the wheat

* Drowning is the typical fate of the Jews in Norris's fiction. Cf. *Vandover* and *McTeague*.

bound for the new markets of the East; thus does imperialism begin to deliver America from the Jews. If, as Norris contended, one of the highest responsibilities of the novelist was to demonstrate that the United States must still pursue the course of Empire, *The Octopus* was a most responsible novel.

With his book all but done, Norris could not finish it without introducing one more character, the semimythical Shelgrim, the "giant figure" of "colossal intellect" who is president of the Pacific and Southwestern Railroad. During one of his last days in San Francisco, Presley calls on Shelgrim in his office. Although it is well past six o'clock in the evening, Shelgrim is still at his desk. Seventy years old, Shelgrim is still powerful and vigorous. "The enormous breadth of the shoulders was what, at first, most vividly forced itself upon Presley's notice. Never had he seen a broader man." Generous as he is strong, Shelgrim is represented as being extremely kind to his office staff and, more importantly, it is made clear that he does not relish the brutal policy decisions which, as president of the railroad, he is forced to make. A man of "vast sympathies," Shelgrim tells Presley he had no personal desire to crush the ranchers, it was his job which constrained him to do so:

> You are dealing with forces, young man, when you speak of . . . railroads, not with men. . . . Men have only little to do in the whole business. . . . If you want to fasten the blame of the affair at Los Muertos on any one person, you will make a mistake. Blame conditions, not men.

Presley is at first dumbfounded, but then agrees that Shelgrim is right.

In the stress of the fierce conflict which had raged through *The Octopus*, Norris had said many bitter things about the business world, but at the end of the novel he felt compelled

200

to absolve the broad-shouldered, indomitable father figure of any blame for what had gone before.

vi

Never before did Norris approach his work "with such trepidations, tear up so many false starts" as he did in writing *The Pit*, the second volume of the trilogy. Planned as the novel of distribution, *The Pit* was to concern the attempt of a single individual on the Chicago grain exchange to corner the world's supply of wheat. But the story of speculation in grain, like the story of its production in *The Octopus*, immediately gave way as soon as Norris began to write, to a more fascinating and more troublesome theme: the relationship between his father and mother and himself.

Norris's first (and last) novel about a businessman is prefaced by an inevitable reminiscence — "Of certain lamentable tales of the round (dining-room) table heroes; of the epic of the pewter platoons, and the romance-cycle of *Gaston le Fox*. . . ." Inevitable because the hero whom Norris, in his shyness, had once transposed to the fourteenth century he now proposed to deal with directly. A wealthy Chicago businessman, Curtis Jadwin has come a long way from the small farm in Michigan where he was born. His schooling as a boy had been meager; although given the chance to go to high school, the boy had preferred getting into business as quickly as possible. Thirty-five years old as the novel begins, Jadwin is still unmarried.

Norris and his mother are scarcely better disguised. Laura Dearborn, the heroine of *The Pit*, is a young woman of "extreme height." A native of "a second-class town of central Massachusetts," she has only recently arrived in Chicago. Consumed with vague ambition to be a great actress of Shakespearean roles, Laura finds the dream world of the opera and the theater infinitely more exciting than the world she must live in.

Laura is also passionately fond of "literature," an interest she shares with Sheldon Corthell, an artist who is very much in love with her. Corthell is "a slightly built man of about twenty-eight or thirty; dark, wearing a small, pointed beard, and a mustache that he brushed away from his lips like a Frenchman." Although he has asked Laura to marry him and has been refused, he continues to pursue her, while she in turn indicates that her first decision has not been a final one.

Once Jadwin is introduced to Laura, however, she is forced to make up her mind immediately, for, once having fallen in love with her, Jadwin will not wait on Laura's whim, as Corthell had been willing to do. Attracted to Jadwin, Laura agrees to come to a decision.

Just why the capitalist should appeal to the would-be actress — as he does — is at first unclear. Jadwin does not like the opera, nor does he care for books; Laura has no enthusiasm either for the Sunday school which Jadwin conducts (he is a follower of Moody, she is an Episcopalian), or for the sport of fishing which is his passion. The murk and grime of the business district in which Jadwin thrives appalls her. The side of Chicago which Corthell represents is the part of the city that Laura understands and loves. Corthell, who "passed his life gently, in the calm, still atmosphere of art, in the cult of the beautiful, unperturbed, tranquil; painting, reading," seems much more Laura's type.

Yet undeniably, she is also attracted by Jadwin's force and drive. Thus her choice is a difficult one: "of the two existences which did she prefer, that of the business man, or that of the artist?" After some hesitation, Laura concludes that the

> figure that held her imagination and her sympathy was not the artist, soft of hand and of speech, elaborating graces of sound and color and form, sensitive and temperamental . . . [but] the fighter, unknown and unknowable to women . . . hard, rigorous, panoplied in the harness of the warrior, who strove among the trumpets, and who, in the brunt of conflict, conspicuous, formidable, set the battle in a rage around him, and exulted like a champion in the shoutings of the captains.

She tells Jadwin she will marry him, but as soon as she gives her decision she feels unsure again; Jadwin doesn't really seem to understand her. What finally sways her toward the businessman is the realization of what material rewards life with Jadwin will bring: a mansion facing Lincoln Park, with a conservatory, an art gallery and a church-sized organ. "I'll have my own carriage and coupé . . . a saddle horse if I want to, and a box at the opera and a country place. . . . Think of it, that beautiful house, and servants, and carriages, and paintings, and, oh, honey, how I will dress the part!" Neither as warrior nor as provider can Corthell compete; Jadwin and Laura are married.

The marriage is not a success. Almost immediately, Jadwin becomes more than ever drawn toward the business world. Finding that his real-estate interests are not enough to keep him occupied, he begins to speculate in grain futures. As his successes multiply, so do his office hours. The excitement of winning keeps him more and more away from home.

Amidst the lonely splendor of her mansion, Laura is bored. Her husband has developed no aesthetic interests since their marriage; on their long-anticipated trip to Europe, he thought the museums and cathedrals which she adored completely dull. Laura argues with Jadwin that he is spending so much time at the office that it is affecting his health, but she cannot move him. Nervous and lonely, Laura begins, toward the end of her first three years with Jadwin, to question whether she should ever have consented to marry this man who, when she does see him, can only talk about bulls and bears and the price of wheat in South Russia or the Argentine.

At this juncture, Sheldon Corthell returns from Europe. Laura invites him to dinner with Jadwin and herself; when Jadwin telephones to say he will be detained at work, they dine alone. After dinner, Corthell and Laura walk together in the art gallery and talk of the paintings of Bouguereau; he darkens the lights in the room and plays Liszt to her on the organ. Laura is greatly moved. "She felt all at once as though a whole new world were opened to her. She stood on Pisgah."

The same evening that Corthell is instructing Laura in the delights of art, Jadwin successfully completes the greatest speculation of his career, a coup which establishes him as the Napoleon of the financial world. Although physically exhausted, Jadwin throws himself back into the fray the following day, for he now believes he can corner the entire world supply of wheat. In the course of pursuing this grandiose scheme, his relations with Laura deteriorate even further. "Whole days now went by when he saw his wife only at breakfast and at dinner."

Laura consoles herself by seeing Corthell; "by slow degrees the companionship tended toward intimacy." When Jadwin begs off from a certain engagement which means a good deal to Laura, she invites Corthell to come to her on that evening; upon his arrival, Laura conducts him to her upstairs sitting room, where she allows him to tell her that he still loves her. A few evenings later, Corthell endeavors to kiss her. "She threw out a defensive hand, but he caught the arm itself to him and, before she could resist, had kissed it again and again through the interstices of the lace sleeve. Upon her bare shoulder she felt the sudden passion of his lips."

Overcome with guilt, Laura feels that she must try once more to win back her husband from his fanatical concentration on his work. The wheat corner, which Jadwin has now achieved, forces him, despite constant headaches and eye-strain, to be at his office almost twenty-four hours a day. Yielding to her persuasion, he agrees to come home early one night and allow her to entertain him. In a scene which Henry James must have had in mind when he remarked that *The Pit* would have been a good satire of Chicago society if Norris had known it was a satire, Laura tries to revive her husband's interest in her by appearing before Jadwin in the darkened gallery room dressed in the sort of costume Bernhardt had worn in the role of Theodora. Startled, Jadwin asks her:

"Whatever put it into your head to get into this rig?"
"Oh, I don't know [she replies], I just took the notion. You've seen me in every one of my gowns. I sent down for this, this morning, just after you left. Curtis, if you hadn't made me love you enough to be your wife, Laura Dearborn would have been a great actress. . . . Ah," she cried, suddenly flinging up her head till the pendants of the crown clashed again. "I could have been magnificent. You don't believe it. Listen. This is Athalia — the queen in the Old Testament, you remember."
"Hold on," he protested. "I thought you were this Theodora person."

But Laura is off in a gale of quotation from Racine. She dashes out and reappears as Bizet's cigarette girl, a red rose in her hair and castanets in her hands. Her final effort is spoiled, however, as Jadwin's broker suddenly enters with news of a crisis on the exchange and Jadwin hastily returns to the business district, leaving the desolate Laura alone once more.

The climax of the novel comes on the night of Laura's birthday. Pinning the future of her marriage on Jadwin's honoring that date, she asks her husband to promise that even "if all La Salle Street should burn to the ground" he will come home to her that evening. He agrees, even though his business affairs have been approaching a state of crisis. For Jadwin's headaches and jaded nerves have affected his fabulous business sense and he has overruled his broker's advice that he stop trying to maintain his corner in the face of the huge world harvest of wheat.

On the morning of Laura's birthday, the world price breaks and the Chicago exchange is deluged with selling orders. Facing financial ruin, Jadwin descends to the floor of the "Pit" in an attempt to stem the tide. "So great had been his power, so complete his dominion, and so well-rooted the fear which he had inspired," that for a moment his appearance is sufficient to strike "consternation into the heart of the hardiest of his enemies." But it is only for a moment. "The Wheat had broken from his control. For months, he had, by the might of his single arm, held it back; but now it rose like the upbuilding of a colossal billow." As it crashes over him, Jadwin's indomitable strength, so long overtaxed, gives way. "Under the stress and violence of the hour, something snapped in his brain." The gallant knight is carried from the field of battle on his shield.

All of this has occurred unbeknownst to Laura. She is only aware that at eight o'clock that evening Jadwin has still not come home. The doorbell rings — but it is Sheldon Corthell, come to bring Laura blue violets on her birthday. At the sight of the flowers, Laura breaks into tears. Corthell tells her he is the only one who has ever understood her; through her tears, Laura reproaches him for not having been strong enough to have won her before. "Why did you leave me only because I told you to go? Why didn't you make me love you then?" Trying to be manly, Corthell takes Laura in his arms and kisses her. "You love me! I defy you to say you do not," he cries. Weeping now himself, Corthell tells Laura he will come for her the following morning to take her away with him. But as Corthell departs, the stricken Jadwin arrives home. Recognizing his plight, Laura's allegiance to Jadwin comes flooding back. In the opportunity to nurse her warrior back to health Laura has at last found her true role.

In the concluding chapter, Jadwin — his health now restored — is shown making plans for moving West. He has taken the loss of all his wealth with godlike indifference and is enthusiastically mapping out plans for a new enterprise in which he will undoubtedly "make two or three more fortunes in the next few years." Through his illness, Jadwin and Laura have become close once again and there is no doubt that she will be going West with him. As for Corthell, he is sailing for Europe. The artist had lost out to the businessman, the father had beaten the son, once and for all time.

The story of Jadwin, Laura and Corthell proved to be Norris's swan song. Having written down what was closest to his heart, there was perhaps nothing more he had to say, in any event. Stricken suddenly with peritonitis, Norris died in San Francisco just four months after completing *The Pit*.

CHAPTER V

The Passion of Robert Herrick

"I suspect," he continued, "that all your life you have been searching for something lost, inside, something that would release you and let you live. . . . Most of us are engaged on that quest."

— ROBERT HERRICK

O F ALL the writers in America at the beginning of the twentieth century who were concerned with the theme of success, none despised the "second generation" more heartily than Robert Herrick. Indeed, so fervent were his feelings about success as to raise them beyond the level of the comparative; Herrick's hates possessed an absolute intensity. His novels are memorable if for no other reason than the passion which burns and scorches every page.

But there is a more important reason why Herrick's books deserve to be remembered. Deeply concerned with the problems of American society, Herrick was not content simply to condemn the present or to wish, as David Graham Phillips did, that the past could be recaptured. Unhappy with the "second-generation" world of 1900, Herrick did not waste his time hoping that the conditions which had given rise to the success myth could be recreated; instead he aspired to be a myth-maker himself; he sought — and the search carried him

208

hither and yon — to provide America with an alternative to success which would be equally viable as a way of life and equally compelling as a vision. His novels, imaginative explorations all, are a chronicle of the terrible quest for that alternative.

ii

To understand the search one must first understand the seeker. But in the case of Herrick this is a difficult feat, and it is Herrick himself who is the source of the difficulty. At once arrogant and shy, Herrick believed in the private life and in "the virtue of reticence." Thus his personal, unpublished memoirs are primarily a "biography of thought" and contain only the barest minimum of personal detail and anecdote. Of his family background, the memoirs tell us simply that his father's people had been small farmers who had lived for more than a hundred years in a village near Salem, Massachusetts, and that his mother was a descendant of the prominent Peabody and Manning families of Salem and the daughter of a Congregational minister whose church was in Weymouth, Massachusetts, and whose horse was the finest in town. Herrick's parents moved to Cambridge shortly after they were married and his father entered a Boston law office. Possibly inspired by the example of her socialite relatives on Beacon Hill, Herrick's mother renounced the church of her forefathers and became an Episcopalian. As for Herrick's early years, the memoirs tell us that he was born in Cambridge, went to the Cambridge public schools, and entered Harvard, the year after his father died, "a very poor boy." That is all. Beyond those few sparse details, the memoirs do not go; and Herrick did not write other reminiscences or collect his letters. Perhaps disheartened by his gift for self-suppression, no biographer has ever undertaken to write a life of Herrick.

Yet his novels are peculiarly personal documents. They are filled with portraits of people he knew, from his closest friends to passing acquaintances; and not only portraits but life histories, for Herrick did not hesitate to include in his fiction — even at the cost of violating the confidences of his friends — "transcripts from the actual record of their lives." In drawing up the dramatis personae of a work in progress, Herrick would occasionally list opposite his characters the names of the actual people on whom they were based. Two novels, *The Real World* and *Waste,* draw especially heavily on autobiographical materials, particularly from the period of Herrick's formative years. Although *Waste* was written twenty-three years later and involved totally different characters and locales, it nevertheless centers around a hero whose childhood experience is identical with that of the hero of *The Real World.* So minutely detailed is the duplication of experience that there is little doubt that the childhood in question is in fact the author's own.

The childhood is characterized by disorder and early sorrow. The hero cannot remember a time when the world did not seem to him "chaotic" and "unreal." Although too young to understand why, he instinctively senses that there is "something wrong with the family," discovering only as he grows older that the trouble is "Money. Sordid disputes about money. There was never enough money." Never enough, that is, for the hero's mother, a woman of "tyrannous temper" and a "savage tongue," who prides herself on her family background and is very aware of social distinctions. Holding herself and her children aloof from the common neighborhood in which they live, she constantly taunts her husband — a descendant of "mere farmers" — for not earning enough to support her in a manner befitting her background or appropriate to her ambitions.

The father, however, stifling between regret for the professional career which marriage had forced him to abandon and his lack of appetite for mere money-making, is unable to maintain even his present economic status. As his affairs disintegrate, the tempo of the quarreling between him and his wife is stepped up and the family skids downhill into genteel poverty.

Of this period of his life, the hero recalls the "rotting peach tree, the untidy yard, the scaling stucco, the shabby maladjusted house," and how the boys at the public school whom "he would have liked to know drew away from him, as if warned at home of his social degeneracy." The social aspirations implicit in the family's attendance at an Episcopalian rather than a Congregational church are bitterly abandoned. Eventually, the hero's father, "sick of defeat in the contest he had waged with life," takes to his bed. "In a kind of exaltation" — which revolts the hero — his mother nurses the father until he dies. With his father's death, the hero's childhood is at an end, and shortly afterwards he leaves home to go to Harvard. Given such a chaotic, unhappy family life, there is little wonder that even long after Herrick had left Cambridge and gone to teach at the University of Chicago he could never bring himself to say very much directly about his formative years. Only behind the mask of fiction could he tell the truth.

Herrick's bitter memories of his childhood and early youth were rendered even more galling by his conviction that the period between his birth in 1868 and his graduation from Harvard in 1890 had been for most Americans an era of unparalleled opportunity, happiness and success. While he grew up in a home torn apart over the failure of his father to get ahead, everyone else's family, he was convinced, was having a wonderful time. If there is a special poignance which suffuses all of Herrick's comments on the period of Alger's heyday, it stems from his acute sense of loss, from his feeling that all the wonder and excitement of a great era had passed his family by.

Thus, whatever reservations Herrick may have had about his own mother, his general opinion of the wives of "the generation of money-earners after the [Civil] War" was that they were above reproach. In the two autobiographical novels, the mother is castigated for goading the father into trying to become a success, but in all his other novels Herrick lauded the women of the postwar period for the part they played in helping their husbands make a fortune. The typical American wife in those days, Herrick said admiringly, waited for her mate just behind the financial firing line, ready "to care for him, to equip him and to hoard his pelf." It was the husband's force that made the money, but "it was *her* thrift and willingness to forego the present ease that created future plenty." Female ambition, which had wrecked his own home life, seemed to Herrick to be precisely the reason why all the other fathers and mothers of the period were so happily married. "Living . . . together for an economic end," their marriages were uniformly blissful.

With the exception of his sick, ineffectual father, American men of the older generation seemed to Herrick to have been giants in the earth. True Alger heroes every one of them, they had all the virtues. They were honest; they were direct; yet these attributes did not in the least prevent them from behaving with the glorious disregard for the law of "condottieri leaders." They were "splendid . . . brigands," who were nevertheless "honorable" and "unselfish" men. Life for these heroes was one long, prolonged battle that "wrung . . . [them] to the last reserve of strength"; yet there was a peacefulness in their souls that was "beyond mere energy." Their employes loved them, even though they methodically fired every man who ever went out on strike. They spent their lives making money, but saw "things larger than dollars on their horizon." They sprang from the people — to become the "best aristocracy that this country has seen." Their coat of arms, Herrick said, "bore the legend: Integrity and Enterprise."

The tragedy to Herrick was that, for all their virtue and strength, these heroic men and women were a vanishing race; in his novels they are all old and waiting to die, their last years made unhappy by the knowledge that their children are not worthy to succeed them. Herrick felt that the new age was witnessing the irrevocable "passing . . . of that period of the towering industrial creators"; modern America had entered an anticlimactic era of "luxury and trusteeship." Cheated by his parents out of a happy childhood in the golden age of success, Herrick the man concluded that he had been cheated again, that the success society in which he was fated to live did not at all resemble the glorious world which he was sure had existed in the past, but was a horrible facsimile of his own family life.

Many American writers at the end of the nineties had begun to notice the tensions between husbands and wives arising out of the efforts of the latter to coerce the former into an ever more furious pursuit of success. Henry James, for example, observed that the typical American husband of the period was "driven" into the economic struggle by his "immitigable womankind, the wives and daughters who float, who splash on

the surface and ride the waves, his terrific link with civilization, his social substitutes and representatives, while, like a
diver for shipwrecked treasure, he gasps in the depths and
breathes through an air-tube." The poetess and newspaper
columnist Ella Wheeler Wilcox considered, "after reading
thousands of letters, and listening to thousands of confessions
from both women and men," that "the majority of men who
are straining every nerve to accumulate great fortunes, instead
of stopping to enjoy comfortable incomes, are stimulated to
this course of action by restless, ambitious and discontented
wives and daughters." For Herrick, however, who as a child
had seen and heard his mother's attempts to stimulate his
father into action, and whose own unhappy marriage finally
terminated in divorce, words like "immitigable" and "discontented" were far too mild to apply to modern American
womanhood. The younger women in his novels are predatory
beasts of prey who stop at nothing to achieve their goals. "Let
some woman get hold of you," Herrick warned the men of
America, "fasten her claws in you, and then you are done for."
The monition was an important theme in his first novel, and in
his last. But it was only in the six full-length portraits of "second-generation" women which make up Herrick's best-known
novel, *Together,* that the full force of his fury was unleashed.

The composite portrait of the heroines of *Together* reveals a
sexually frigid woman who resents pregnancy for what she
fearfully imagines is its bad effect upon her complexion, and
who regards children as a calamitous intrusion upon her freedom. Spurning motherhood, she fills up her life with woman's
club meetings and trashy novels, with outspending her husband's income, inconclusive flirtations with other men and
endless daydreams of even greater success in some "larger
future." But these things are not enough; nothing engages her,

nothing absorbs her. There is, as Herrick had said of an earlier heroine, "a restless, savage beast" inside her which nothing in her useless life can satisfy or appease. "Ever trying to find something beyond the horizon," she drifts from experience to experience in the hope of discovering something to do. You will find her, Herrick wrote, "overfed, overdressed, sensualized, in great hotels, on mammoth steamers and luxurious trains, rushing hither and thither on idle errands." Frantically bored, she is the easy victim of "the fearful modern disease of nerves"; the "Queen" of the American success society is, for all her power, "a neurotic slave." Neurosis, however, is no excuse; Herrick's final judgment of the American woman showed absolutely no mercy. If her image were to be struck on a coin, he wrote, it would reveal a "Vampire, sucking at the souls of men."

Nor did his denunciation of modern American women soften Herrick's condemnation of their husbands. American men at the turn of the century, said Herrick, generally fell into one of two categories: either "they lacked ability and grit, or were frankly degenerate — withered limbs." Herrick felt that of the two types the latter was the more depraved, being composed of men who had substituted social-climbing for business ambition, preferred playing polo to working, and superciliously jeered at anyone who did not share their tastes.

Even those members of the "second generation" who went into business were a far cry from what their fathers had been. Their very physical appearance was different — and a change for the worse. Whereas in the seventies the American entrepreneur had been an "angular, hard-headed" man with sharp, flashing blue eyes, the "image of modern power" had a "lean, hungry, seamed face, surmounted by a dirty-gray pall." Bribery of government officials and the plundering operations of the trusts had replaced honest competition; the gambling spirit had superseded the ancient and honorable "gospel of work"; the urge "to develop and civilize" the country had given way to a "shamefully, rapaciously, swinishly" conducted exploitation. "The best aristocracy this country has seen" had been succeeded by "the most unblushing the world had ever seen." If *condottieri* leaders and splendid brigands obviously knew something about plunder, or if the contention that America had undergone "development" in 1870 but was enduring "exploitation" two decades later was a dubious distinction, these considerations did not at all affect Herrick's wholesale condemnation of the new businessman.

Herrick's gloomy view of the society he saw around him was made even darker by his refusal to believe, as David Graham Phillips did, that there were any easy political solutions to what ailed America. For while the Declaration of Independence might have been written in the "spirit of conquest and greed" and the Constitution might celebrate organized self-ishness in the name of freedom, the worship of success was "woven," Herrick said, "out of tradition" as well as of law; in America, Horatio Alger was Burke as well as Locke. Therefore, voting new laws, electing new candidates, or throwing out the Constitution and writing a new one, were not sufficient to destroy success.

This insight made Herrick a political pessimist. Thus, although he hated the trusts, he found Theodore Roosevelt's trust-busting activities "besotted vanity and colossal ignorance." T. R.'s conservation policies Herrick considered as having only a vote-getting significance; in his view, Roosevelt didn't "give a tinker's dam about waterpower or all the rest of the progressive bunk, but it's popular, it's the coming thing, and Teddy is the greatest band-wagon climber you ever saw."

Indeed, the whole progressive movement seemed to Herrick not a "crusade of right against might," but simply the "ancient revolt of the little hogs against the big hogs." And Wilson's New Freedom was no better. Regardless of the brand name, Herrick regarded the effort to regulate American society by political means as "almost farcical."

Nor did he believe with Jack London that economic revolution would solve anything. This was not, however, because Herrick did not consider the possibility of revolution a likely one. Like many other Americans of his time, Herrick feared that revolution was just around the corner. His novels resound with such warnings as, "The good people of Chicago are running things on a wrong basis, and someday they will wake up with forty thousand Polacks and other impetuous citizens tearing down their houses." But while Herrick was convinced that the greedy folly of the "second generation" was leading the country straight to revolution, he was equally sure that the overthrow of the existing order would only replace greed with greed. "There would be merely a row, some shooting; and back again to the same old game of grab." Herrick was pessimistic about the efficacy of revolution because he was sure that industrial labor — the strongest potential revolutionary group — was as firmly committed to the success dream as any other element in American society. The leaders of organized labor were, he said, "hungry for the fleshpots." It is significant of his view of labor that in his fictionalized account of the bitter Pullman strike of 1894, which Herrick considered a kind of French revolution in miniature, he slanderously assigned the failure of the strike to a sellout by Debs and the other officials of the American Railway Union to the railroads.

No political or economic change, in short, could work any sea change in America, Herrick felt, "so long as the spirit of man was untouched." Until such time as it was touched, success would remain in the eyes of the American people "the one glorious prize of life." Success would never be overcome by social change, only by inner reform. Religion alone could save America.

iii

Herrick's roots were Puritan. He, however, could not accept the faith of his ancestors, not even in one of the various diluted forms in which it was presented at the close of the nineteenth century. Indeed, conventional religion of any sort was unacceptable to Herrick. Yet if he was devoid of religion, a religious hunger remained; Herrick could shake off Congregationalism, but he could not exorcise his Puritan hankering for the ideal. His insistence that man's spirit must be touched before America would abandon its worship of success is the statement of an unalterably religious person. The problem for Herrick was, where to find the new religion which could touch the spirit of modern man?

The Gospel of Freedom, Herrick's second novel, is the story of his discovery of that new faith. The protagonist, Adela Anthon, is the daughter of a great American entrepreneur who had made a fortune in the brick business after the Civil War. Adela has her father's energy and his common sense, but she cannot accept his success ideal as her own. When her marriage to a rather unprincipled businessman of the newer type fails, her dissatisfaction with life in a success society becomes intolerable. Restless, unhappy, she takes up with an art critic, Simeon Erard, whom she had known in Paris before she was married. Erard's contempt for the business world, for democ-

racy, for everything American, matches her mood and she returns to Europe with him.

Conducting her through the museums and churches of
France and Italy, Erard endeavors to instruct her in "values."
The values are those of *fin-de-siècle* aestheticism, the credo of
"beauty is truth" and "art for art's sake" with which Herrick
had become acquainted as an undergraduate at Harvard and
then again in Florence, where he spent the winter and spring
of 1896. Erard worships art, not success; his values are utterly
opposed to the work-and-win, strive-and-succeed maxims of
American civilization. Adela's happiness with him in Europe,
the delight she takes in his company and his conversation,
strongly suggests, at this point in the novel, that Herrick had
come upon the new ideal he was looking for. Art for art's sake,
he seemed to suggest, was the antisuccess religion and Erard
the art critic was its prophet.

Simeon Erard, however, is a vicious caricature, the most
vicious of all the nasty portraits of his friends and acquaintances which Herrick included in his fiction. Based in all probability on the art critic Bernard Berenson,* who had been an
under·raduate at Harvard at the same time as Herrick — they
served together as editors of the *Harvard Monthly* — Erard is,
as Herrick develops him, a mincing, precious figure. Part of
the novelist's hatred of his character is anti-Semitism:
spawned in some "dull back alley in Jersey City," Erard is a
"little Jew" with a flattened face that is "almost repulsive."
The greater part of Herrick's animus, however, stemmed from
the simple fact that although the disciples of what he sneer-
ingly called "ultra-aestheticism" hated the success society of

---

* Herrick denied that Erard was based on Berenson. The resemblances
are, however, too close for coincidence — e.g., Erard's theory of "prehen-
sile values" is obviously a nasty variation on Berenson's "tactile values."

the American nineties as much as he did, Herrick infinitely preferred the latter to the former.

Finally understanding Erard for what he is, Adela rejects him and turns to the man who represents the true ideal she has been searching for. He is Thornton Jennings, who advises Adela that the only genuine alternative to success is peace of soul, a "state of spirit in the face of our Lord the Master." The only way to bring the soul to peace, he informs her, is "to accept the world as it comes to our hands, to shape it painfully, without regard for self." Despite the religious cast of his conversation, Jennings is not a minister; he is the exemplar of the new religion through which, Herrick hoped, America would save its soul. Jennings is that characteristic figure of Herrick's fiction, the man who, whether he appears as doctor, lawyer, engineer or architect, is the hero of all Herrick's novels: the Professional Man. How could the spirit of man be touched? Through single-minded dedication to an intellectual discipline. Herrick's new church was the university, its priest was the professionally trained student.

iv

The Gospel of Freedom was published in 1898, at the close of two remarkable decades in American education. The period between 1878 and the publication of Herrick's novel was the great seedtime of the higher learning in America: the number of colleges and universities in this country increased in these twenty years from three hundred and fifty-odd to nearly five hundred; the combined student body nearly doubled. No statistics can measure the increase in enthusiasm which Americans felt for higher education, but Lord Bryce, visiting the

United States in the eighties, observed that "Nothing more strikes a stranger who visits the American universities than the ardour with which the younger generation has thrown itself into study, even kinds of study which will never win the applause of the multitude." John D. Rockefeller had scorned a college education in favor of getting an early start in the business world, but in the eighties and nineties increasing numbers of young men not only desired a college education, but graduate training as well. The absence of graduate schools in universities at home at first caused young American scholars to go to Germany for their training; in the eighties, over two thousand Americans were enrolled at Berlin, Leipzig, Heidelberg, Jena or Halle. But the establishment of Johns Hopkins primarily as a training ground for graduate students, quickly followed by the opening of graduate schools at Harvard, Yale, Chicago and elsewhere, meant that by 1898 there were nearly five thousand students doing graduate work in the United States. The phenomenon was, as one historian has said, "something different, something which never before had had so ample an expression in American life: a passion for truth born of knowledge. . . ."

Possibly most significant of all, these were the years when the standards of professional training were raised to a far higher level than ever before. In 1878, diploma selling was a regular business; for a price, one could become a doctor, a lawyer or a theologian without any trouble. The curriculum requirements at even the most reputable universities were farcically low. "At most institutions in 1878 a medical student, after absorbing atmosphere in a doctor's office for a time and taking a lecture course of four or five months, repeating it the second year, could obtain his degree. . . ." The law schools were, if anything, worse. But by the end of the century, the situation had changed considerably. It was no longer possible to buy diplomas and the universities had jacked up their entrance conditions, lengthened their course programs and made them more rigorous.

Included in the flood tide of young Americans in the nineties who scorned the idea of business and preferred instead to have a professional career was Robert Herrick. Upon graduation from Harvard, he decided to become a teacher. Hired by the Massachusetts Institute of Technology, he spent three years there teaching English to future engineers and scientists. In 1893, Herrick moved on to Chicago, where William Rainey Harper, the president of the just-opened University of Chicago, was endeavoring to establish the most distinguished educational institution, both on the undergraduate and professional levels, in the United States.

At Chicago, one of Herrick's colleagues was Thorstein Veblen, whose *The Theory of the Leisure Class* appeared a year after Herrick's *Gospel of Freedom* and became the most celebrated indictment of the "second generation" of success ever to be written by an American. The teacher of English and the section man in economics were of one mind about the rich. But the most interesting, and significant, point of similarity between Herrick and Veblen lies not so much in the common cause they made against the "second generation," but in their apotheosis of the Professional Man.

The excited conviction that man's knowledge was now sufficient to enable him to control his environment was one of the great forces behind the flowering of American universities and professional training schools in the last decades of the nineteenth century. But it was not until the first decades of the new century that that conviction found, in the books of Thorstein Veblen, its most fully developed expression. In book after book — *The Theory of Business Enterprise, The Instinct of Workmanship* and *The Engineers and the Price System* — Veblen proclaimed that it was at last possible for society to be efficiently run — if only its direction were assumed by the one kind of man who understood its modern complexity: the professionally trained engineer, the aloof, ascetic scientist, contemptuous of financial success, who had no other interest than the technological problems of his work. Herrick's conception of the Professional Man was cut from the same cloth as his colleague's ideal of the engineer. Herrick thought of his hero as the priest of a new monasticism, a man who renounced all ease and luxury, was dedicated to his work, and who defined success as a job well done, not as money earned.

But in 1898 Herrick's hero still existed largely in his mind; Thornton Jennings had appeared but briefly in *The Gospel of Freedom;* the novels glorifying the Professional Man lay in the future. Only as he actually came to write them did Herrick encounter the imaginative difficulties which were to make his hero such a far less consistent, and yet in some ways such a more significant, figure than Veblen's engineer.

For Herrick, after all, was a novelist; there were exigencies of his trade confronting him with which the economist-sociologist Veblen did not have to cope. Veblen described his engineer's role in a modern industrial plant, or predicted the methods he would employ to improve the operation of society once he was in control, and let it go at that. Being a novelist, Herrick could not restrict himself to such abstractions; he had to describe his hero in human as well as technological terms; he had to show him paying the rent and falling in love; he had, in sum, to tell about his life. When the novelist did so, he ran into trouble which, ultimately, proved too great for his imagination to surmount.

223

The baffling difficulties which Herrick encountered with this hero on whom he was counting so much began with the very first novel which was mainly devoted to the Professional Man — *The Web of Life*. The hero, Howard Sommers, is a young surgeon who, as the story opens, is attached to the staff of a Chicago hospital. Born poor, Sommers has lived ascetically all his life and is wholly dedicated to his work — at which, like all of Herrick's Professional Men, he excels. His one concession to the world of success is his romantic interest in a young Chicago debutante. She, however, believes in success, while Sommers of course despises it, and they quarrel.

The symbolic clash of values is thus fairly launched — only to sink from sight almost at once when Sommers accepts a lucrative offer to join the staff of a fashionable society doctor with offices in the Loop. The antisuccess hero suddenly, in mid-novel, becomes an Alger hero, his consecrated career a rags-to-riches story. For Herrick's protagonist is a man possessed of great skill, will power, and an immense capacity for work, but far from distinguishing him as the antisuccess hero, these qualities are precisely those glorified by the success myth. When one of Alger's bootblacks was so endowed, he was inevitably destined to rise, and so, ironically, is the hero of *The Web of Life*. The phenomenon which Veblen the economist was able to ignore, but which Herrick the novelist could not, was that a highly trained and skillful Professional Man in American society was very apt to become a financial success. Herbert Hoover, whom Herrick supported for the Presidency in 1920 ("It is the sheer intelligence of the man . . . that has won my allegiance."), and who in the year of *The Web of Life* was well on his way, thanks to his engineering ability, to a fortune of more than a million dollars, was the ironic, real-life version of Veblen's ideally impoverished engineer.

Having stumbled upon the baffling fact that Veblen's version of the American hero was not at all opposed to Alger's, but only a scientific variation on the theme of mill boy-to-millionaire, Herrick found *The Web of Life* a good deal more difficult to write than he had bargained for. In the next phase of the novel, Herrick depicted the young surgeon as desperately unhappy about his increased income, perhaps in the hope that if his protagonist were shown as angry at how much money he was earning, he would seem less like just any other Alger hero. It is for this reason, too, that Sommers redoubles his scorn for the world of society — although he increasingly frequents it.

Finally, Sommers makes an all-out rebellion against success, an action which marks both the turning point of the novel and the author's major imaginative effort to free himself from the horns of the dilemma which impaled him. The rebellion is sweeping; the surgeon not only quits his job with the fashionable doctor, but turns his back on all his society friends; he stops seeing the debutante altogether and goes to live with a married woman on the South Side of the city. Just as the debutante had embodied the values of the success society, so his liaison with the married woman is the symbol of his renunciation of that society. Sommers's affair with the latter is the first of many instances in Herrick's fiction which make sexual radicalism the symbol of a more general social rebellion: "That night they escaped the world with its fierce cross-purposes . . . the brutality of human success, the anguish of strife. . . . Outside the peaceful rain fell ceaselessly, quenching the flame and the smoke and the passion of the city."

As a final rejection of the world he had known, Sommers and the woman flee Chicago for a small village, far away from "the city with its horrible clatter of ambitions." His flight, the surgeon is sure, is not temporary; he intends his escape to be a "return to the soil," where he will "live like the primitive peasant without ambition." The woman, however, knows better; she knows that Sommers cannot for very long stand the dull little village, with its "unpainted, stuffy-looking houses," and, indeed, after only a few months of rural boredom he is ready to return to Chicago.

The rebellion has become less drastic, but it has not yet been put down. Still avoiding the people he had previously known, Sommers and the woman set up rather Spartan housekeeping in an abandoned temple left over from the World's Fair of 1893. Sommers is quite confident that he has irrevocably thrust "the world into the background," but again the woman demurs. "A man like him," she thinks, "could never be happy, standing outside the fight with his equals." Once again she is proved right, this time for economic as well as psychological reasons. Not only cannot Sommers adjust temperamentally to the ascetic life, but he is unable, despite his brilliant medical talent, to put together a neighborhood practice sufficient to support the two of them, even on the modest scale suitable to a new monasticism. Herrick attempted various explanations of Sommers's inability to earn any money, but none of them proved adequate; finally Herrick did not explain it at all — only insisted upon it. The reason for the breakdown of Herrick's explanations is that the real explanation of Sommers's curious economic failure lies entirely outside the novel; it is contained in the fact that Herrick was as bored with the young surgeon in his monastic role as he showed Sommers to be.

Herrick could not bear to see his hero wasting all his talent on the desert air; a dreary neighborhood practice was an inadequate outlet for the talents of a trained specialist in whose strong, Professional Man's hands the destiny of a whole nation deserved to be placed. Nor could he bear to see that talent unattested to by the very standard of success to which the surgeon presumably was antipathetic, lest that talent be called into question. The problem in *The Web of Life* thus became one of restoring Sommers to the great world of success without his having to go back on his resolve to renounce that world forever. The face-saving excuse Herrick adopted for his hero was the device of circumstances-beyond-his-control. Herrick forthwith depicted Sommers's life not only as dull, but impossible. Through no fault of his own, Sommers's decision to devote his life to his profession and not to making money led not to the good, ascetic life, but to starvation. To starvation and tragedy; for good measure, Herrick added the suicide of the woman to the list of Sommers's misfortunes. Her death is the last straw; his meeting her had signified the beginning of his revolt and her death represents its termination.

Poor and lonely, the surgeon has no choice but to re-enter "that web of life from which they had striven to extricate themselves . . . that fretwork, unsolvable world of little and great, of domineering and incompetent wills, of the powerful rich struggling blindly to dominate and the weak poor struggling blindly to keep their lives. . . ." His return to the success society instantly results in the re-recognition of his medical talents; he serves for a time on the staff of a large New York hospital, then as a medical officer in the Spanish-American War. With the defeat of Spain, he returns to Chicago and marries the long-suffering debutante.

That this incident smacked strongly of the cliché-ending of hundreds of success novels, Herrick was aware. In a last-ditch effort to stave off this disastrous comparison, Herrick had his hero insist that neither he nor his bride should share in the will of her wealthy father. Sommers's belief that "for many reasons their lives would be happier without the expectation of un-earned wealth" was, Herrick hoped, proof of his hero's con-tinued contempt for success, but in fact it was the classic ges-ture of the Alger hero who, in Sommers's words, wants "to start with the crowd at scratch, not given a handicap."

With his antisuccess hero acting and talking like Mark the Match-Boy, Herrick cut his losses and simply abandoned the novel. Three pages after the surgeon's marriage, *The Web of Life* comes to a startlingly abrupt halt. In those three pages, we are informed that the surgeon has taken over the practice of an older doctor, which, "if not lucrative, was sufficiently large and varied to satisfy [him]." Sommers's wife, we are further informed, has had a child, and the curtain falls with the surgeon holding the baby in his arms and murmuring about the goodness of "life." The blurred details of Sommers's financial status and the vague effort at affirmation of life on the final page were the result of Herrick's final desperate at-tempts to conceal just how badly his novel had fallen short of all that he had hoped it would accomplish.

Having failed with a doctor as hero, Herrick tried a lawyer in his next novel; after that he tried an architect; again and again Herrick attempted to write the great American antisuc-cess novel. But however promising each new version of the Professional Man seemed at the start, he never proved satis-factory. For all their confident beginnings, Herrick's novels kept breaking down in the middle, while the endings were uniformly hasty, confused and irresolute. The conclusion of *The Common Lot*, for example, finds the architect hero taking his place beside the common people who, he asserts, have no interest in success (and therefore presumably superior archi-tectural taste), although the main purport of the novel has been to show that the common people worshiped success and had abominable taste. In the last chapters of *A Life for a Life*, the hero expresses his disdain for the world of success by giving up his high-salaried job to go back "into the ranks." When someone points out to him that by returning to the bottom he is merely starting out for the top all over again, the hero perplexedly admits that this is so. Before the implications of this interesting admission can be explored, however, the hero loses his life in a fire and the novel is broken off.

Conflagrations became, in time, almost a trademark of Herrick's fiction — they were, after all, one way to bring novels to a conclusion when they actually had no conclusion. But Herrick's most satisfactory device for avoiding the embarrassment of endings was to transpose the locale of his novels to the West in the closing pages.

The first time he tried it was in *The Real World*. In this novel, the hero is a lawyer who has risen — "by power of the will" — from poverty to a job with a large New York law firm. This is the juncture at which Herrick usually ran into trouble. But the West gave him a way out. When the law firm offers to take in the hero as a partner, he refuses, and his tone of assurance indicates how confident Herrick was in his new-found device: "I don't believe I want merely money, or position, or professional reputation." With that, the hero packs his bags and heads for Mound City, Iowa, where, "fired with the sense of freer life and creative purpose," he becomes the lawyer for a western railroad and leads it in a successful fight against Wall Street control. In contrast to so many other Herrick novels, *The Real World* concludes on this vigorous, affirmative note.

Affirmative because by dint of transporting his hero to the West, Herrick was enabled to accomplish everything in his novel which he had set out to do. The hero's rise from poverty to New York law firm was proof that he was thoroughly capable of competing in a success society, while his refusal to join the firm, plus his scorn for the money-grubbing aura of Wall Street, was proof of his qualification as the antisuccess hero. But whereas Herrick was usually unable to let either the rise or the refusal prevail, with the consequent dissolving effect on the latter part of his novels, in *The Real World* the flight to the West allowed Herrick to have his cake and eat it, too: to have both the refusal prevail and the rise re-enacted.

Yet, alas, this happy solution was not without its fatal flaw. By moving to Iowa the hero had, after all, merely replaced a career in the success society of New York with one in its Midwestern counterpart; the Professional Man was still an Alger hero. If life in Mound City, Iowa, appeared more palatable to Herrick than life in New York, it was not because it was qualitatively different, but only because the raw, new Midwestern town symbolized in Herrick's mind the vanished success society of the post-Civil War period which he so admired. For when the hero of *The Real World* arrives in Mound City, he steps across the threshold into the past; moving westward in space has taken him backward in time; Iowa in 1901 is the New York of 1870. In the West, Herrick's lawyer hero is in effect a member of the first, not the second, generation, a representative of the best aristocracy, not the worst, in sum, an Alger hero moving up the ladder in the golden dawn-age of the success myth.

Because the West represented the past to Herrick, his hero's arrival in Mound City did not really furnish his novel with an ending, but with a second beginning. A second beginning, however, was better than no ending at all, and Herrick soon learned to rely heavily on this device. Those novels in which he employed it are all characterized by the high, clear, confident tone of their conclusions and are the most nearly integrated books that Herrick ever wrote. But it is highly ironic that the man who had hoped to create an antisuccess myth should have found himself obliged to transform his novels of the Professional Man into a kind of Western version of the Alger stories.

v

Like his heroes, Herrick himself found the professional life not wholly satisfying. For a period of many years, he suffered from a "long downward course of health," which was largely the product of neurasthenia. In an effort to regain his health, he spent more and more time away from his teaching duties at Chicago. (There was not much to hold him at the university in any event. The scholar's life, which Herrick had imagined as "lean, lonely, unlovely, wholly absorbed in its devotion to immaterial things, its reward an inner reward," had turned out to be infected with "the spirit of the . . . market place," characterized on the one hand by the "feverish desire" of the professors to make money out of their knowledge and on the other by the students' definition of education as preparation for a "good job" after graduation.) He gave up not only teaching, but America; for six months of every year Herrick lived in Europe. But across the decade 1900–1910, the period of his greatest productivity as a writer, Herrick's health did not improve.

His case was puzzling, but not unusual; it was, indeed, quite typical of the experience of an increasing number of Americans of the time. Indeed, so rapidly did the rate of physical and mental breakdowns advance that the phenomenon became a public as well as a medical question: Was life in a success society too hectic for the human organism to bear? Orison Swett Marden, the editor of *Success,* observed that "Anxiety and care may be read on nearly every American face, telling the story of our too serious civilization. . . . We have not yet learned, as a people, that grief, anxiety, and fear, are the great enemies of human life." Ella Wheeler Wilcox testified that her "mountain of mail" was a "volcano of seething unrest." With Freud still beyond the American horizon, cures sprang up by the thousands. Herrick reported that the Chicago of his day swarmed with "osteopaths, faith healers, mind healers, physical culturists, Swamis, Exodites, Introdites, masseurs, etc., etc. — working cures by mind or muscle — prophets of the soul or of the belly."

One of the principal prophets in the Chicago area was William S. Sadler. For a time, Sadler had served as a professor at the Post Graduate Medical School in Chicago, but eventually gave it up for the more lucrative fields of lecturing and writing on medical subjects. One lecture, "Faith and Fear," was delivered by Sadler more than one thousand times. His numerous books — called the "Sadler Classics" — included such titles as *Worry and Nervousness: or The Science of Self-Mastery* and *The Truth About Mind Cure.* Sadler's principal thesis was that high tension was the dominant characteristic of modern social and commercial life, particularly among the American people. "It was this fact," Sadler wrote, "that led to the coining of the term *Americanitis,* which it was intended should stand for this restless, tense, high pressure life which is characteristic of the average American citizen." The cure which Sadler offered to the casualties of the "great race" for the top of the success heap was what he termed "the master key to mental medicine": a nondoctrinal version of Protestant Christianity, dressed up in the language of medical science. It is not surprising, given Herrick's own illness and the general concern at the time with the problem of mental breakdown, that Herrick's greatest effort to create a new myth in America should have centered around a medico-religious figure very much like Sadler.

Thus in *Together*, written toward the end of his worst period of ill health, the principal character is a young society woman who is afflicted with "Americanitis." Failing to obtain a cure from ordinary doctors, she turns to a Doctor Renault who, although a surgeon, nonetheless insists that religion, not medicine, affords the only way out of her nervous depression. Impressed by Renault, she decides to join him at the hospital-retreat he has established in rural Vermont. Possessed of "a power of the old saints who worked miracles," Renault is engaged in restoring his patients' health by "pure force of will." After several months of working in Renault's hospital and listening to him talk (" 'Life is GOOD — all of it — for every one.' He held her eyes with his glance while his words reverberated through her being like the CREDO of a new faith."), the heroine is completely rehabilitated. Renault's Sadlerian techniques have, we may assume, freed her from submission to the furious round of the success society and given her some better credo to live by.

But they have not. Rejoining her husband — from whom she had been estranged — she quits New York and moves to Texas, where they go into railroading. The credo of the new faith has not, in other words, become a way out of the world of success, but a therapeutic remedy enabling one to resume living in the same old way. Far from being antisuccess, Renault's medical religion is nothing else than a means of repairing the nervous damage wrought by the rugged competition of American life and of restoring men and women to fighting trim. One of Sadler's books was entitled *What Every Salesman Should Know About His Health; Together* might very easily have been called *What Every Woman Should Know About Her Nerves.*

Yet the novel is not quite so easily dismissed; there remains, after all, the figure of Renault himself. While it is true that the purpose of his therapy is to return his patients to the world of success as fast as he can repair them, he himself, by his own deliberate withdrawal from the big-time, fee-splitting world of New York medicine to the plain, spare discipline of his country hospital, seems the embodiment of the heroic ideal for which Herrick had been searching. Renault, although a minor figure in the novel, gave his creator confidence that in the "medical priest" he had (at last!) found the authentic antisuccess hero.

Emboldened, Herrick wrote *The Master of the Inn,* one of his shortest books and one of his few bestsellers. The inn is a retreat near Stowe, Vermont; its master is a doctor who "heals both body and soul." To the inn come men "from the clinic or the lecture-room, from the office or the mill — wherever men labor with tightening nerves," to work in the fields, bathe in the pool and be confessed by the master. Giving neither drugs nor pills, the master takes hold of these shattered Americans and makes them "fall in love with *life.*" The novel is an eighty-page, antisuccess idyl; if its conclusion is tragic and sudden, it is only because Herrick wished to avoid introducing some flaw that would spoil the tone. Before anything can go awry, the inn burns down and the master dies in the blaze.

Encouraged by the fact that the novelette had done just what he wanted, and by the deluge of letters which came to

234

him from people demanding to know where the inn had been located and who the master was, Herrick next projected a much more ambitious novel with a medical priest as protagonist. *The Healer* carried with it the highest hopes of Herrick's career.

Like all of his novels, *The Healer* begins surely and confidently. Frederick Holden, the hero, has had a rags-to-riches youth which has carried him from poverty and ignorance through medical school and training abroad to a lucrative urban practice. But such a life proves to be disastrous to his personality and to his medical talent; success robs him of his celebrated power of the "will," with which he has always cured people. In despair, he forsakes his practice and returns to the north woods where he had been brought up as a boy. As the novel opens, a vacationing millionaire's daughter has fallen ill in a nearby camp and Holden is called in to treat her. Finding his will power restored — the result of his having left the success world — he is able to cure her.

His eventual marriage to the heiress does not soften, as was so often the case in Herrick's novels, the determination of the hero to avoid the world of success. It is his firm intention to stay in the north woods and cure people who come to him, and he persuades his bride that in this remote world, far from the everlasting pursuit of money, she will be happier, too. She does stay with him; Holden begins to cure people; it is *The Master of the Inn* all over again, but on a major scale.

That major scale, however, was Herrick's undoing, because at this idyllic point in the novel Herrick had reached not the end, but only the middle of his story. The second half of the novel is all irony. Holden's will power is enormous; his cure is infallible; he becomes famous. In a short time, his remote north-woods home becomes a mecca for thousands of men and women, burned out in the "great race" and in need of help. In exchange for helping them "to make money by the aid of the spirit," they make Holden a wealthy man. The great irony of *The Healer* is that although Holden is the antisuccess hero par excellence, a man who is dedicated to his craft and who lives far away from the great world, his professional competence utterly destroys the kind of life he had envisaged. In the north woods, Holden is busier with patients than he had ever been in the city; and he is also making more money.

And with his financial comeback, he naturally again loses his will power, his power to heal; Holden eventually has to rely on mere medicines, just like any ordinary doctor. Too late to save him from the deleterious consequences of his own ability, a fire wipes out his sanitarium. Holden, the supreme embodiment of Herrick's hopes for "a new priesthood of healing," bitterly refuses to rebuild his hospital; he admits that the success society is unavoidable, and would as soon make his way in the city as in the north woods. The end of the novel finds him the director of a large, metropolitan institute for the study and cure of nervous diseases. The ashes of Holden's north-woods retreat spelled the calamitous end of Herrick's hopes that he could create a new myth in America.

vi

With the fiasco of *The Healer,* Herrick was a desperate man. His dislike of "this creed of *success*" became an obsessional hatred. The glorious, exhilarating race for the top which Alger had celebrated had been condemned by Herrick in 1900 as "a brutal game . . . a good deal worse than war," and the comparison was to prove significant. A decade and a half and many novelistic failures later, nothing could shake Herrick's conviction that the only way for America to throw off its slavish submission to success was by going to war.

War as a purgative to rid the American system of the success poison, war as a superior form of activity to money-grubbing, was an idea which engaged many Americans of the period. Jack London hailed military conflict as providing the occasion for a "pentecostal cleansing" of American civilization, while Theodore Roosevelt declared to his friend Henry Cabot Lodge that "this country needs a war." Herrick had first felt the attraction of this idea during the Spanish-American War. Van Harrington, the protagonist of his novel *The Memoirs of an American Citizen*, expressed Herrick's hopes for what Santiago Bay and San Juan Hill might portend:

> The sick spirit of our nation needed just this tonic of a generous war, fought not for our own profit. It would do us good to give ourselves for those poor Cuban dogs. The Jew spirit of Wall Street doesn't rule this country, after all, and Wall Street doesn't understand that the millions in the land long to hustle sometimes for something besides their own bellies. So, although Wall Street groaned, I had a kind of faith that war would be a good thing, cost what it might.

When the war with Spain failed to have the hoped-for cathartic effect on American society, Herrick turned to his architects and doctors once more. But with the final failure of the Professional Man in *The Healer* (1911), he again lifted his eyes hopefully towards the gods of war. The incident at Sarajevo was viewed by Herrick as a calamity, but it was also the answer to his prayers.

At the invitation of the French government, Herrick toured the Western Front in 1915. The vividly pro-Allies book *The*

World Decision which came out of this trip was published early in 1916 and played a part, albeit a small one, in swaying American public opinion toward participation in the war. But the book was far from being merely a journalistic or propagandistic report; *The World Decision* was first and foremost an allegory, a projection on the scale of world war, of Herrick's private war with success.

Ignoring England's participation entirely, Herrick saw the conflict as a struggle between the Latin civilization — France and Italy — on the one hand and the Teutonic civilization on the other. The Latin world, in Herrick's account, stood for "a larger, finer interpretation of life than economic success" — such things as "beauty, sentiment, tradition, all that give color and meaning to life" — while Germany, which had elevated "greed and the lust of power to the dignity of a philosophical system," seemed, in Herrick's analysis, to be dedicated to some sort of German translation of the success myth. The war's outcome was thus crucial for America because the conflict between these rival ideas was in fact a struggle for the minds and hearts of the American people. Upon the war's outcome, Herrick warned, depended "the form which our national character is to take ultimately." He foresaw a triumphant Germany as insuring in this country, through "peaceful penetration" of the German philosophy, the final, ineradicable victory of the success ideal. America's duty, to herself and to the world, was clear.

Herrick in *The World Decision* was also in full agreement with London and Roosevelt that an infusion of the military spirit would have a beneficent effect on the country. The slaughter of modern war, Herrick declared, was better than "the aimless selfishness in which our American youth are brought up." Patriotism, "the supreme loyalty to life of the individual," alone was capable of making America renounce its loyalty to success. Consequently, Herrick believed, the whole nation, women as well as men, "should be made to feel the obligation of national service," for only in this way could Americans learn to forget themselves and subordinate their personal ambition to that transcendent loyalty. When the Congress did in fact declare war, Herrick's last hopes were running high.

But, as with all of his other dreams, this one, too, turned to nightmare. The conflict which was to have saved the American people from "the sodden self-interest, the sodden comfort-getting, to which they had sunk," led merely to the success-mad twenties. "The great cleansing Cause" turned out to be "the greatest insanity in human history." America, "the least lovely civilization on God's earth," was now utterly beyond salvation.

His hopes blasted, Herrick took out the defeat of his quest for an alternative to success in invective and denunciation. Passionate affirmation of the possibilities of American life became passionate rejection of its realities. In the middle of the twenties, when he came to write his novelized autobiography, there was no other possible title for the book than *Waste*. If Herrick's novels usually suffered from a vagueness of tone and attitude, particularly in their closing pages, there is no mistaking the savage frustration, the mordant self-laceration, of *Waste*'s end. It is perhaps the darkest conclusion in American autobiography: "He had," said Herrick of himself,

a sense of corruption working at the very roots of life, turning it into some obscene joke, a meaningless tale told in the void. Money, possession, the will to dominate, a cringing fear of the blind herd, set loose the mainsprings of human puppets. . . . All was one inextricable weave, one vast nexus of squalor in which the human spirit wallowed helpless. All!

Conclusion

As Americans born in the late sixties or early seventies of the last century, the five men who comprise this study were all brought up on the success myth; as American writers who launched their literary careers in the nineties, they were keen observers of the life which they saw around them. Almost inevitably, therefore, the fiction of these men was concerned with certain common problems.

There was, for example, the problem of poverty. To be poor in a status society meant that a man's life was hard, but at least it was not shameful; if he made the best of a bad bargain, that was all that was expected. But in the fluid, mobile world of American society, a poor man was supposed to rise; not to do so was a sign of weakness, if not a badge of immorality. The ferocity of this proposition was glossed over in the mythic America of the Alger stories by reason of the fact that heroes always won the race for the top. But in the real America, heroes sometimes lost, and it was their recognition of this appalling fact which caused all these five writers to be haunted by the specter of failure. Dreiser and Herrick were witnesses to the psychological havoc which failure wreaked on their fathers, while Dreiser's own inability to succeed led him to the very brink of suicide. London's illegitimacy and his family's poverty cast a shadow of fear and shame across his entire life. For Norris's autobiographical hero, Vandover, failure meant social ostracism, physical disease and moral degradation; for Phillips's Susan Lenox, it meant a descent into prostitution. These writers knew that the road downward in a statusless society had, in Dreiser's words, "but few landings and level places," and the horror which they felt at this fact was conveyed by their employment of death as the primary symbol of American failure. The suicide of Hurstwood in *Sister Carrie,* the electrocution of Clyde Griffiths in *An American Tragedy,* the bloody slaughter of the ranchers in *The Octopus,* the tragic life and death of Wolf Larsen in *The Sea-Wolf,* were the morbid nightmares which troubled their sleep.

Yet if these writers knew how calamitous it was to lose the race for the top, they were also conscious that there were horrors attached to winning. Dreiser's Cowperwood, London's Martin Eden and the professional heroes of Herrick's fiction were rags-to-riches figures who discovered to their dismay, after they had reached the top, that success was not what the myth had cracked it up to be. The company of millionaires and blue-blooded debutantes, which had seemed so desirable to them when viewed from afar, proved, as they might have learned from Norris's *Blix* or Phillips's *Joshua Craig,* to be both frivolous and dull. Sister Carrie found that success completely robbed life of the drama of succeeding, while the hero of London's *Burning Daylight* made the even more distressing discovery that not only did success take the tang out of life, it did not even provide a letup from the race — the struggle to *maintain* one's position at the top of the heap was just as demanding as the struggle to get there. The pace that killed had to be kept up, but the enthrallment and the exhilaration attendant upon the rise were now replaced by monotony, boredom, exhaustion — and death. Failure caused Hurstwood to take his own life, but it was success which drove Martin Eden to suicide; when Dreiser thought to kill himself he was penniless, but when London swallowed a lethal dose of morphine he was earning sixty thousand dollars a year.

If poverty was psychologically more hazardous in a success society than in a status society, so too was marriage. In a status society, a woman marrying a store clerk had no other expectation than that her husband would always remain a clerk, and that she would remain a clerk's wife. In America, no such assured expectations existed; marriage was a gambling matter, a pari-mutuel mobility bet. The husband gambled that his wife would be able to rise right along with him, would be capable of accommodating herself to the successive tasks of entertaining the boss's wife and then of being the boss's wife. The gamble made by the American wife was that the store clerk she married would eventually become a storeowner. As always in gambling, not everyone won his bet. Thus in Dreiser's *The Titan*, the breakdown of Cowperwood's marriage to Aileen Burke was traceable to her inability to make the transition to the expansive, socially prominent life which his success had made possible for them. The marital quarrels, separations, and divorces which litter the pages of Herrick's novels all grew out of quarrels about money. But the risky nature of American marriage was reflected in the personal lives of the authors as well as in their novels. Dreiser, London and Herrick were all divorced by their wives; in addition, the unhappy marriage of Norris's parents finally terminated in divorce and Herrick's mother and father must surely have thought about such a solution to their marital battles.

If the conditions of life in America disrupted the marriage bond, they also corrupted sexual relationships. As Sister Carrie knew, the dispensation of her favors was a potent means for getting ahead, and therefore she viewed the act of love as a marketable commodity to be coldly bargained over; when she needed Drouet's help in Chicago she became his mistress, but when her husband failed in New York she refused to let him touch her. In Norris's *McTeague* the sado-masochism of McTeague's and Trina's relationship arose directly out of their quarrels about money, while the most perverted act in a novel of perversion occurred the night that Trina spread the gold pieces between the sheets in her bed and slept all night upon the money.

And then there was the problem of the children of success, the "second generation." Many of the spoiled brats in the novels of Phillips and Herrick seemed utterly beyond redemption; snobbish, effete, lazy, they created a whole new series of tensions within the life of the family. The crude solution worked out by Alger for saving the souls of such children, which was to arrange for them to become poor suddenly (thereby transferring them from the second generation back to the first), was not improved upon by any of these writers. London's rich young men and women went to the Arctic or to the coast of Siberia for therapy; Norris's society boys were shanghaied onto ships; Phillips's brats were written out of their father's wills and forced to go to work; Herrick's children left the East and went West. The inappropriateness of such solutions was reinforced by the false assumption which these writers shared with their society that the "second-generation" problem was all the children's fault; Norris's life should have been proof that parents were partly responsible for the way their sons and daughters turned out.

The unhappiness engendered by life in a materialist culture was responsible for the interest of these writers in immaterialist religion. Dreiser dabbled in Christian Science and mesmerism; London attended occult séances, read Madame Blavatsky and wrote prophecies; Herrick succumbed to the mystique of the scientist. In doing so, they were seeking — like many of their contemporaries — to discover some ideal in life beyond the success myth, something which would free them from the problems which plagued them. They found, however, that they could not escape success by means of religion, for religion was itself infected with the Alger virus. Dreiser's Cowperwood used the techniques of mesmerism to enhance his bank account and his sex life; the occult mysteries failed to divulge to London how an antisuccess Utopia could possible operate; Herrick's dedicated scientists could not avoid, even in the remote north woods, becoming Alger heroes. Far from supplying a solution to the baffling problems of modern American life, religion was itself a source of confusion and dissatisfaction.

London the economic revolutionist and Phillips the political reformer demonstrated that success could not be overthrown by violence or legislated out of existence any more than it could be transcended by religion. The leaders of the working class, as London portrayed them, believed in the mythology as much as any banker, a fact which goes far toward explaining the signal failure of radical groups at the turn of the century to appeal to the bulk of the American people. The socialist philosophy of Ernest Everhard was so shot through with success as to make it seem like Tweedledum to the Iron Heel's Tweedledee. Yet this is not to imply that American radicals would have come to power if they could only have freed themselves from success; London's socialist novels, and the Socialist Party in the days when he was a member, were palatable to Americans precisely because they *were* shot through with success. And the failure of the Moscow-dominated Communist Party in our own time may be explained by its complete eschewal of a myth to which such an overwhelming percentage of Americans — including the proletariat — subscribe.

Phillips's novels showed that the similarity between opposing political forces in this country grew even more pronounced as one moved toward the center of American political life and the two great parties. Both the Republicans and the Democrats at the turn of the century stood on a platform of success; the former talked of the full dinner pail, the latter of removing the economic crown of thorns from the brow of the people. For the party out of power — in Phillips's time, the Democrats — this similarity posed an agonizing problem: how was it possible to develop an effective counter-program to the party in office when there was so little real difference between the parties? The pathetic solution proposed by Phillips's political Messiahs was to have the party out of power assert that its devotion to the common ideal of success was superior to that of the party in power, and to prove its assertion by a political platform whose announced goal was the re-creation of the conditions of American life which had existed at the time of Horatio Alger. If, in the dream world of fiction, Messiahs won elections on such a platform, the absurdity of nostalgia as a political idea was inadvertently proved by Phillips's inability to portray his heroes in office. In real life, of course, the party of William McKinley went right on winning, a fact which produced among the political out-groups of the time more and more reckless attempts to gain power. The anti-Semitism and antiforeignism of the ranchers in Norris's *The Octopus*, their eager embrace of the imperialist adventure, the war fever which inflamed both London and Herrick, were all exploited by the out-groups in a hysterical attempt to win political victory, regardless of the cost. In sum, the universal acceptance of success in America tended, as these writers have shown, to prevent intelligent thought on public issues by depriving the opposition of a clearly discernible program, thus producing a reliance on political absurdities and hysteria. Yet, it can be argued, the universal acceptance of success made the absence of intelligence from American politics less crucial than it might otherwise have been. As long as Bryan and McKinley both believed in the success myth, why worry who won?

The monotony of our political life was true of our literature as well, and it was the all-dominating success myth which once again created the problem. When Henry James complained that in America there were "no castles, nor manors, nor old country houses, nor parsonages, nor thatched cottages, nor ivied ruins" he was talking about the lack of differentiation in American life, which, he felt, was the major cause of the impoverishment of the literary imagination in this country. For all the great length and breadth of the nation, its sectional flavors, its polyglot people, there was a dreary sameness about our efforts to rise and our dreams of success that posed definite problems for our literary artists. Certainly the five writers in this study found that sameness imaginatively stultifying, a fact which is most clearly exemplified by the common difficulty they had in bringing their novels to a significant conclusion. Frank Cowperwood, the sham-smasher and transvaluer, tried desperately to set himself apart from the common herd, but the more he tried the less he succeeded, and so Dreiser had to go on writing more and more pages of his seemingly endless trilogy in the vain attempt to make Cowperwood something more than an Alger hero. The smoke and violence which shrouded the ending of London's *The Iron Heel* simply obscured the fact that London had no idea as to how he could make Utopia seem attractive. Phillips's Messiahs always disappeared from sight just as they were about to change the political and economic face of America. Norris's novels generally ended with his heroes about to set off for somewhere — New York, the Arctic, Cuba, India — where, they insisted, life would be different, but the heroes only asserted this and their assertions were never proved dramatically. Conflagrations, departures for the Far West and bleak despair were the signs of Herrick's calamitous inability to conclude his novels satisfactorily. Success kindled the American imagination, certainly, but it stifled it as well.

That the five writers in this book were concerned, both personally and literarily, with the manifold problems created by life in a society dedicated to the success myth seems by now obvious; yet it has not always been so clear. William James's brilliantly acidulous remark that "the exclusive worship of the bitch-goddess SUCCESS . . . is our national disease" has been for half a century the keynote, ironically enough, of literary and social historians of American civilization, who yet have refused to grant that the worship was exclusive or that the disease was national. Distrusting the business classes, these historians have adopted James's remark as a weapon with which to belabor American businessmen, but have refused to concede that our writers as well as our industrialists have exalted the bitch-goddess, thereby completely missing the real significance of James's statement. Thus in 1915, Van Wyck Brooks, a democratic socialist, excoriated American writers in a famous diatribe for their failure "to move the soul of America from the accumulation of dollars," but by this he did not mean to imply that they worshiped success; hoping that someday socialism would replace success, and recognizing the vital role played by literature in cultural revolutions, Brooks could not afford strategically to make such a damaging admission; he wished to criticize the failure of our writers to attack the business enemy more severely, but the last thing in the world he wished to say was that they were in the camp of the enemy. Brooks criticized the important writers of the American past for being highbrows, for being unconcerned with the brutal injustices inflicted on our society by the minority class which both worshiped and represented success, but he did not even hint that the reason these writers had not attacked success was because they believed in it. For Brooks's book (*America's Coming-of-Age*) was a call to arms. To the American writers of the future, Brooks guaranteed immortality if they would but participate in the coming victory of socialism. "The happiest excitement in life," he told them, "is to be convinced that one is fighting for all one is worth on behalf of some clearly seen and deeply felt good and against some greatly scorned evil." He not only assured them about the future, but about the past, and here we reach the crux of Brooks's strategy: to give future writers the encouraging sense that their opposition to success would be in the great tradition of our literature, that they would be *"working in a great line,"* Brooks asserted that our most important writers of the past had all been opposed to success. They just hadn't been opposed hard enough, was all. The five books which, from *The Flowering of New England* to *The Confident Years,* make up Brooks's monumental study of our literary tradition, take as their main purpose this task of encouragement. Like many another American political strategist, Brooks found a usable past indispensable to his hopes for the future; in order to convert young American writers to the cause of democratic socialism, Brooks insisted that "the American imagination had been on the side of the 'Left' since Jefferson's days."

Brooks's influence on literary criticism in this country has been enormous. Vernon L. Parrington, whose political roots were in the Populist movement and who profoundly distrusted the financial and industrial interests of the East, wrote his great *Main Currents in American Thought* in order to show that the best American writers and intellectuals from the beginning to the present have fought on the side of the people against the tyrannical property interests. The political opponent of the business community, Parrington enlisted history on his side by maintaining that our literary tradition consisted of a Manichean struggle between the good writers, who loved the people and hated success, and the bad businessmen and politicians — plus a few renegade writers — who hated the people and loved success. The Marxist critics of the 1930's, men like Granville Hicks and V. F. Calverton, also endeavored to prove the Manicheanism of our literary past in order to hasten the Marxism of our economic future; the New Deal critics — Henry Steele Commager, Alfred Kazin, Walter Fuller Taylor, to mention a few — attempted to buttress the political program of Franklin D. Roosevelt by insisting that American writers have been historically opposed to success. Commager spoke for all the New Deal critics, indeed, for the whole reach of our literary criticism since Brooks, when he asked, "Who, in the half-century from Cleveland to Franklin Roosevelt celebrated business enterprise or the acquisitive society . . . ?" Answering his own question, Commager added, "Never before in American literature and rarely in the literature of any country had the major writers been so sharply estranged from the society which nourished them and the economy which sustained them as during the half-century between *The Rise of Silas Lapham* and *Grapes of Wrath*."

Yet Theodore Dreiser, Jack London, David Graham Phillips,

Frank Norris and Robert Herrick were not estranged from their society; they were molded by that society, took their values from it, lived out their lives in it. Far from scorning the bitch-goddess, they grew up on the success myth and in their maturity accepted it as the key to the meaning of American life. The society which was portrayed in their fiction was not one which was split into two warring camps, Left versus Right, good versus evil, or what you will, but a society which, as William James had said, exclusively worshiped a common deity, which was *locked* in the struggle to get ahead, not separated by a struggle between opposing ideals.

It is well that we now begin to see the error of the Manichean interpretation of our literature and our culture. For the success myth is still the great American myth, as vivid today as it was when Dreiser wrote *Sister Carrie;* the psychological, social and literary problems with which these five writers were concerned remain the great unsolved questions of our contemporary society. In our own time, the politicians out of power for a long period have been the Republicans, not the Democrats, but they have invoked the nostalgic good old days of Horatio Alger as repetitiously as the Democrats did in Phillips's day; if the xenophobia of Norris and London has disappeared as a form of political hysteria in this country, other forms have risen to take its place. The problems engendered by marriage in a success society seem, if anything, to be more acute now than they were in the fiction of Dreiser and Herrick. The specter of failure still haunts us; our writers still wrestle with the monotony of American life.

And if the Alger stories have long since disappeared from the family library, Alger's name and his immortal image of the ragged newsboy are still very much with us — with all of us. The American Schools and Colleges Association annually presents a series of "Horatio Alger Awards" to Americans whose "success stories are concrete evidence that America is still the land described by our forefathers as the place where equality and opportunity are synonymous." One of the most popular song hits of 1953 was something called "Rags to Riches." A biographer of Herbert Hoover praises the ex-President by saying that "Mr. Hoover's was a Horatio Alger story such as Alger never dared write," and the *Nation* eulogizes Harry S. Truman by declaring that "there is a Horatio Alger quality" to his rise from haberdashery to the White House. A Boston sportswriter, seeking to convey to his readers his awe at the exploits of a local athlete, writes that "the Ted Williams story is the old Horatio Alger theme brought up to date and given a baseball setting"; a professor at Harvard, wishing to vivify Marlowe's *Tamburlaine the Great* for a mid-twentieth-century American audience, remarks of the play's hero that "the novelty, the unique individuality of Tamburlaine, lay in the fact that his was a success story"; the Secretary of the Treasury, George M. Humphrey, mystified by the popularity of Hemingway's *The Old Man and the Sea*, asks, "Why would anybody be interested in some old man who was a failure and never amounted to anything anyway?" Whittaker Chambers finds it significant that, in contrast to the "glittering Hiss forces," the loyal men like Thomas Murphy and Richard Nixon who backed him came, most of them, "from the wrong side of the railroad tracks." What Chambers forgot to add, however, was that the man he sent to jail was named for America' great mythmaker.

But if Alger is still very much with us, if his name is still invoked every day on every side, his mythic interpretation of the American experience is nonetheless almost ninety years old, and in America that is very old indeed. His simple, but enormously compelling, vision of a fluid society which infallibly rewarded the plucky and lucky with fame and fortune had, in the opportunistic scramble after the Civil War, a solid basis in fact. But such was the rate of complication and diversification of American life that even within Alger's own lifetime his vision began to lose contact with the social situation it endeavored to describe. The disparity between myth and reality which suddenly opened under the feet of Americans at the end of the nineties is apparent everywhere in the novels and stories of the five writers who make up this study — indeed, in the work of every American writer of the period. In the complex multiverse which is the United States in the middle of the twentieth century, Alger's version of the success myth seems primitive and naïve, hopelessly inadequate to the task of ordering and interpreting our social experience to ourselves. Alger preached the gospel that hard work was the *sine qua non* of success, yet in contemporary America the "Protestant ethic" has given way to personality-selling as the classic means of rising in the world. The fact that men and women still do rise in the American world attests to the continued validity of Alger's belief in social mobility; but while the fact that American society is still fluid and open goes far toward explaining why Alger continues to exert a powerful pull on the American imagination, Alger's simplistic conception of mobility does no more than begin to comprehend the manifold processes which make for fluidity in modern American society. More obsolete than the Model T, Alger continues to be our mythmaker; until we show some of the same sort of ruthlessness about discarding outworn mythologies as we do about outdated motorcars, we shall never be able to get at the unprecedented meaning of American civilization today.

Sources

For readers who wish to check my references, a slightly longer and fully annotated version of this book is on deposit in the Harvard College Library. The following is simply a list of the sources, exclusive of the writings of Dreiser, London, Phillips, Norris and Herrick, from which I have quoted directly.

Introduction
Alfred Whitney Griswold, "The American Cult of Success" (unpublished Ph.D. thesis, Yale University, 1933); Herbert Mayes, *Alger: A Biography Without a Hero* (New York, 1928); Henry Nash Smith, *Virgin Land: The American West as Symbol and Myth* (Cambridge, Mass., 1950).

Chapter I
Honoré de Balzac, *Père Goriot* (Paris, 1834); Edmund Bergler, M.D., *Money and Emotional Conflicts* (Garden City, N. Y., 1951); Helen Dreiser, *My Life with Dreiser* (New York, 1951); Mary Baker G. Eddy, *Science and Health with a Key to the Scriptures* (Boston, 1891); Robert H. Elias, *Theodore Dreiser: Apostle of Nature* (New York, 1949); Alfred Whitney Griswold, "The American Cult of Success" (unpublished Ph.D. thesis, Yale University, 1933); William Manchester, *Disturber of the Peace: The Life of H. L. Mencken* (New York, 1951); Orison Swett Marden, *How They Succeeded: Life Stories of Successful Men Told by Themselves* (Boston, 1901); Orison

Swett Marden, *Pushing to the Front or, Success Under Difficulties* (Cambridge, Mass., 1895); F. O. Matthiessen, *Theodore Dreiser* (New York, 1951); H. L. Mencken, *A Book of Prefaces* (New York, 1917); H. L. Mencken, *The Philosophy of Friedrich Nietzsche* (Boston, 1908); C. Wright Mills, *White Collar: The American Middle Classes* (New York, 1951); Burton Rascoe, *Theodore Dreiser* (New York, 1926); Arthur M. Schlesinger, *The Rise of the City 1878-1898* (New York, 1933); Stuart P. Sherman, *On Contemporary Literature* (New York, 1917); Alexis de Tocqueville, *Democracy in America* (2 vols., New York, 1945); Lionel Trilling, *The Liberal Imagination* (New York, 1950).

Chapter II

Aneurin Bevan, *In Place of Fear* (London, 1952); Oscar Handlin, "American Views of the Jew at the Opening of the Twentieth Century" (*Publications of the American Jewish Historical Society*, XL, June, 1951); Ira Kipnis, *The American Socialist Movement, 1897-1912* (New York, 1952); Nadezhda K. Krupskaya, *Memories of Lenin*, translated by E. Verney (New York, n.d.); Algernon Lee, ed., *Essentials of Marx* (New York, 1946); Charmian London, *The Book of Jack London* (2 vols., New York, 1921); Joan London, *Jack London and His Times: An Unconventional Biography* (New York, 1939); H. L. Mencken, *Prejudices. First Series* (New York, 1919); Bailey Millard, "Jack London, Farmer" (*The Bookman*, XLIV, October, 1916); Joseph Noel, *Footloose in Arcadia: A Personal Record of Jack London, George Sterling, Ambrose Bierce* (New York, 1940); Upton Sinclair, "Is This Jack London? His 'Spirit' Talks with Upton Sinclair" (*The Occult Review*, LII, December, 1930, and LIII, January, 1931); Irving Stone, *Sailor on Horseback: The Biography of Jack London* (Cambridge, Mass., 1938); Anna Strunsky Walling, "Memoirs of Jack London" (*The Masses*, IX, 1917).

Chapter III

Claude G. Bowers, *Beveridge and the Progressive Era* (Cambridge, Mass., 1932); F. Scott Fitzgerald, *This Side of Paradise*

(New York, 1920); Richard and Beatrice Hofstadter, "Winston Churchill: A Study in the Popular Novel" (*American Quarterly*, II, Spring, 1950); Alfred Kazin, *On Native Grounds: An Interpretation of Modern American Prose Literature* (New York, 1942); Isaac F. Marcosson, *David Graham Phillips and His Times* (New York, 1932); Elting E. Morison and others, eds., *The Letters of Theodore Roosevelt* (5 vols., Cambridge, Mass., 1952); Upton Sinclair, *The Jungle* (New York, 1938); Booth Tarkington, *The Magnificent Ambersons* (Garden City, N.Y., 1922); Booth Tarkington, *The Turmoil* (Garden City, N.Y., 1922); John Tebbel, *George Horace Lorimer and The Saturday Evening Post* (Garden City, N.Y., 1948).

Chapter IV

Horatio Alger, Jr., *Fame and Fortune; or, The Progress of Richard Hunter* (Boston, 1868); Horatio Alger, Jr., *Mark, the Match Boy; or, Richard Hunter's Ward* (Boston, 1869); Claude G. Bowers, *Beveridge and the Progressive Era* (Cambridge, Mass., 1932); Oscar Handlin, "American Views of the Jew at the Opening of the Twentieth Century" (*Publications of the American Jewish Historical Society*, XL, June, 1951); Oscar Lewis, ed., *Frank Norris of "The Wave." Stories and Sketches from the San Francisco weekly, 1893 to 1897.* Foreword by Charles G. Norris (San Francisco, 1931); Isaac F. Marcosson, *Adventures in Interviewing* (New York, 1919); Orison Swett Marden, *Architects of Fate or, Steps to Success and Power* (Boston, 1895); Orison Swett Marden, *Pushing to the Front or, Success Under Difficulties* (Cambridge, Mass., 1895); Carey McWilliams, *California: The Great Exception* (New York, 1949); Franklin Walker, *Frank Norris: A Biography* (New York, 1932).

Chapter V

Richard Hofstadter, *The American Political Tradition and the Men Who Made It* (New York, 1948); Henry James, "American Letter" (*Literature*, II, March 26, 1898); Charmian London, *The Book of Jack London* (2 vols., New York, 1921); Orison Swett Marden, *Architects of Fate or, Steps to Success and Power* (Boston, 1895); Blake Nevius, "The Novels of Robert Herrick: A Critical Study" (unpublished Ph.D. dissertation, University of Chicago, 1947); William S. Sadler, *Americanitis — Blood Pressure and Nerves* (New York, 1925); William S. Sadler, *The Truth About Mind Cure* (Chicago, 1928); Arthur M. Schlesinger, *The Rise of the City 1878-1898* (New York, 1933); Ella Wheeler Wilcox, "The Restlessness of the Modern Woman" (*The Cosmopolitan*, XXXI, July, 1901).

Conclusion

Boston Herald (May 6, 1952); Van Wyck Brooks, *The Confident Years: 1885-1915* (New York, 1952); Van Wyck Brooks, *Three Essays on America* (New York, 1934); Whittaker Chambers, *Witness* (New York, 1952); Henry Steele Commager, *The American Mind: An Interpretation of American Thought and Character Since the 1880's* (New Haven, 1950); David Hinshaw, *Herbert Hoover: American Quaker* (New York, 1950); Henry James, *Hawthorne* (New York, 1879); Henry James, ed., *The Letters of William James* (2 vols., Boston, 1920); Harry Levin, *The Overreacher: A Study of Christopher Marlowe* (Cambridge, Mass., 1952); *Life* (34, January 19, 1953); *The Nation* (176, January 24, 1953); *The New Yorker* (May 16, 1953).

Acknowledgments

I should like to thank John F. Huth, Jr., of Cleveland, Ohio, for his generosity in making available to me his collection of Dreiserana, particularly his copies of *Ev'ry Month*, an almost unobtainable magazine. Louis Hartz's seminar on American political theory, which it was my privilege as a Harvard student to audit in the fall of 1951, considerably influenced my thinking about the success mythology and I record his influence with gratitude. William R. Taylor has given me aid and encouragement in my endeavors on innumerable occasions during the past three years. Carl Kaysen read the chapter on Phillips to my profit. The chapter on Herrick was subjected to the rigorous analysis of Perry Miller, and both I and the chapter have since been the better for it. Kenneth B. Murdock read the entire manuscript and made many helpful suggestions, particularly with regard to tone and language. His advice as to what changes should be made — and should not be made — in preparing the book for publication was of great service to me. Edward Weeks and Seymour Lawrence helped me to improve the book in many ways, but more importantly, they had faith in it; I shall always be grateful to them for that fact. My greatest debt of all is to Oscar Handlin. His assistance was important at every step of the way; from the largest conceptual questions to the smallest editorial details, he gave me the benefit of his wisdom, which is as kind as it is great. Valerie Lynn

259

performed the dreary tasks of typing and proofreading the manuscript with unfailing good humor. If this is an incomplete catalogue of her contributions, it is because they defy enumeration.

INDEX

INDEX

INDEX

Cleveland, Grover, 250
Commager, Henry Steele, 250
The Common Lot, 228-229
Communist Manifesto, 86, 151
Communist Party, 245-246
The Confident Years, 249
Cooper, James Fenimore, 7, 8
Cosmopolitan, 116, 128
The Cost, 131-132, 133, 142, 143, 144
Coxey's Army, 80
Curtis, Cyrus H. K., 125

A Daughter of the Snows, 90, 92
Delineator, 37
The Deluge, 133
DePauw University, 141, 152
Designer, 37
Dickens, Charles, 162
Divorce, 9, 165, 243. *See also* Robert Herrick
Donnelly, Ignatius, 97
Doubleday, Mrs. Frank. *See* Neltje Blanchan
Doubleday, Page, 15
"The Dream of Debs," 98
Dreiser, Helen, 73-74
Dreiser Looks At Russia, 69, 71, 72
Dreiser, Theodore, values of, 13; childhood, 16; character of father, 16-17; character of mother, 17-18; poverty of family, 17-18; reads *Pluck and Luck* and other pulp magazines, 18; reads *Self-Help*, 18; dreams of success, 18; goes to Chicago, 18-19; tries to get ahead, 18-19; newspaper days, 20-22; dreams of success, 20-21; fears failure, 21-22; tries and fails to become successful writer, 22; becomes editor of *Ev'ry Month*, 22-23; writes editorials, 23-24; opposed to political and economic reform, 24; works for Marden, 24-26; writes *Sister Carrie*, 27; his coldness of

temperament, 28; his feelings of social superiority, 29; *Sister Carrie* suppressed, 36; sinks into poverty and contemplation of suicide, 36; begins and abandons *Jennie Gerhardt*, 36-37; becomes editor of Butterick "Trio," 37; invests money, 37-38; resigns from editorship and resumes writing *Jennie*, 38; opinion of Rockefeller, 39-40; begins the Cowperwood trilogy, 42; writes *The "Genius,"* 42; reads Mencken's *Nietzsche*, 42-43; responds enthusiastically, 43; fascinated by Christian Science, 45; belief in mental telepathy, 46-56; publishes autobiographical and travel books, 61; writes *An American Tragedy*, 61; period of affluence, 67-69; opinion of New York, 68-69; for intellectual aristocracy, 69; visits Soviet Union, 69; writes *Dreiser Looks At Russia*, 69; opposed to Communism, 69-71; reaction to the depression, 71-74; writes *Tragic America*, 71; financial security wiped out, 72; writes *America Is Worth Saving*, 72; writes *The Bulwark* and *The Stoic*, 73; buried at Forest Lawn, 74; anti-Semitism of, 192*n.*; mentioned, 10, 241, 242, 243, 245, 247, 250, 251
Dresser, Paul, 22, 22*n.*, 52*n.*
du Maurier, George, 49

EDDY, MARY BAKER, 45, 46
Edison, Thomas A., 25-26, 35
Education in America, 220-222, 231
Emerson, Ralph Waldo, 46, 75
The Engineers and the Price System, 223
Ev'ry Month, 24, 25, 32, 71

264

INDEX